Financial and Management Accounting

Third Revised and Enlarged Edition

Volume II

C.L. Tyagi
Madhu Tyagi

ATLANTIC
PUBLISHERS & DISTRIBUTORS (P) LTD

Published by
ATLANTIC
PUBLISHERS & DISTRIBUTORS (P) LTD
7/22, Ansari Road, Darya Ganj, New Delhi-110002
Phones : +91-11-40775252, 40775214, 23273880, 23275880
Fax : +91-11-23285873
Web : www.atlanticbooks.com
E-mail : orders@atlanticbooks.com

First Edition, 2003
Second Revised and Enlarged Edition, 2017
Third Revised and Enlarged Edition, 2022

Printed & bound in India by Atlantic Print Services

Preface to the Third Edition

Seeing the overwhelming response of the previous edition, the third revised edition of the book is being presented to the students. It could not be brought out on anticipated time due to COVID-19 pandemic. Now, it is ready for the students with new updates. Additional matters are added in the topics like Break-even Analysis, Operation Research, and Accounting Changing for Price Level. New topics such as Human Resource Accounting, Inflation Accounting, and Management Accounting in Non-Profit Organisations are included. The reason is that there is no agreement among writers as to which topics should be included in a book on Management Accounting because of its wide scope. Various definitions of this discipline have ended in emphasizing some of its facets only to the exclusion of others.

The book has been designed with a specific objective of fulfilling the needs of graduate and post-graduate students of Indian universities. Students appearing for C.A., I.C.W.A., and I.C.S.I. examinations may also find it useful.

We hope that the book will come to the expectations of the students. Errors and deficiencies pointed out by the readers are welcome. We thank Atlantic Publishers and Distributors Pvt. Ltd., New Delhi, without whose efforts the book would not have seen the light of the day.

C.L. Tyagi
Madhu Tyagi

Contents

12
Standard Costing and Variance Analysis

Not all controls are quantitative controls and not all quantitative controls are accounting controls. The accounting controls consist of the following (i) technical standards, (ii) performance standards, (iii) resource allocations, (iv) profitability measures, (v) investment centre measures. Two main accounting control techniques are known as budgetary control and standard costing. A standard is "a thing serving as basis of comparison" and it represents what 'should be' i.e., a standard of efficiency. A standard cost is a predetermined cost of a single unit or a number of product units during a specified period in the immediate future. A standard cost has two components: a standard and a cost. As standard is a norm and whatever is considered normal can be generally accepted as standard. The standard can be expressed in money, time or percentage. The standard rate may be expressed in money, physical inputs and physical outputs.

BUDGETARY CONTROL AND STANDARDS COSTING

In the early stages, the two techniques developed separately. Standard costing was applied in the workshop to the production costs. Budgetary control was applied to the financial aspect of the business. Later it was realized that both were complementary to each other as both were applications of the same principle. The budgets normally incorporate the standards. Budgets relate to the whole business and standards costing may only relate to cost centre activity only. Standard costs are useful in the construction of a budget. Budgeted costs are total costs and standard costs are unit costs. Former is possible without the later, but later is not possible without the former. Budgetary control covers financial control of all activities of a firm. But control of performance may be either through standards or through resource allocation. Standards can be regarded as goals or objectives to be aimed for. But neither control nor standards are static.

Types of Standard

The standard may be used in either of the following senses:

1. Past performance standards.
2. Basic or bogey or bulletin standards.

3. Currently attainable standards.
4. Ideal standards, or theoretical standards.
5. Expected actual standards.
6. Normal or long run standards.
7. Super standards.

Eric L. Kohler defines a standard as "a desired attainable objective, a performance, a goal, a model".

A past performance standard codifies in standard form the firm's experience as regards material, labour and facility usage. The standard price component of standard cost may be past-oriented, but it is more likely to represent present factor prices with standard usage component reflecting past experience. They are easy to be constructed, but may establish a standard cost to ferret out inefficiencies. Basic or bogey standard is like past performance standard except that their use is extended indefinitely. A base period efficiency and price may become a criteria. They lose their utility for control purposes because they become out of date. However, an adjustment may be made by index number to make it uptodate. Under currently attainable standards an attempt is made to express in standards what can be attained by individuals and groups working a high levels of efficiency. Their use provides an incentive. But their use may give numerous unfavourable variances because they are set on high side showing efficiency of better workers on their better days. They are widely used because they have the most desirable motivational impact and used for financial planning and departmental performance.

An ideal standard, assuming use of present facilities, assumes that standard will be established so as to reflect what could be accomplished under the most favourable conditions. This standard is unrealistic and self-defeating.

Expected actual standards, under conditions of control, represents what performance will be in the coming period utilizing present work force and facilities and assuming the normal operating of motivational devices and control efforts. What is wanted as a standard is the average efficiency for the period as will be expressed in the final actual cost of goods sold figure. These standards are revised annually so as to motivate.

For the operation of a standard cost system the operations, for which standard costs are derived, are standardized. The system of responsibility accounting is practiced and there is good budgeting system. There is qualified personnel and there is well-developed communication and reporting system.

All the above type of standards can be classified in three categories: (a) strict or tight standards, (b) attainable standards and (c) loose or lax standards. The first type is set at a maximum level of efficiency, representing conditions that can seldom, if ever, be attained. The attainable or normal standards can be achieved with reasonable effort. With loose standards, there may be a tendency to indulge in self congratulation.

Advantages of Standard Cost Accounting

Standard costs were initially developed as a means of reducing or minimizing cost. As standard cost systems evolved, other objectives were sought in their utilization, e.g., as an aid to product data pricing and convenience in accounting for inventories. Standard costs provide useful for control over cost, in the costing of inventories, for finding interim profits, in planning and budgeting, in the study of alternatives and in the pricing of products. The most important advantages of standard costing may be summarized as follows:

(a) *Management by exception*: Standard cost accounting follows the principle of "management by exception". Actual results that correspond with the standards require little attention. The exceptions are, however, emphasized. In actual or historical cost accounting, it is sometimes difficult to separate the exceptions from the flow of data being processed. Furthermore, many of the measurements may not be made until after it is too late to take corrective action.

(b) *Motivation and measures of efficiency*: It is useful as a basis for evaluating various operations. There are check points so that variations from the standards can be detected and brought under control. While operations are in progress, comparisons of actual results with the standards can be made and unfavourable conditions can be brought to attention and corrected before losses accumulate. Thus, it provides a framework for judging performance.

(c) *Income determination*: Losses can be reduced or eliminated entirely in a system that provides for an immediate reaction to any tendency to stray from predetermined standard. Output valued at standard costs and estimated earnings are also based on standard selling prices of output. The difference between standard cost and standard selling prices give estimated earnings to be realized during a given period.

(d) *Policy formation and profit planning*: It helps the management in preparing the price list for production orders, for contracts and bides, planning production of new products and new styles and furnishing cost estimates. While defining standard costing J. Betty says, "It is a system which is designed to show in detail how must each product should cost, produce and sell when the business in operating at a stated level of efficiency and for a given volume of output."

(e) *Inventory valuation*: Inventory is valued at cost or market price whichever is lower. Here the cost may be a standard cost instead of determining it by LIFO or FIFO or average cost. Institute of Cost and Management Accountants, London says, "Its main purpose are to provide base for control through variance accounting for the valuation of stock and work-in-progress and in exceptional cases selling prices."

SETTING OF STANDARDS

There are several ways to estimate standards for prices and quantities needed to produce a product. The most common are: engineering methods (including time and motion studies) and managerial estimates based on experience and knowledge of the production process. These methods apply to determine quantity standards.

The steps in setting the standard costing are: (1) predetermination of cost, (2) actual costs are compared with standard costs, (3) difference between actual and predetermined costs (variance) are found and causes are determined, (4) managerial action to prevent unfavourable variance, (5) standards are reviewed from time to time. The standard should be for a definite period, should be based on sound accounting information and should take into account the inflation prevailing. But much depends on how the managers behave and cooperate.

A standard cost may represent any of the following: (1) ideal conditions of productions activity, (2) a forecast of what costs should be under normal conditions, (3) a representative of average cost conditions, (4) a predetermined cost representing budget forecast of expected production, (5) a reasonably attainable expectation of plant operation, (6) a replacement cost computed at latest market or replacement value.

The Standard Hour

There may be a problem as how to express the production achieved. There should be a common measurement in which the output differently measured can be expressed. The most common unit of measurement is time, based on "standard hours" which is a measure of the work content of a clock hour. The measurement of the work produced in terms of standard hour is, therefore, a calculation irrespective of the time actually taken to produce the work in the factory.

The Standard of Attainment

The fixing of standard is time and money consuming task. They should be fixed for use over a reasonable period without change. But they should be revised as well. The objective of standard costing is cost control. The currently attainable standard is the level of attainment normally adopted. Following example may be cited:

Theoretical Maximum standard	Expected standard (90%)	Normal standard
$\frac{\text{Total cost}}{\text{Standard hours}} = \frac{₹\ 10,00,000}{5,00,000 \text{ hrs.}} = ₹\ 2$	$\frac{₹\ 10,00,000}{4,50,000 \text{ hrs.}} = ₹\ 2.22$	$\frac{₹\ 10,00,000}{4,00,000 \text{ hrs.}} = ₹\ 2.50$

The Level of Activity

The basis for establishing standard costing is usually the normal capacity i.e., average for the financial year. The normal capacity is calculated on any two basis: (a) the average capacity to produce, (b) the average capacity to produce and sell. The second basis is more realistic because it takes into account plant availability and marketing experience and forecasts. A standard cost sheet is prepared to give full information on quantities, qualities, time etc., of the elements of cost.

Three ratios may be mentioned here that have relationship with variance analysis and are based on different levels of activity.

(a) *Activity ratio*: It is the ratio of number of standard hours equivalent to the work produced expressed as a percentage of budgeted standard hours. This ratio, also called production volume ratio, is calculated by the formula:

$$\frac{\text{Standard hours for actual output}}{\text{Budgeted production in terms of standard hours}} \times 100.$$

(b) *Efficiency ratio or productivity ratio*: It is the ratio of standard hours equivalent to the work produced expressed as a percentage of the actual hours spent in producing that work. Formula:

$$\frac{\text{Standard hours for actual output}}{\text{Actual hours worked}} \times 100.$$

(c) *Capacity ratio*: It is the ratio of actual hours worked expressed as a percentage of budgeted production in terms of standard hours. Formula:

$$\frac{\text{Actual hours worked}}{\text{Budgeted production in terms of standard hours}} \times 100.$$

Example 1

Actual hours worked = 4,000

Standard hours for actual production = 3,600

Budgeted production in terms of standard hours = 4,400

(a) Activity ratio $= \frac{3,600}{4,400} \times 100 = 90\%$

(b) Efficiency ratio $= \frac{3,600}{4,000} \times 100 = 81.8\%$

(c) Capacity ratio $= \frac{4,000}{4,400} \times 100 = 90.9\%.$

Learning Curves

In the setting standards for labour and labour related inputs, one important consideration is the effect on performance of learning phenomena. In many production situations opportunities will arise for improvements in performance because of "built in" learning which occurs as the same tasks is carried out a large number of times. The result could be that the average labour times per unit of output declines, at least during the early stages of a new process. The concept is not a new one and the applications of the idea were made in the American air frame industry as early as 1925. It was on the basis of these early studies that an 80% learning model was developed. The simple application is as follows:

Every time the output level is doubled, the average labour hours per unit are 80% of the previous value. Therefore, if the first unit took 125 hours to produce, the average for the next two would be 100 hours per unit, i.e., 200 hours in total. Four units would take 100 (0.8) = 80 hours average per unit and so on. Note that the marginal hours for the third and fourth are (320 – 200) = 120.

Learning curve information is relevant for pricing decision, man power planning (work scheduling and motivation) and cash flow forecasting (capital budgeting). It can be shown by a graph as under (Exhibit 12.1):

LEARNING CURVE

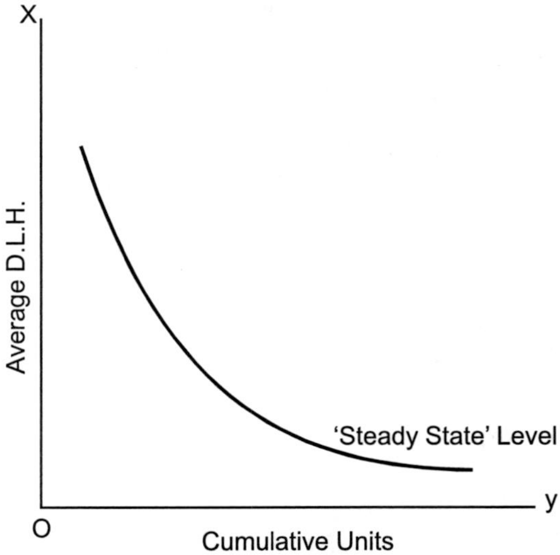

Exhibit 12.1

When learning effects are expected, they cannot be ignored in relation to labour standard setting. The standard set at 'steady state' level may produce unjustifiable and unfavourable feedback during intermittent reporting periods and so sacrifice commitment to eventually making the standard. Alternatively standard which do not take into account of potential learning effects may lead to easily attainable goals which could also be demotivating and lead to a 'levelling off' of performance at productivity levels below expected 'steady state' inputs. The same dysfunctional reaction could result from the following performance down the learning curve with the standard.

Mathematically, the learning curve can be expressed as

$$y = ax^b$$

y = average number of hours required for X units
a = number of labour hours required for the first unit
x = cumulative number of units produced
b = index of learning, equal to log of the learning rate divided by the log of 2.

Thus, if the first unit took 250 hours and it was estimated that an 80% learning curve effect would occur; to estimate the average hours for 2 units:

$$y = 250\ (2)^b \qquad \text{where} \quad b = \frac{\log 0.80}{\log 2} = -0.322$$

$$\therefore\ y = 250\ (2) - 0.322 = 200$$

and total number of hours for X units is given by:

$$YX = a \times b + 1$$
$$= 250\ (2)^{0.678} = 400.$$

As a demonstration of the use of learning curves, the following is a brief example relating to pricing situation in which reducible curves are involved.

LEARNING CURVE TABLE

Following is the relationship between cumulative volume (X) and cumulative average price of elements subjects to the learning curve (Y) at 80%.

X	Y (%)
1.0	100.0
1.1	96.9
1.2	93.3
1.3	91.7
1.4	89.5
1.5	87.6
1.6	86.1
1.7	84.4
1.8	83.0
1.9	81.5
2.0	80.0

In this case it is assumed that $X = 1$ refers to the units in the first order, i.e., no learning effects took place in the first batch.

Example 1

Anurag Ltd. have just completed an initial order of 160 units of product A for Praveen Ltd. The cost and prices were:

Direct Material

8 meters of x at ₹ 3.50 per meter

12 kg of y at ₹ 1.00 per kg.

Conversion Costs: (including labour hours and related overheads). (Reducible by learning)

Deptt. 2,50 hours at ₹ 2.80 per hour

Deptt. 3,15 hours at ₹ 2 per hour

Conversion costs (Non-reducible)

Deptt. 1,4 hours at ₹ 3.50 per hour

Profit margins:

Direct material cost + 2½%

Conversion cost + 12½%

Therefore, the price for the initial order was:

	₹
Direct materials	40
Reducible conversion costs	170
Non-reducible conversion costs	14
Total cost	224
Profit margin:	
2½% on direct materials	1
12½% on conversion costs	23
Profit per unit	248

Anurag Ltd. have been asked to quote for an additional order of 80 units. Praveen Ltd., have stipulated that the learning curve effects should be taken into account expecting a reduction in price. Using the above table, the revised selling price would be as under:

Additional order for 180 units

Cumulative units	240
Ratio initial batch	1.5
Learning curve factor	0.876
Unit reducible cost	₹ 170
Reduced unit costs	₹ 148.92 (₹ 170 × 0.876)
Cumulative cost	₹ 35,741 (240 × ₹ 148.92)
Cost of initial batch	₹ 27,200 (160 × ₹ 170)
Marginal cost of standard order	₹ 8,541 (35,741 – 27,200)
Marginal cost per unit	₹ 106.76 (8,541 ÷ 80)

Non-reducible conversion

	₹
Cost per unit	14
Direct material cost per unit	40
Revised total cost per unit	₹ 106.76 (106.76 + 14 + 40)

Profit margins

2½% on direct materials	₹ 1 (2½% × ₹ 40)
12½% on conversion costs	₹ 15.1 (12½% × ₹ 120.76)
Revised selling price per unit	₹ 176.86

Therefore, the unit price can be reduced from ₹ 248 to ₹ 176.86—a reduction of about 29%.

ANALYSIS OF VARIANCE

Even though standard costs may be carefully set and revised as conditions change, actual costs will vary from standard costs. The differences between standard costs and actual costs are called variances. These variances occur in direct materials, direct labour and factory overhead. They are the results of many causes and these causes must be analysed. In most cases standard costs and cost variances are recorded in the accounts.

If the actual costs incurred are less than standard costs, the variance is **favourable** (F). If the actual costs are more than the standard costs, the variances is **unfavourable or adverse** (U or A). The total variance for a particular period is ordinarily a composite of a number of variances, some of which may be favourable and some unfavourable. One single variance will not give accurate results. Therefore, variance analysis be done with care and it merely brings out items for investigation. Interpretation of variances is not always straightforward and is not a medicine.

The problems are the following:

1. *Difficulty in measuring results accurately*: Actual costs may be badly organized so the results obtained will be inaccurate. So the cost accounting system must be efficient. Implementation, prediction or measurement may be wrong.

2. *Interdependence between variances*: An adverse variance from standard may be the consequence of a decision by the management to obtain a favourable effect in some other respect e.g., reduce the price for increasing sales or use cheaper raw material of lower quality.

3. *The type of efficiency standard in operation*: Efficiency standard depends upon the efficiency level. This level may be ideal, expected or attainable standard. The variance will differ in each case.

4. *Inflation*: If the standard cost is based on current price level, the effect of inflation will be to create ever increasing adverse price variance.

5. *The opportunity cost of variance*: It is explained in a later section of this chapter.

6. *The controllability of variance*: It means that the time when variance should be investigated is to be appropriate.

7. *Cost/benefit analysis of variance investigation*: The expected costs of investigation and control of variance should be compared with expected benefit from control action. Statistical quality control and control charts are used for investigating variances.

PRODUCTION VARIANCES

Ordinarily, a manufacturing firm will establish standard costs for each of its product. Each standard cost consists of a standard direct material cost, a standard direct labour cost and standard factory overhead cost.

The standard cost for direct materials in manufacturing a finished product is the product of two factors: standard quantity and standard price. The standard cost of direct labour in making finished unit is also the product of two elements: standard time and standard rate.

To determine the standard cost for factory overhead, fixed and overhead rates must be calculated for a given level of activity, usually the normal capacity for operations. A cost formula is developed for the purpose of budgeting overhead costs.

Variable costs for direct labour and direct materials are on a unit basis. The variable overhead, mostly shown as total, an hourly cost or unit cost can be found from the total. In absorption costing fixed costs are budgeted in total and then absorbed into standard unit cost on a machine hour basis or direct labour hour basis. It is sometimes difficult to draw a distinction between variable overhead incurred and variable overhead absorbed, only it is known at a later time.

Production Variances are divided into following types:

(A) *Direct material cost variance*. It is further subdivided into (i) Direct material price variance, (ii) Direct material quantity variance, (iii) Direct material mix and (iv) Yield variance.

(B) *Direct labour rate variance*. It is further subdivided into (i) Direct labour rate (wages variance), (ii) Direct labour time or efficiency variance and (iii) Direct labour mix variance.

(C) *Overhead cost variances*. They are further classified into variable overhead cost variances and fixed overhead cost variances and calender sub-variance. They are further subdivided and are explained on page 295.

Assume that a product x is made in only one workshop. The monthly fixed overhead cost for the workshop is ₹ 30,000 and the variable overhead incurred @ ₹ 1 per direct labour hour. The normal capacity is 10,000 hours in making the product. The monthly overhead budget would be as follows: Total factory overhead = Total fixed overhead + (variable overhead per unit × volume).

₹ 40,000 = ₹ 30,000 + (₹ 1 per direct labour hours) × 10,000 direct labour hours.

The standard factory overhead rate, at Normal Capacity, of 10,000 DLH, would be ₹ 4 i.e., standard variable factory overhead rate ₹ 1 plus standard fixed factory overhead rate (₹ 30,000 ÷ 10,000 DLH) ₹ 3.

Example 3

The standard cost for direct material and direct labour are as follows:

		₹
Direct material (2 kilos @ ₹ 1 per kilo)		2
Direct labour (1 hour @ ₹ 4 per hour)		4
Factory overhead (on basis of D.L.H. shown above)		
Variable	₹ 1	
Fixed	₹ 3	4
Total standard cost per unit of product *X*		10

During the month of February, the workshop produced 9,800 units of product *X* and there are no opening and closing work-in-process and one unit takes one hour to produce. The actual costs were:

		₹
Direct materials (20,600 kilos @ ₹ 1.05 per kilo)		21,630
Direct labour (9,700 hours @ ₹ 4.20 per hour)		40,740
Factory overheads	₹	
Variable	8,730	
Fixed	30,000	38,730
Actual cost in February		1,01,100

The relevant materials, labour and overhead variances, with formulas, are explained below. Figures are based on above example.

(a) *Direct materials cost variance*: It consists of two variances—materials price and materials quantity variance.

Direct Material Cost Variance

Direct materials cost variance = Standard costs – Actual costs
= (Standard price × Standard quantity) – (Actual price × Actual quantity)
= (₹ 1 × 19,600 kilos) – (₹ 1.05 × 20,600 kilos)
= ₹ 19,600 – 21,630 = ₹ 2,030 (U)

It is subdivided into two:

(i) Direct materials price variance:

Formula: (Standard price × Actual[1] quantity) – (Actual price × Actual quantity)

Or

(Difference in unity price of inputs) × (Actual input used)

= (₹ 1 × 20,600 kilos) – (₹ 1.05 × 20,600 kilos)

= ₹ 20,600 – ₹ 21,630 = ₹ 1,030 (U)

(ii) Direct materials efficiency usage or quantity variance:

Formula: (Standard[2] price × Standard quantity) – (Standard price × Actual quantity)

Or

(Inputs actually used) – (Inputs that should have been used) × Standard price

= (₹ 1 × 19,600) – (₹ 1 × 20,600)

= ₹ 19,600 – ₹ 20,600 = ₹ 1,000 (U)

Verification = D.M. usage variance + D.M. price variance

Total D.M. variance = ₹ 1,000 (U) + ₹ 1,030 (U) = ₹ 2,030 (U)

Combined or joint price efficiency variance = Difference in prices × Difference in quantity = 0.05 × 1,000 = ₹ 50 (U).

In case of usage variance, we multiplied the standard price by differential of quantities and in price variance actual quantity was multiplied by differential of prices. Price standard helps to check the performance of purchasing department and effect of price increase or decrease on company's profits. Quantity standard should be set after taking into account the size, shape and quality of the product and the result expected from the use of various types of materials.

(b) *Direct Labour cost variance*: It is like material variances also.

Direct Labour Cost Variance

Formula: (Actual hours × Actual rate) – (Standard hours – Standard rate)

(9,700 × ₹ 4.20) – (9,800 × ₹ 4)

₹ 40,740 – 39,200 = ₹ 1,540 (U)

It is also subdivided into two types:

(i) Labour wage (rate) variance

Formula: Actual hours (Actual rate – Standard rate)

= 9,700 (₹ 4.20 – ₹ 4) = ₹ 1,940 (U)

(ii) Labour efficiency (time) usage or quantity variance

Formula: Standard rate (Actual hours taken – Specified standard hours)

---

1. If we multiply by standard quantity, it is called PURE price variance.
2. Some authors call it pure quantity variance. Only for quantity variance, we multiply by actual price. This is done because variance may be calculated either at purchase or at the time of use.

= ₹ 4 (9,800 – 9,700)
= ₹ 400 (F)

Verification = Wage variance – Efficiency variance
= ₹ 1,940 (U) – ₹ 400 (F) = 1,540 (U)

Labour rates variances are not too frequent because rates are usually established by bargaining or fixed by legislation. If they occur, they are due to unusual short-term conditions existing in the industry. Efficiency standards are fixed by engineers and are based on actual performance. It is of limited use in case of work done by machine or where operating times are strongly influenced by factor which cannot be standardized.

Note: Material mix and yield variance and labour mix variance are explained on page 304.

(c) *Factory overhead variances*: The total factory overhead variances may be analysed into three: (i) expenditure or spending (Budget), (ii) efficiency and (iii) capacity, i.e., they relate to costs, and output time respectively. At the outset, it should be noted that this is not the only analysis because there can be so many overhead calculations. Moreover, here we assume a flexible budget for explaining the example that follows. The term "volume" may be used sometimes by some people for capacity. Remember that in case of variable factory overhead there is no capacity or volume variance. For convenience we discuss factory overhead variance under three headings:

(A) Variable factory overhead cost variances
(B) Fixed factory overhead cost variances
(C) Calendar sub-variance

(A) *Variable factory overhead cost variances*: It should not be further subdivided unless there are reasonable grounds. Controllable or variable factory overhead variance is also called flexible budget variance.

Formula: Actual variable overhead cost – Standard variable overhead costs for actual production.

OR

(Standard hours for actual output × Standard overhead rate per hour) – Actual overhead.

₹ 8,730 – ₹ 9,800 = ₹ 1,070 (F)

It is subdivided into two types:

(i) *Expenditure or spending or budget variance*

Formula: Actual variable cost – Budgeted cost allowance.

Or

(Budgeted Variable Actual inputs × Actual prices) – Flexible budget on actual inputs. Budgeted Cost allowance is calculated by multiplying actual level of activity by standard cost per hour/unit i.e., standard variable overhead for actual production.

₹ 8,730 – (₹ 1 × 9,700 hours) = 970 (F)

(ii) *Variable efficiency variance*

Formula: Actual hours – Standard hours allowed for actual production × Variable factory overhead standard rate

Or

= Actual inputs[1] at actual prices – Budgeted inputs allowed for actual output achieved

= 9,700 – 9,800 × ₹ 1 = ₹ 100 (F).

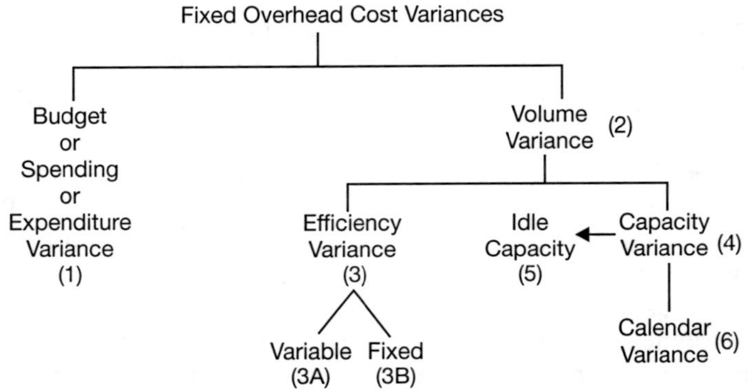

Notes: (a) Some authors use two-way variances. It means No. 1 and No. 2 above. Some authors use three-way variances. It means No. 1, No. 3 and No. 4 above.

(b) Students should be careful in understanding the difference between standard costs and budgeted costs.

Some authors use Four variance method

It means (1) Spending or Expenditure Variance + Variable efficiency variance + Fixed efficiency variance and Idle capacity variance

It represents idle capacity or unused capacity i.e. difference between budged (normal) capacity and actual capacity [1 + 3A + 3B + 5].

Chart

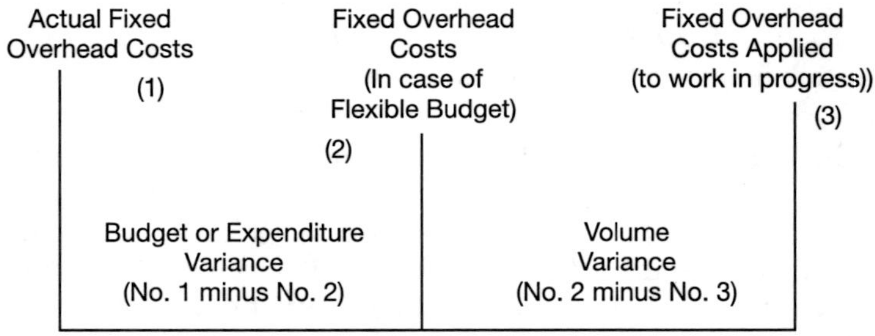

1. Actual hours are an input concept. Standard hours are an output concept.

(B) *Fixed factory overhead cost variances*

Formula: Actual fixed costs – Fixed costs recovered or Total standard cost.

₹ 30,000 – 29,100 = ₹ 900 (U)

(9700 hours × 3 = 29100)

It can be subdivided into two types:

(i) Spending or expenditure/budget or controllable variance

Formula: Actual fixed cost – Budgeted fixed cost

(In the problem, budgeted production is not given, so assume it 9800 units.)

₹ 30,000 – ₹ 29,400 = 600 (U)

(ii) Volume or denominator variance. It relates to fixed expenses only.

Formula: Recovered overhead costs – Budgeted overhead costs

OR

Standard Rate (Actual production – Budgeted production)

₹ 29,100 – 29,400 = ₹ 300 (U)

This variance be further divided into two as follows:

(a) Capacity variance. Capacity variance = (Standard capacity hours – Budgeted hours) × Standard fixed overhead rate

= (10,000 – 9,800) × ₹ 3 = 600 (U)

(b) Fixed efficiency variance.*

Formula: (Actual hours – Standard hours allowed for actual production) × Standard fixed overhead rate

= (9700 – 9800) × ₹ 3 = 300 (F)

Note: The formula for total efficiency variance is: Fixed efficiency variance plus variable efficiency variance

₹ 300 + ₹ 100 = ₹ 400 (F)

If the overhead rate is expressed per unit of output instead of per standard hour, the treatment will be as under:

---

* Denominator activity i.e. budget hours minus applied hours i.e., standard hours allowed.

If standard hours allowed exceed denominator activity, the denominator variance is favourable or *vice versa.* In our example, denominator activity is 10,000 hours. Actual hours are 97,00. Suppose standard hours allowed (for application of overhead) are 9,800. The denominator variance is:

(10,000 – 9,800) × ₹ 3 = ₹ 600 (U). But here we have favoured not the standard hours applied but actual hours. This denominator variance is ₹ 900 (U). The remaining variance of ₹ 300 is fixed overhead efficiency variance. Charles T. Horngren is of the opinion that such refinement is unnecessary in most cases.

Suppose standard output for 40 hours per week = 1,400 units.

Actual hours worked 32 and actual fixed overhead ₹ 1,500, the **variances** will be as follows:

(i) Volume variance = Standard O.H. rate per unit × (Actual production in units or quantity – Budgeted production in units or quantity)

(1,200 – 1,400) × ₹ 1 = ₹ 200 (U)

(ii) Capacity variance = Standard O.H. rate per unit × (Standard quantity – Budgeted quantity)

(1,120 – 1,400) × ₹ 1 = ₹ 280 (U)

(iii) Efficiency variance = standard O.H. rate per unit (standard production – actual production)

(1,120 – 1,200) × ₹ 1 = ₹ 80 (F)

Volume variance = Capacity variance + Efficiency variance

(C) *Calendar subvariance.* The number of days planned in budget may be different from number of days available for production. It is a part of capacity variance.

Suppose actual possible hours = 9,700. Budgeted hours 9,750. O.H. rate ₹ 3.

(9,750 – 9,700) ₹ 3 = 150 (U)

Example 4

Calculate the calendar variance from following data.

Standard data	**Actual Production data**
Standard for the period = 2,400	Hours worked = 2,500
Standard no. of days = 25	Days worked = 27
Standard production = 1,500 units	Fixed O.H. = ₹ 1,300
Standard fixed O.H. = ₹ 1,200	Actual production = 1,600 units

Solution

$$\text{Standard O.H. rate per hour} = \frac{₹\ 1{,}200}{2{,}400} = 0.50 \text{ per hour}$$

$$\text{Standard O.H. rate per unit} = \frac{₹\ 1{,}200}{1{,}500} = 0.80 \text{ per unit}$$

Calender variance:

(a) If standard O.H. rate per unit is taken:

$$\left(\begin{array}{l}\text{Revised budget quantity i.e.}\\ \text{Budgeted quantity on the basis} - \text{Budgeted production}\\ \text{of actual working days}\end{array}\right) \times \text{Standard rate per unit}$$

(1620e[1] – 1,500) × ₹ 0.80 = 120 × 0.80 = ₹ 96 (F)

e[1] in 25 working days the standard production is 500 units. In 27 working days it will be 1620.

(b) If standard O.H. rate per hour is taken:

$$\left(\begin{array}{l}\text{Budgeted hours on the basis} \\ \text{of actual working days}\end{array} - \text{Budgeted Hours}\right) \times \text{Standard rate per hour}$$

(2592e[2] – 2,400) × ₹ 0.5 = 96 (F)

e[2] in 25 working days total standard hours are 2400, then in 27 working days these hours will be 2,592 hours.

While calculating overhead variances, one should prepare a chart of budgeted standard and actual cost. Suppose the actual and budgeted data is as follows:

	Budgeted	**Actual**
Cost	₹ 1,00,000	₹ 1,20,000
Production (units)	50,000	40,000
Hours	2,50,000	30,000
Days	20	21

A budgeted costs cover the entire activity or operation, whereas standard cost shows cost per unit. In case of above data thus standard rate per unit in ₹ 2 (100,000 ÷ 50,000) and standard rates per hour is ₹ 4 (1,00,000 ÷ 25,000) and one unit is produced in half an hour. The standard cost then will be 4000 × ₹ 2 = ₹ 80,000 and standard hours will be 40,000 × 1/2 = 20,000 hours. Since the number of days is 21, therefore revised budgeted units and revised budgeted hours will be calculated

$$\frac{50,000}{20} \times 21 = 52,500 \text{ units}; \frac{50,000}{20} \times 21 \doteq 52,500 \text{ hours.}$$

If revised budgeted production is not given, then budgeted production will be taken.

Following will help to remember the formulae:

Actual (1) Standard (2) Budgeted (3)

(1) Total F.O.H.V. (Costs Amount)	1–2
(2) Total V.O.H.V. (Costs Amount)	1–2
(3) F.O.H. expenditure V. (Costs Amount)	1–3
(4) V.O.H. expenditure (Costs Amount)	1–3
(5) Volume (Production units)	1–3 (Only for F.O.H.)
(6) Capacity (Production units)	2–3 (Only for F.O.H.)
(7) Efficiency (Time Hours)	1–2 (For both V. and F.O.H.)

STANDARD COST AND PREDETERMINED OVERHEAD RATES

The method employed in allocating factory overhead may be based on direct labour hour costs or direct labour hours or machine hours or units of production. The estimated overhead are divided by the basis selected (machine hours, direct labour hours etc.) to find overhead rate.

There are two approaches to deal with overhead rates.

(A) *Normal Absorption Approach*

Example 5

We assume the following data:

Estimated factory overhead ₹ 60,000 P.A. Direct labour cost ₹ 1,00,000 P.A. In one month the direct labour cost was ₹ 8,000.

Then ₹ 4,800 $\left(₹\ \frac{60,000}{1,00,000} \times 8,000\right)$ is overhead and will be applied as follows:

Work-in-process A/c	Dr.	₹ 4,800	
To Factory Overhead A/c			₹ 4,800

Factory Overhead Account

			₹
Indirect materials	—	Applied	4,800
Indirect labour	—		
Other overhead	—		

Work-in-Process

Direct material	—	Balance to finished goods Account
Direct labour	—	
Applied overhead	4,800	

Some accountants transfer applied (absorbed) overhead from work-in-process to factory overhead applied account and from factory overhead applied account to factory overhead account. The result is same.

Disposition of variances: Factory overhead account will show a debit or credit balance; which means overheads are under applied or over applied (under/over absorbed) (called variance).

Monthly balances are carried forward on balance sheet. An under applied is a deferred charge (liability) and over applied is a deferred credit. At the end of the year, the balances may be treated in two ways: (a) Theoretically the year end balance of factory overhead account is apportioned among cost of goods sold account, finished goods inventory account and work-in-process inventory account on some basis. Under-applied will be debited to these accounts and over-applied to be credited. (b) Practically, the full amount be carried to cost of goods sold account.

Suppose under-applied costs are ₹ 300. Then entries in each case will be:

(a) Cost of goods sold A/c (50%) – Dr. ₹ 150
Finished goods inventory A/c (30%) – Dr. ₹ 90
Work-in-process A/c – Dr. (20%) – ₹ 60
To Factory Overhead ₹ 300

(b) Cost of goods sold – Dr. ₹ 300
To Factory Overhead ₹ 300

(B) *Standard Absorption Costing Approach*

If standard costing is used, then there are three methods. Under the first method work-in-process account is debited with actual quantities at actual prices.

The above methods can be shown as follows:

First Method

Work-in-Process

Actual quantity × Actual price (AQ × AP)	Standard quantity × Standard price (SQ × SP)

Second Method

Under this method actual quantity with standard price is debited.

Work-in-Process

AQ × SP	SQ × SP

Third Method

Under this method standard quantity with actual price is debited.

Work-in-Process

SQ × AP	SQ × SP

Under first method all variances are reflected in work-in-process account. Under second method price variances are determined before costs are transferred to work-in-process account. Under third method all variances are determined before the costs are transferred to work-in-process account.

Example 6

Standard cost: Raw material A 2 units @ ₹ 10 per unit.

Raw material B 3 units @ ₹ 6 per unit

Direct labour: 100 hours @ ₹ 3 per hour

Overhead: 100 hours @ standard rate overhead

Standard overhead rate was:

$$\frac{\text{Normal capacity}}{\text{Direct labour hours}} = \frac{₹\ 9{,}000}{10{,}000} = 0.90 \text{ Paise per D.L.H.}$$

Fixed cost	₹ 4,000
Variable cost	₹ 5,000

Actual costs: Raw material B 27 units @ 6.04 per unit
Raw material A : 188 units @ ₹ 9.95 per unit
Direct labour: 8,980 hours @ ₹ 3.06 per hour
Overhead: ₹ 10,920

Units produced: 90, sale price ₹ 600, units sold 50.

			₹	₹
(A)	Work-in-process A/c	Dr.	41,924.36	
	To Raw materials (Actual)			3,525.56
	To Direct labour (Actual)			27,478.80
	To Overheads (Actual)			10,920.00
(B)	Finished goods inventory A/c	Dr.	38,520	
	To Work-in-process A/c			38,520
(C)	Work-in-process (standard cost)	Dr.	10,920	
	To Factory overhead			10,920

(D) For the units sold the cost of goods sold account will be debited by standard cost (50 × ₹ 428) and finished goods will be credited.

Note: The actual cost is transferred to factory overhead account and standard cost is transferred to Work-in-process Account.

Work-in-Process A/c

	₹		₹
Direct Material A (Actual)	1,870.60	Material A (standard)	1,800.00
B (Actual)	1,654.96	Material B (standard)	1,620.00
Direct labour (Actual)	27,478.80	Labour (standard)	27,000.00
Overhead (Actual)	10,920.00	Overhead (standard)	8,100.00
Actual cost	41,924.36	Standard cost (per unit ₹ 428)	38,520.00
Variance = ₹ 3,404.36			

Finished Goods Inventory A/c

	₹		₹
Work-in-process A/c (standard cost)	38,520	Cost of Goods A/c	21,400

Cost of Goods Sold A/c

	₹	
Finished goods Inventory A/c	21,400	

Disposition of variances: Variances from standard costing, when monthly or other interim statements are prepared, are ordinarily carried forward on the balance sheet, with net unfavourable variances being shown as deferred charges and net favourable variances being shown as deferred charges and net favourable variances being shown as deferred credits. Year-end variances are generally closed out. This is done in two ways:

(a) Theoretically, each variance should be closed proportionately to the cost of goods sold account and related inventory accounts. Add if unfavourable and *vice versa.*

(b) Practically, a variance is usually closed in its entirety directly to the P & L account. In this case variances are shown as deducted from gross margin (if unfavourable) and added (if favourable) before setting and administrative, expenses are deducted. See the following. Figures are imaginary

First Method (Variance Prorated)

			₹
(1)	Sales		30,000
(2)	Cost of goods sold (standard cost)	21,400	
	Plus unfavourable variance between cost of goods sold and inventories (say 5/9 of ₹ 3404.36)	1,891.31	23,291.31
(3)	Gross Margin		6,708.69
(4)	*Less* Selling and Admn. Exp.		5,000.00
(5)	Net Income		1,708.69

Second Method

(variance closed directly to P & L A/c)

1.	Sales	30,000
2.	Cost of goods sold (at standard cost)	21,400
	Gross Margin (based on standard cost)	8,600
	Adjustment for variances:	
	Add favourable variances	—
	Less unfavourable variances	3,404.36
3.	Gross Margin Adjusted	5,195.64
	Less Selling and Admn. Exp.	5,000.00
	Net Income	195.64

The difference between net income under two methods is equal to the amount of unfavourable variance adjusted to the cost of goods sold account proportionately i.e. 4/9 × 3404.36. This the amount of goods in inventory that were not sold.

The variances in factory overheads arise because of volume of production attained and expenditure that are made and recorded. The first is called 'volume or capacity variance'. This arises only in case of fixed costs.

It is the difference between actual production and predetermined capacity. The second variance is budged or spending variance that arise from the difference in actual expenditure and budgeted allowance. It arises in variable costs as well as in fixed costs. Some authors doubt the usefulness of volume variance.[1]

In absorption costing system volume variance or (capacity or idle capacity or sometimes called activity or denominator variance) arise. The first step in analyzing fixed overhead is to calculate the under or over-applied overhead. Then under or over-applied is subdivided into budget and volume variance. One author[2] uses the term denominator variance or production volume variance for idle capacity variance. He uses the term volume variance only for the variance between Master (static) budget and flexible budget amounts. Denominator variance does not arise in direct costing method, because no fixed overhead is applied to product. Denominator variance is not useful for planning and control. He uses the term flexible budget variance for budget variance.

MIX AND YIELD VARIANCES

These variances have no meaning unless they are a guide to control action. Mix variance occurs in direct materials and direct labour, while yield variance occur in direct materials only. Mix variance of discrete items should not be calculated. When more than one material is used in the manufacture of a product, the mixture of the inputs to the process may be different from the standard mix, and to the extent that the materials in the mix are priced differently, a direct material mix variance can be calculated. This variance is a part of material usage variance. The difference in actual mix and standard mix may take two forms.

(a) Standard weight of mix and actual weight of mix may be the same, but actual weight of the different materials used may differ.

(b) Standard weight and actual weight may be different.

Formula

(i) Material mix variance = Standard price (Revised standard quantity – Actual quantity)

$$\text{Revised standard quantity} = \frac{\text{Total weight of actual mix}}{\text{Total weight of standard mix}} \times \text{Standard quantity}$$

OR

$$\text{(ii) Material mix variance} = \begin{pmatrix}\text{Actual} \\ \text{quantity of} \\ \text{materials} \\ \text{inputs in} \\ \text{standard} \\ \text{proportions}\end{pmatrix} - \begin{pmatrix}\text{Actual} \\ \text{quantity of} \\ \text{materials} \\ \text{inputs in} \\ \text{actual} \\ \text{proportions}\end{pmatrix} \times \begin{pmatrix}\text{Standard} \\ \text{price per} \\ \text{unit of} \\ \text{material}\end{pmatrix}$$

---

1. *Managerial Accounting*, Dominiak and Louderback, p. 372.
2. *Cost Accounting*, Charles T. Horngren.

Example 7

If the actual weight of different components differ, and total weight is same.

Material	Standard price per unit	Actual units used	Standard quantity units
A	₹ 10	100	96
B	20	20	24
		120	120

Product X is produced by mix of A and B

The actual products produced: 95 units of product X standard wastage = 5%

Materials mix variance:

Revised standard quantity: $A = \frac{120}{120} \times 96 = 96$ units

$$B = \frac{120}{120} \times 24 = 24 \text{ units}$$

Variances:

	₹
A ₹ 10 × (96 – 100) =	40 (U)
B ₹ 20 × (24 – 20) =	80 (F)
	40 (F)

Note: In such a case the material usage variance and mix variance are same.

Example 8

If the actual total weight and standard total weights of materials components also differ, besides the actual and standard weights of mix:

A product X is made of two materials, A and B. Following are details:

	Standard units	Standard price ₹	Actual units
Material A	60	5	80
Material B	40	10	40
	100		120

Materials mix variance:

Revised standard quantity $A = \frac{120}{100} \times 60 = 72$ units

$$B = \frac{120}{100} \times 40 = 48 \text{ units}$$

Mix variance:

	₹
A = ₹ 5 (72 – 80) =	40 (U)
B = ₹ 10 (48 – 40) =	80 (F)
	40 (F)

Yield Variance: Yield variance is calculated on the basis of output. The formula is:

(i) Standard cost per unit (Standard production – Actual production)

OR

(ii) $\begin{pmatrix}\text{Actual}\\\text{quantity of}\\\text{materials}\\\text{inputs in}\\\text{standard}\\\text{proportions}\end{pmatrix} - \begin{pmatrix}\text{Actual material}\\\text{output grossed up}\\\text{to allowance for}\\\text{standard wastage}\\\text{in standard}\\\text{proportions}\end{pmatrix} \times \begin{pmatrix}\text{Standard}\\\text{price per}\\\text{unit}\end{pmatrix}$

This variance is also a part of material usage variance. The yield difference is priced at standard price. Taking Example 6, the yield variance can be found as follows:

		₹
Material	A = ₹ 10 (96 – 80) =	160 (U)
	B = ₹ 20 (24 – 20) =	80 (U)
		240 (U)

Note: Wastage is 5% and 95 units are produced. So actual units used are:

$$95 + \frac{(5 \times 95)}{95} = 100 \text{ units.}$$

The standard proportion of A is 80% and B is 20%. Hence of 100 units A's actual production is 80 units and of B 20 units.

OR

For 120 units used, the standard output should be 114 units of *X* i.e., for 114 units of *X*, standard input is 120 units of A and B.

For 95 units of *X*, standard input should be 100 units of *X*.

Labour Mix Variance

It is a part of labour efficiency variance.

Formula: Labour mix variance =

(i) (Standard cost of actual composition – Standard cost of standard composition)

OR

(ii) (Actual hours × Standard rate of actual mix) – (Actual hours × Standard rate of standard mix)

OR

Standard labour rate (Actual hours of labour employed at standard mix) – (Actual hours of labour employed at an actual mix).

Example 9

The budgeted labour force for product *X* is as follows:

15 skilled labour @ 60 Paisa per hour for 50 hours
10 semi-skilled labour @ 45 Paisa per hour for 30 hours

Actual labour force was as under:

12 skilled labour @ 60 Paisa per hour for 50 hours
15 semi-skilled labour @ 45 Paisa per hour for 30 hour

Standard cost of actual mix:

		₹
12 skilled labour @ 60 Paisa per hour for 50 hours	=	360.00
15 semi-skilled labour @ 45 Paisa per hour for 30 hours	=	202.50
		562.50

Standard cost of standard mix:

		₹
15 skilled labour @ 60 Paisa for 50 hours	=	450.00
10 semi-skilled labour @ 45 Paisa for 30 hours	=	135.00
		585.00

Mix variance = ₹ 562.50 – 585.00 = ₹ 22.50 (F)

Note: Idle time variance, also a part of efficiency variance, can be found by formula:

Idle hours × standard hourly rate.

Example 10

Standard labour hours and production rate of an article are as follows. You are to calculate labour mix and labour sub-efficiency variances.

	Standard			Actual		
	Hours	Rate	Amount	Hours	Rate	Amount
		₹	₹		₹	₹
Skilled worker	5	15	75	4,500	20	90,000
Unskilled worker	8	5	40	10,000	4.50	45,000
Semi-skilled worker	4	7.50	30	4,200	7.50	31,500
			145	18,700		1,66,500

Article Produced 1,000 units.

Solution

LABOUR MIX VARIANCE

(Revised standard mix of actual hours worked – Actual mix) × St. Rate

			₹
Skilled worker	(5,500 – 4,500)	× 15	= 15,000 (F)
Un-skilled worker	(8,800 – 10,000)	× 5	= 6,000 (A)
Semi-skilled worker	(4,400 – 4,200)	× 7.50	= 1,500 (F)
			10,500 (F)

$$\frac{\text{Standard Mix}}{\text{Total Standard Hours}} \times \text{Total actual hours}$$

(1) $\dfrac{5,000}{17,000} \times 18,700 = 5,500$

(2) $\dfrac{8,000}{17,000} \times 18,700 = 8,800$

(3) $\dfrac{4,000}{17,000} \times 18,700 = 4,400$

Note: 1,000 units × 17 total standard hours = 17,000 hours

Labour Sub-efficiency Variance

Formula = (Standard hours for actual production – Revised Standard hours) × S.R.

			₹
Skilled worker	= (5,000 – 5,500)	× 15	= 7,500 (A)
Un-skilled worker	= (8,000 – 8,800)	× 5	= 4,000 (A)
Semi-skilled worker	= (4,000 – 4,400)	× 7.50	= 3,000 (A)
			14,500 (A)

Example 11*

A company uses three materials x, y and z and standard are as follows:

		₹
5 kilo of x @ 0.70	=	3.50
3 kilo of y @ 1.00	=	3.00
2 kilo of z @ 0.80	=	1.60
10 kilo of standard mix input @ 0.81		8.10

But this mix process 9 kilos of finished product at a standard cost of ₹ 8.10 ÷ 9 kilo = ₹ 0.90 per kilo.

* Adapted from C.T. Horngren, *Cost Accounting*.

The actual result were as follows in a month:

		₹
45,000 kilos of x @ ₹ 0.80	=	36,000
33,000 kilos of y @ ₹ 1.05	=	34,650
22,000 kilos of z @ ₹ 0.85	=	18,700
100,000 kilos		89,350

This 100,000 kilos produced 92,070 kilos at standard cost of 0.90 = ₹ 82,863.

Find yield and mix variances.

Yield variances:

To produce 92,070 kilos, materials needed is 1,02,300 kilos

$$\left(92{,}070 \times \frac{10}{9}\right)$$

So the proportion of x, y, z will be:

x = 1,02,300 × 5/10 = 51,150 kilos
y = 1,02,300 × 3/10 = 30,690 kilos
z = 1,02,300 × 2/10 = 20,450 kilos

Apply the formula:

	₹
x = (51,150 – 45,000) × 0.81 =	4,981.50 (F)
y = (30,690 – 33,000) × 0.81 =	1,871.10 (U)
z = (20,000 – 22,000) × 0.81 =	1,247.40 (U)
	1,863.00 (F)

OR

	₹
Output 92,070 kilos @ 0.90 =	82,863
Input 100,000 kilos @ 0.81 =	81,000
	1,863

OR

Actual production exceeds standard yield of input by 2,070 kilos (92,070 – 90,000) and at standard material cost is 0.90. So yield variance is 0.90 × 2,070 = ₹ 1,863.

Mix variance:	₹
x = (51,150 – 45,000) × (0.70 – 0.81) =	676.50 (U)
y = (30,650 – 33,000) × (1.00 – 0.81) =	438.90 (U)
z = (20,460 – 22,000) × (0.80 – 0.81) =	15.40 (F)
	1100.00 (U)

OR

x = (5,000 × 0.70) =	3,500 (F)
y = (3,000 × 1.00) =	3,000 (U)
z = (2,000 × 0.80) =	1,600 (U)
	1,100 (U)

SALES VARIANCES

The variances in revenues of a single product are due to volume and price. In case of multi-product the variances are the result of price, efficiency and sales volume. The sales volume may further be divided into quantity variance and sales mix variance. The variances can be found thus:

Sales price variance = (i) (Actual price – Standard price) × (Actual sales in units)

OR

(ii) Actual sales amount – Actual sales at standard price

Volume variance: (i) Budgeted sales – Standard sales

Budgeted sales = Standard or budgeted sales quantity × Standard selling price

Standard sales = Actual quantity of sales × Standard selling price

OR

(ii) (Flexible budget units – Static budget units) × Budgeted unit contribution margin

OR

(iii) Actual sales at standard prices – Standard sales.

Note: Some authors, like R.S. Kaplan, call volume variance as sales – activity variance and what we name as quantity variance, they call it volume variance. The term cost/price/efficiency variance = Sales price + Variable cost + Fixed cost variances. Sales volume variance can also be found by following formula:

(Actual sales in units – Standard sales in units) × Standard average gross profit per unit.

Example 12

From the following calculate sales price and sales volume variance. The production and sales are same and there is no opening or closing stocks.

	Actual	Static Budget	Flexible budget at various levels		
Units	10,000	12,000	10,000	12,000	14,000
Sales	7,20,000	8,40,000	7,00,000	8,40,000	9,80,000
Variable cost	5,46,600	5,52,000	4,60,000	5,52,000	6,44,000
C/M	1,73,400	2,88,000	2,40,000	2,88,000	3,36,000
Fixed costs	1,72,000	1,76,000	1,76,000	1,76,000	1,76,000
Income	1,400	1,12,000	64,000	1,12,000	1,60,000

Budgeted Amount Per Unit

	₹
Sales	70
Variable cost	46
C/M	24

Solution

Sales price variance = ₹ 7,20,000 – 7,00,000 = ₹ 20,000

OR

= (₹ 72 – ₹ 70) × 10,000 units = ₹ 20,000 (F)

Sales volume variance = (10,000 – 12,000) × ₹ 24 = ₹ 48,000 (U)

Quantity variance

Formula = (i) Budgeted sales – Revised standard sales

$$\text{Revised standard sales} = \frac{\text{Budgeted sales of a product}}{\text{Total budgeted sales}} \times \text{Total actual sales}$$

OR

(ii) (Actual volume in units – Static budget volume in units) × Budgeted average contribution margin per unit.

Mix variance: The accounting literature on variance analysis of multiple products case is too much and is confusing.

Formula: (i) Revised standard sales – Actual sale at standard price

OR

(ii) (Actual volume in units – Static budget volume in units) × Budgeted individual contribution margin per unit – (Budgeted average contribution margin per unit)

OR

(iii) (Actual sales at standard prices – Actual sales at standard costs) – Actual sales at standard average gross profit.

Example 13

From the following data, find sales quantity, sales mix and sales volume variances.

Budgeted

	Product A			Product B			Total		
	Units	Price ₹	Total	Units	Price ₹	Total	Units	Price ₹	Total
Sales	1,000	10	10,000	9,000	2.50	22,500	10,000	3.25	32,500
V.C.	1,000	6	6,000	9,000	2.00	18,000	10,000	2.40	24,000
C/M	1,000	4	4,000	9,000	0.50	4,500	10,000	0.85	8,500

Actual

Product	Units sold ₹	Price per unit ₹	V.C. ₹	C/M
A	2,000	10.25	6	4.25
B	5,000	2.50	2	0.50
	7,000			

Solution

Budgeted average contribution margin per unit = ₹ 0.85

Weighted average contribution margin per unit =

	₹
A 2,000 × 4 =	8,000
B 5,000 × 0.50 =	2,500
7,000 units	10,500

= ₹ 10,500 ÷ 7,000 = ₹ 1.50

Sales quantity variance:

	₹
For A = (2,000 – 1,000) × ₹ 0.85 =	850 (F)
B = (5,000 – 9,000) × ₹ 0.85 =	3,400 (U)
	2,550 (U)

Sales mix variance:

	₹
For A = (2,000 – 1,000) × (₹ 4 – 0.85) =	3,150 (F)
B = (5,000 – 9,000) × (₹ 0.50 – 0.85) =	1,400 (F)
	4,550 (F)

Sales volume variance:

	₹
For A = (2,000 – 1,000) × ₹ 4 =	4,000 (F)
B = (5,000 – 9,000) × ₹ 0.50 =	2,000 (U)
	2,000 (F)

Note: In the quantity variance formula instead of actual volume we can take flexible budget volume figure because both physical volume are the same. The sales mix variance can also be found as follows:

Weighted average contribution – Budgeted average contribution margin × Actual margin units sold i.e. ₹ 1.50 – ₹ 0.85 = ₹ 0.65 × 7,000 units = ₹ 4,550.

Example 14

From the following data, calculate sales price, sales volume, sales quantity and sales volume variances:

Product	Budgeted			Actual		
	Quantity	Price ₹	Total ₹	Quantity	Price ₹	Total ₹
x	1,200 units	20 =	24,000	1,200 units	16	19,200
y	2,000 units	8 =	16,000	1,600 units	10	16,000
	3,200		40,000	2,800		35,200

Solution

Standard sales i.e. Actual quantities × Standard price:

	₹
x = 1,200 units × ₹ 20 =	24,000
y = 1,600 units × ₹ 8 =	12,800
	36,800

Revised standard sales

$$x = \frac{24,000}{40,000} \times 100 = 60\%$$ 60% of 36,800 = ₹ 22,080

$$y = \frac{16,000}{40,000} \times 100 = 40\%$$ 40% of 36,800 = ₹ 14,720

(i) Prices variance

	₹
x = 24,000 – 19,200	4,800 (U)
y = 12,800 – 16,000	3,200 (F)
	1,600 (U)

(ii) Volume variance

x = (24,000 – 24,000)	Nil (U)
y = (16,000 – 12,800)	3,200 (U)
	3,200 (U)

(iii) Quantity variance

x = (24,000 – 22,080)	1,920 (U)
y = (16,000 – 14,720)	1,280 (U)
	3,200 (U)

(iv) Mix variance

x = (22,080 – 24,000)	1,920 (F)
y = (14,720 – 12,800)	1,920 (U)
	Nil

Note: Price + Volume = Values variance = ₹ 4,800 (U) Quantity + Mix = Volume variance = 3,200 + 0 = 3,200.

Example 15

From the following information calculate sales volume variance and sales mix variance:

Standard		Sales		Cost	
Product	Quantity units	Unit price ₹	Total ₹	Unit cost ₹	Total ₹
A	100	50	5,000	25	2,500
B	200	40	8,000	30	6,000
	300		13,000		8,500
Actual					
A	200	49	9,800	26	5,200
B	125	42	5,250	25	3,125
	325		15,050		8,325

Solution

$$\text{Average gross profit} = ₹\ \frac{4,500}{300} = ₹\ 15 \text{ per unit}$$

(i) Sales volume variance

Standard sales units	=	300
Less actual sales units	=	325
Difference in units	=	25
Sales volume variance	=	25 × ₹ 15 = ₹ 375

OR

		₹
Actual sales at average gross profit = 325 × ₹ 15 =		4,875
Standard sales =	₹ 13,000	
Cost of standard sales =	₹ 8,500	4,500
Difference		375

(ii) Sales mix variance:

Actual sales at standard prices	15,000
Actual sales at standard costs	8,750
Difference	6,250
Actual sales at average gross profit	4,875
Favourable mix variance	1,375

Net volume variance = ₹ 1,375 – 375 = ₹ 1,000

Example 16

The details of two products S and R are given below. You are to find the missing information.

	R	S
Sales and Qty. in units:		
Standard	X	400
Actual	500	X
Price per unit in ₹		
Standard	12	15
Actual	15	20

Sales price variance	X	X
Sales volume variance	1200 (F)	X
Sales value variance	X	X

Sales mix variance for both products is ₹ 450 (F)

Solution

PRODUCT R

Sales price variance = (AP – SP) × AQ = (15 – 12) × 500 = ₹ 1,500 (F)

Sales volume variance = Suppose SQ is x then (AQ – SQ) × SP

= 1,200 (F) given then (500 – x) × 12

₹ 1,200 (F) value of x = 400

Sales value variance = Price variance + Volume variance = 1,500 (F) + 1,200 (F) = 2,700 (F)

In order to find out the actual sales quantity of product S, a new table is prepared. Suppose actual quantity of product S = x units

	Standard			Actual		
	Qty.	Rate ₹	Amount	Qty.	Rate ₹	Amount
R	400	12	4,800	500	15	7,500
S	400	15	6,000	x	20	$20x$
	800		10,800	$500 + x$		$7,500 + 20x$

Sales mix variance = R = (SQ – AQ) × SP = $\left\{250+\frac{x}{2}-500\right\}\times 12$

$= 3,000 + 6x - 6,000$

$= (-)\ 3,000 + 6x$

$$S = \left[\left(250\times\frac{x}{2}\right)-x\right]\times 15$$

$= 3,750 + 7.50x - 15x = 3,750 - 7.50x$

for both R & S sales mix variance is given ₹ 450 (F). Thus:

$450 = [-300 + 6x] + [3750 - 7.50x]$

$450 = 750 - 1.50x$

$x = 800$

Sales price variance = (20 – 15) × 800 = 4000 (F)

Sales volume variance = (800 – 400) × 15 = 6000 (F)

Sales value variance = 4,000 + 6,000 = 10,000 (F)

Columnar Approach for Sales and Mix Variances

Example 17

Baboo Ltd. makes and sells two products A and B. The budget for 2015 is as follows:

	A	B	Total
Units	2,000	18,000	20,000
	₹	₹	₹
Selling price (per unit)	10	2.50	
Sales	20,000	45,000	65,000
Standard variable cost	12,000	36,000	48,000
Standard contribution	8,000	9,000	17,000
Actual Results			
Units	6,000	14,000	20,000
Sales	60,000	42,000	1,02,000
Variable cost	37,500	27,250	64,750
Actual contribution	22,500	14,750	37,250

It is assumed the firm does not hold any stocks. Calculate the sales quantity variance and sales mix variance.

Solution

The sales price variance is only in case of B of ₹ 7,000 (F). The variable cost variance of A is ₹ 1,500 (U) and of B ₹ 750 (F). The net volume variance is for A ₹ 16,000 (F) and for B ₹ 2,000 (U). It is found by formula Standard contribution per unit × (Budgeted sales – Actual sales).

In theory it is a good approach if contribution is taken into account for calculating variance. But this can be done if variable costs can be identified. However, the total contribution variance is ₹ 20,250 (F).

Coming to the quantity and mix variances, there are two methods (a) unit basis or margin (b) turnover basis (monetary basis).

Formulae

Unit basis: (i) Quantity variance

(Budgeted sales units – Actual sales units) × Budgeted average weighted contribution per unit.

(ii) Mix variance

(Difference between budgeted and actual units) × Budgeted average contribution unit – Budgeted individual contribution per unit.

The weighted contribution per unit is $= \dfrac{17{,}000}{20{,}000 \text{ units}} =$ ₹ 0.85 per unit.

Turnover basis

The calculations under monetary (turnover) method will be:

(a) *Quantity variance* = (Budgeted turnover – Actual turnover) × Budgeted average weighted contribution per Rupee of turnover. Both the turnover will be at standard price. The average weighted contribution will be

$$₹\ \frac{17,000}{65,000} = ₹\ 0.26$$

(b) *Mix variance*

(Differences between budgeted and actual units and actual turnover) × (Budgeted average contribution per Rupee of turnover – Budget individual contribution per Rupee of turnover). The calculations under two methods are shown below:

First method

(Quantity variance)		(Mix variance)
Product A = (2,000 – 6,000) × 0.55	= 3,400 (F)	(2,000 – 6,000) × (0.85 – 4) ₹ = 12,600 (F)
Product B = (18,000 – 14,000) × 0.85	= 3,400 (U)	(18,000 – 14,000) × (0.55 – 0.50) = 1,400 (F)
	₹ Nil	₹ 14,000 (F)

Second method

Product A = (20,000 – 60,000) × .26	= 10,400 (F)	(20,000 – 60,000) × (0.26 – .40) = 5,600 (F)
Product B = (45,000 – 35,000) × .26	= 2,600 (U)	(45,000 – 35,000) × (0.26 – 0.20) = 600(F)
Total	₹ 7,800 (F)	Total ₹ 6,200 (F)

The actual mix produced a weighted contribution per unit of ₹ 1.55 and weighted contribution per Rupee of ₹ 3.26 at standard prices, as shown below:

	Actual Sales Price		Budgeted Contribution		Total Contribution
	Units	Standard Price ₹	Per unit ₹	Per rupee	₹
Product A	6,000	60,000	4.00	0.40	24,000
Product B	14,000	35,000	0.50	0.20	7,000
	20,000	95,000			31,000

The mix variance in units represent 20,000 units sold at an average weighted unit contribution on ₹ 0.70 higher than the standard i.e. ₹ 14,000 (F) and mix variance in rupees represent ₹ 95,000 of total sales achieved at standard prices at an average weighted contribution per rupee, approximately ₹ 0.066 higher than budget.

If we add quantity and mix variances, it is equal to volume variance. Under both the methods volume variance will be same. The above example can be shown in a columnar approach:

	Actual quantity in Actual mix at actual Prices			Actual quantity in actual mix at Standard prices			Actual quantity in Standard mix at Standard prices			Budgeted quantity in Standard mix at Standard prices		
	Units	Turnover	Contri-bution	Units	Turnover	Contri-bution	Units	Turnover	Contri-bution	Units	Turnover	Contri-bution
Product A	6,000	60,000	24,000	6,000	60,000	24,000	8,000	20,000	8,000	2,000	20,000	8,000
Product B	14,000	42,000	14,000	14,000	35,000	7,000	12,000	45,000	9,000	18,000	45,000	9,000
Total	20,000	102,000	38,000	20,000	95,000	31,000	20,000	65,000	17,000	20,000	65,000	17,000

Sales price variance ₹ 7,000 (F) | Sales mix variance ₹ 14,000 (F) | Quantity variance NIL

OPPORTUNITY COST APPROACH TO VARIANCE

Prof. Joel S. Demski (1966) suggested a different approach to variances. The approach compares what a firm actually accomplishes during some planning period with what it deems of the basis of hind sight it should have accomplish. He says that it is necessary what realistically have been achieved during a period, rather than what possibly out of date budget plan intended be achieved. This implies that proper standard to be used in supplying variance information a standard based on actual conditions, i.e. those that would have been incorporated in the original plan if the actual conditions had been known in advance. This is called export or currently attainable standard. The opportunity cost considers actual results, budgeted results and 'export' optimum results.

Marginal cost variances are calculated in opportunity cost approach, i.e. sales volume variance are valued at contribution foregone. There is no fixed cost volume variance. This is because contribution foregone, in terms of extra expenditure of lost revenue, is nearest equivalent to opportunity cost. Charles T. Horngren suggested that contribution foregone approach to reporting capacity variance would be preferable to traditional absorption costing capacity variance. So he suggests that in management control reports the capacity variance should indicate the opportunity cost for failing to work at production. Horngren makes a distinction between marketing variance and production variance. The same argument can be applied to efficiency variance.

Michael Bromwich (1969) developed some of Demski ideas to suggest a practical approach to opportunity cost variance reporting. He says that the causes of variance might be two:

(a) adverse operational performance.

(b) in accurate planning or faulty standards.

Harvey Thompson (1978) developed the ideas of Bromwich to distinguish between planning variance which are (a) possibly avoidable so as to increase profit (i.e. opportunity cost variance), (b) unavoidable, planning errors which have resulted in a bad budget, but which have not attained realistic profit expectations.

VARIANCE INVESTIGATION

The simplest method of testing variance significance is to apply a percentage rule where any variance outside a fixed percentage from standard is investigated. If a variance is recorded inside the fixed percentage limit, the probability that the process in control is assumed to be 1.0. Similarly, if the variance falls outside the limit, the probability that the process is out of control is assumed to be 1.0. If the variance is within the limit, there is an 80% chance that the process is in control. The management should investigate, as long as the probability that the process is out of control multiplied by the benefits from investigation is greater than the cost of investigation, i.e.

$$(1 - P)\ B > C$$

where P = probability that process is in control. B = benefits resulting from investigation. C = cost of investigation. For example, if a firm operates "materiality test" on variances based on 10% limit either side of the standard with one particular process it is estimated that, if the reported variance is in excess of 10% unfavourable, there is a 15% chance that the process is in control. Elimination of variance would save ₹ 1,200 in future. The cost of investigation would be ₹ 750. The gain from the investigation would be:

(1 – 0.15) (₹ 1,200) – (₹ 750) = ₹ 270.

Another way of looking at the problem is to compare the expected cost of carrying out the investigation and of not carrying out the investigation. In this example the expected cost of not investigation are (0.85) (₹ 1,200) = ₹ 1,020. Therefore, the net advantage is ₹ 270.

Example 18

The probability that the process is out of control is 0.20. The cost of investigation estimated ₹ 4,000 and cost of correction in cost of "out of control" estimated ₹ 3,000. If no correction is made the total cost will be ₹ 23,750. Decide, should the management investigate the variance?

Solution

The expected cost of investigation = (0.80) (₹ 4,000) + (0.20) (₹ 7,000) = ₹ 4,600

The expected cost of non-investigation = (0.20) (₹ 23,750) = ₹ 4,750.

The decision should be to investigate. Here decision could be tested by sensitivity analysis. In that case the critical factor would be the probability estimate that the process in control, which would equate the cost of both alternatives:

P (₹ 4,000) + (1 – P) (7,000) = (1 – P) (₹ 23,750)
4,000 P + 7,000 – 7,000 P = ₹ 23,750 – 23,750 P
₹ 20,750 P = ₹ 16,750
P = 0.807 (approx.)

Only a marginal increase in the probability that the process in control could reverse the decision to investigate.

Variance Investigation Criteria: Statistical Control Charts[1]

Statistical control charts depend on the determination of confidence limits the random deviation around the standard which would be based on the mean value of the observations. The variance (or dispersion) of observations while the process was in control would also need to be known.

1. 'The Accountancy Tuition Centre,' London, *Management Accounting* Level 2, p. 147.

If it is assumed that the mean values of any sample are normally distributed around the true mean, then the average of the sample means will be unbiased estimated of the true means as long as the size of the random samples are large enough. In the setting of standard a number of samples would therefore need to be taken and the average of the sample averages used as a standard. This assumes that the result of our value would be acceptable as a performance target. Actual performance records would then represent additional samples, the result of which would be compared with the mean and variance based on previous observations of the process in control. For example, if a series of observations had been carried out on the time taken to assemble a component, the average of the sample averages could have been calculated at 1 hour per unit. Similarly, on the basis of the original observations of the process in control the variance could have been estimated as 0.04 hour. If a recently taken sample for example monthly performance record, indicated a mean time of 2.3 hours, then the properties of the normal curve can be used to estimate the probability of 0.3 hour deviation or more, on the assumption that the process is in control. If the variance based on the original sample was 0.04, then the standard deviation is 0.4 = 0.2 hour. The reported deviation is, therefore, 1.5 standard deviations higher than the mean. Using normal distribution tables it can be seen that the probability of observing a value 1.5 or more standard deviations from the mean is approximately 0.067. This implies that, for a process in control with a mean of one hour and a standard deviation of 0.2 hour, there is relatively small chance of a 0.3 hour deviation occurring.

Suppose the management sets the warning limit as 2 S.D. and action limit at 2.5 standard deviation. For convenience we take 1.96 and 2.57 then are critical would therefore be:

Warning limits	:	Upper 1 hour + (1.96 × 0.20) = 1.392 hours
		Lower 1 hour – (1.96 × 0.20) = 0.608 hours
Action limits	:	Upper 1 hour + (2.57 × 0.20) = 1.514 hours
		Lower 1 hour – (2.57 × 0.20) = 0.486 hours

This information can be shown in a statistical control chart but for inefficient sample information.

Standard Costing Operating Statements

There are various forms of operating statements, but the best one is that produces a meaningful reconciliation possible between budgeted profit and actual profit within the standard costing system framework.

Example 19

Madhur company operates budgetary control and standard costing system. The following information is available:

(a) Only one product called "Vim" is produced and no stocks are carried.

(b) The budgeted sales and production for a month were 900 units. After a reduction in selling price by ₹ 1 below budget to ₹ 10, and unbudgeted advertising of ₹ 500, sales and production were up by 1/9 the over budget x. The standard cost per unit of product is as follows:

Materials: 4 kilos of A at ₹ 1 per kilo.

Labour: 6 hours of labour @ 0.50 P. per hour. The variable production overheads ₹ 5,400 and fixed production overheads ₹ 16,200. The firm uses absorption costing system and labour hours are used as a basis. The overheads were as per the budget. The budgeted labour hours are 54,000. The actual costs for that month are ₹ 39,000 materials, labour ₹ 34,000, for fixed production overheads ₹ 18,000 and for variable production overheads ₹ 6,000. The administrative overheads were ₹ 2,000 and ₹ 600 above budget. The use of material was 41,000 kilos and labour hours 61,000 in that month.

Calculate profit variance, sales margin variance and total cost variances.

Solution

	Budgeted ₹	Actual ₹
Sales	99,000	1,00,000
Production Costs:		
Material	36,000	39,000
Labour	27,000	34,000
Variable overheads	54,000	6,000
Fixed overhead	16,200	18,000
Total production cost	84,600	97,000
Administration cost	1,400	2,000
Advertising	—	500
Cost of sales	86,000	99,500
Profit	13,000	500

Profit variance = ₹ 500 – ₹ 13,000 = 12,500 (U)

Standard production cost per unit = Material + Labour + Variable overhead + Fixed overhead (4 + 3 + 0.60 + 1.80) = ₹ 9.40.

Cost variance = Budgeted cost – Actual cost

= [(Unit produced × Standard cost per unit) + Admn. cost] – Actual cost

= (10,000 × ₹ 9.40 + 1,400) – 99,500 = ₹ 4,100 (U)

Sales margin variance = Budgeted sales margin – Actual sales margin

= (9,000 × 1.6) – (10,000 × 0.6) = ₹ 8,400 (U)

	₹
Material price variance	2,000 (F)
Material usage variance	1,000 (U)
Material cost variance	1,000 (F)
Labour rate variance	3,500 (U)
Labour efficiency variance	500 (U)
Labour cost variance	4,000 (U)
	₹
Variable overhead expenditure variance	100 (F)
Variable overhead efficiency variance	100 (F)
Fixed overhead expenditure variance	1,800 (U)
Fixed overhead efficiency variance	300 (U)
Fixed overhead capacity variance	2,100 (U)
	₹
Administration cost variance	600 (U)
Advertising cost variance	500 (U)
Sales volume variance	1,600 (F)
Sales price variance	10,000 (U)

The above can be presented in two ways. First is by adding all favourable variance to the Budgeted profit and deducting the unfavourable variances.

		₹
Budgeted Profit		13,000
Less: Unfavourable variances	18,300	
Add: Favourable variances	5,800	12,500
Actual Profit		500

The alternative presentation can be on "input basis". It helps to distinguish between direct and indirect costs.

		Budget	Variances	
			Unfavourable	Favourable
		₹		
Sales		99,000		
Direct costs		68,400		
Contribution		30,600		
Less: Indirect cost		17,600		
Net profit		13,000		
Sales variances:				
Price		(10,000)		
Volume				1,600
Direct cost variances (total)		(5,100)		2,100
Fixed cost variances (total)		(3,200)		2,100
Total variance	12,500	(18,300)		
Actual net profit	500			

1. Details items can be shown such as material price, usage, labour rate/efficiency and variable overhead variances etc.
2. Separate costs like fixed overhead expenditure, efficiency and capacity can be shown.

Reconstruction of standard costs: Reverse process: Sometimes it may be necessary to compute budgets or standards using actual data and variances instead of normal procedure of calculating variances from the actual and the standard. This is merely academic exercise than the practical one.

Example 20

The standard cost information is lost of a firm manufacturing product Z. For the period 2015, the following information is available. Reconstruct the detailed standard cost card:

(a) Fixed production overhead was ₹ 53,000, giving unfavourable expenditure variance.

(b) The standard absorption rate for fixed production overhead was ₹ 1.25 per direct labour hour. A fixed overhead volume variance of ₹ 10,000 (F) is disclosed.

(c) Two raw materials P and Q, are used for the product. Total 1,44,000 kilos materials was bought. There was no usage variance. 94,000 kilos of Q were bought, 2,000 less than budgeted amount. Material price variances arose of 10 Paisa per kilo (unfavourable) for P and 25 Paisa (favourable) for Q, representing 5% and 8.33% respectively of standard price per kilo.

(d) Actual direct labour payroll was ₹ 1,30,050 and 1,200 direct labour hours were lost representing 300 finished units lost to production. Actual average loss of wages per direct labour hour was ₹ 2.55. Total direct labour cost variance is ₹ 10,050 (U).

(e) Total actual productive overhead was ₹ 24,480, variable overhead expenditure variance was ₹ 420 (F). Standard rate per hour for variable overhead is based on direct labour hour.

Solution

	₹
(1) Fixed production overhead	53,000
Less: Unfavourable expenditure variance	3,000
Budgeted overhead	50,000

Representing $\frac{50,000}{1.25}$ = 40,000 direct labour hours.

Labour idle time variance is equivalent to 300 finished units per 1,200 hours i.e. 4 hours per unit.

Therefore, 40,000 hours must represent 10,000 budgeted units. Standard fixed overhead cost is ₹ 5 per unit.

(2) Fixed overhead volume variance is stated to be ₹ 10,000 (F) at ₹ 5 per unit, this represents 2,000 units. Actual production for the year was therefore, 10,000 + 2,000 = 12,000 units.

(3)

Material	*P*	*Q*
Price variance	10 P	25 P
Representing % of standard	5%	8.33%
Therefore, standard price	₹ 2	₹ 3
Quantity purchased (no usage variance)		1,44,000
Standard quantity of *Q* was 94,000 + 2,000 =		96,000
Standard quantity of *P* therefore 1,44,000 – 96,000 =		48,000
Standard mix therefore is in 1 : 2 ratio of *P* & *Q*.		
1,44,000 kilos for 12,000 units = 12 kilos per unit		
or in standard mix	*P*–4 kilos	*Q*–8 kilos

(4)

Direct Labour	₹
Actual cost	1,30,050
Less: Total labour cost variance	10,050
Standard cost	1,20,000
For 12,000 units	10 per unit
Wages	1,30,050

Average ₹ 2.55 i.e. $\frac{1,30,050}{2.55} = 5{,}100$ hours paid

(5)

Variable overhead	₹
Actual cost	24,480
Add: Favourable expenditure variance	420
Standard expenditure	24,900
Production hours	51,000
Less: Idle time	1,200
	49,800

Variable overhead rate per hour is therefore:

$$₹\ \frac{24,900}{49,800} = 50 \text{ P. per hour of } ₹\ 2 \text{ per unit}$$

Standard cost card—Reconstituted

	Per Unit ₹
Direct labour—4 hour @ ₹ 2.50	10
Direct material	
P–4 kilos @ ₹ 2	8
Q–8 kilos @ ₹ 3	24

Variable overhead 4 hours @ 50 P.	2
Fixed overhead (expenditure budget of ₹ 50,000)	5
Total standard cost per unit	49

Example 21

Sharp company makes a product and following standard have been set:

	Standard quantity/Hours	Standard Rate	Std. cost
Direct Materials	3 feet	₹ 5 per foot	₹ 15
Direct Labour	X hours	X per hour	X

During March, 2021, the company purchased materials costing ₹ 55,650, all of which were used in the production of 3,200 units of product. Direct labour hours worked were 4,900 hours. Following variances have been computed:

(a) Material quantity variance ₹ 4,500 (U)
(b) Labour efficiency variance 800 (U)
(c) Total labour variance 1,650 (F)

Find (i) material price variance and actual cost of materials
(ii) standard direct labour rate per hour and standard hours allowed per unit of product.

Solution

(a) SP (AQ – SQ) = Material quantity variance
₹ 5 (AQ – 9,600 feet) = ₹ 4,500 (U)
₹ AQ – ₹ 4,800 = ₹ 4,500 (U)
₹ AQ = ₹ 52,500
AQ = 10,500 feet
₹ 55,650 ÷ 10,500 = ₹ 5.30 per foot.

(b) AQ (AP – SP) = Material price variance
10,500 (₹ 530 – ₹ 5) = ₹ 3,150 (U).

(c) AH (AR – SR) = Labour rate variance
4,900 HRS (₹ 750 – SR) = ₹ 2,450 (F)
₹ 36,750 – 4,500 SR = ₹ 2,450 (F)
4,900 SR = ₹ 39,200
SR = ₹ 8.

(d) SR (AH – SH) = Labour efficiency variance
₹ 8 (4,900 HRS – SH) = ₹ 800 (U)
₹ 8 SH = ₹ 38,400
SH = 4,800 HRS.

Example 22

At a 60,000 direct labour hour level, budgeted variable overhead is ₹ 30,000 and budgeted direct labour is ₹ 4,80,000. The following are the results of a month:

(a)	Variable overhead budget variance	₹ 10,500 (U)
(b)	Variable overhead efficiency variance	9,500 (U)
(c)	Actual direct labour cost incurred	₹ 5,74,000
(d)	Material price variance	₹ 16,000 (F)
(e)	Material efficiency variance	9,000 (U)
(f)	Fixed overhead incurred	₹ 50,000
(g)	Fixed overhead variance	2,000 (U)

The standard cost per kilo of materials is ₹ 1.50. The standard allowance is one kilo of direct material for each unit of finished product. 90,000 units were made. No W-I-P in the beginning or end. The purchase price variance was ₹ 0.10 per kilo. The actual average wage exceeded the standard average rate by ₹ 0.20 per hour.

Calculate: (1) Total kilos of direct materials purchased
(2) Total number of kilos of excess material usage
(3) Total number of actual hours of input
(4) Total number of standard hours allowed for finished units produced.

Solution

1. ₹ 16,000 ÷ ₹ 0.10 = 160,000 kilos
2. ₹ 9,000 ÷ ₹ 1.50 = 6,000 kilos
   ₹ 10,500 – ₹ 9,500 = ₹ 1,000 (U) variable overhead spending variance.
3. Standard rate = ₹ 4,80,000 ÷ 60,000 = ₹ 8.00
   Actual rate = ₹ 8.00 + ₹ 0.20 = ₹ 8.20
   Actual hours = ₹ 5,74,000 ÷ 8.20 = 70,000 HRS
4. Standard rate = ₹ 30,000 ÷ 60,000 = ₹ 0.50 per hour
   Efficiency variance of ₹ 9,500 ÷ 0.50 = 19,000 excess hours
   Actual hours – Excess hours = standard hours allowed
   70,000 – 19,000 = 51,000 hours.

Example 23

S.V. Ltd., manufactures a simple product, the standard mix of which is:

Material	*A*	60% at ₹ 20 per kg.
Material	*B*	40% at ₹ 10 per kg.

Normal loss in production is 20% of input. Due to shortage of Material *A*, the standard mix was changed. Actual results for March, 2010 were:

Material	A	105 kg. at ₹ 20 per kg.
Material	B	95 kg. at ₹ 9 per kg.
Input		200 kg.
Loss		35 kg.
Output		165 kg.

Calculate:

(i) Material Price Variance, (ii) Material Usage Variance, (iii) Material Mix Variance and (iv) Material Yield Variance.

Solution

(i) Material Price Variance:

= Standard price – Actual price) × Actual quantity

A: = (₹ 20 – ₹ 20) × 105

= Nil

B: = (₹ 10 – 9) × 95

= ₹ 95 Fav.

(ii) Material Usage Variance:

= (Standard quantity for actual output – Actual quantity) × Standard price

A: = (123.75 – 105) × ₹ 20

= ₹ 375 Fav.

B: = (82.50 – 95) × ₹ 10

= ₹ 125 Adv.

Total ₹ 250 Fav.

(iii) Material Mix Variance:

= (Standard proportion of actual input – Actual proportion) × Standard price

Standard proportion of actual input:

$$\frac{\text{Standard proportion} \times \text{Total actual input}}{\text{Total standard quantity}}$$

A: $\frac{120 \times 200}{200} = 120$

B: $\frac{80 \times 200}{200} = 80$

A: (120 – 105) × ₹ 20

= ₹ 300 Fav.

B: (80 – 95) × ₹ 10
₹ 150 Adv.
Total ₹ 150 Fav.

(iv) Material Yield Variance:

= (Standard yield – Actual yield) × Standard cost per unit

Actual input	200 kg.
Less: Normal loss @ 20% of input	40
Standard yield	160 kg.

$= (160 - 165) \times \frac{3,200}{160}$

= 5 × 20

= ₹ 100 Fav.

Example 24

From the following data for the month of January, compute the variable overhead variances:

Budgeted production for the month	150 units
Budgeted variable overhead	₹ 3,600
Standard time for one unit	10 hours
Actual production for the month	125 units
Actual hours worked	2,250 hours
Actual variable overhead	₹ 3,500

Solution

Standard overhead for actual production:

For 150 units	overhead is ₹ 3,600
For 125 units	$\frac{3,600 \times 125}{150}$ = ₹ 3,000

Standard hours for actual production:

For 1 unit	10 hours
For 125 units	1,250 hours

Standard rate per hour:

For 1 unit	10 hours
For 150 units	= 1,500 hours
For 1,500 hours	overhead is ₹ 3,600
For 1 hour	= ₹ 2.40

Standard production in actual hours:

For 10 hours	1 unit
For 2250 hours	= 225 units

Variable Overhead Cost variance;

= (Standard overhead for actual production – Actual overhead)

= ₹ 3,000 – ₹ 3,500 = ₹ 500 Adv.

OR

= (Standard hours for actual output × Standard overhead rate per hour) – Actual overhead

= (1,250 × ₹ 2.40) – 3,500

= ₹ 3,000 – ₹ 3,500 = ₹ 500 Adv.

Variable Overhead Expenditure Variance:

= (Standard variable overhead rate per hour – Actual variable overhead rate per hour) × Actual hours

$$= \left(\frac{12}{5} - \frac{3,500}{2,250}\right) \times 2,250$$

= ₹ 1,900 Fav.

OR

= (Actual hours × Standard variable overhead rate per hour) – Actual overhead

$$= \left(2,250 \times \frac{12}{5}\right) - 3,500$$

= 5,400 – 3,500 = ₹ 1,900 Fav.

Variable Overhead Efficiency Variance:

= (Standard hours for actual output – Actual hours) × Standard variable overhead rate per hour

= (1,250 – 2,250) × ₹ 2.40

= ₹ 2,400 Adv.

OR

= (Standard production in actual hours – Actual production) × Standard variable overhead rate per unit

= (225 – 125) × 3,600/150

= ₹ 2,400 Adv.

Example 25

In Department X, the following data are submitted for the week ended 8th January:

Standard output for 40 hours per week		1,400 units
Standard fixed overhead	₹ 1,400	
Actual output		1,200 units
Actual hours worked		32
Actual fixed overhead	₹ 1,500	

Calculate (a) Overhead cost variance, (b) Overhead expenditure variance and (c) Overhead volume variance.

Solution

Standard overhead for actual production:

For 1,400 units of standard output, standard cost is ₹ 1,400

1,200 units of actual output

$$= \frac{1,400 \times 1,200}{1,400} = ₹\,1,200$$

Standard hours for actual production:

For 1,400 units of standard output, standard hours = 40

1,200 units of actual output

$$= \frac{40 \times 1,200}{1,400} = \frac{240}{7} \text{ hours}$$

Standard production in actual hours:

For 40 standard hours, standard cost is ₹ 1,400

For 1 Unit ₹ 1

Standard overhead rate per hour:

For 40 standard hours, standard cost is ₹ 1,400

For 1 hour = ₹ 35

Fixed Overhead Cost variance:

= (Standard overhead for actual output – Actual overhead)

= (₹ 1,200 – ₹ 1,500) = ₹ 300 Adv.

OR

= (Standard hours for actual output × Standard overhead rate per hour) – Actual overhead rate per hour

$$= \left(\frac{240}{7} \times 35\right) - 1,500$$

= ₹ 1,200 – ₹ 1,500 = ₹ 300 Adv.

Fixed Overhead Expenditure or Budget Variance:

= (Budgeted fixed overhead – Actual fixed overhead)

= ₹ 1,400 – ₹ 1,500 = ₹ 100 Adv.

Fixed Overhead Volume Variance:

= (Budgeted production – Actual production) × Standard overhead rate per unit

= (1,400 – ₹ 1,200 = ₹ 200 Adv.)

OR

= (Standard hours for actual output – Budgeted hours) × Standard overhead rate per hour

$$= \left(\frac{240}{7} - 40\right) \times ₹\,35$$

$= \frac{240 - 280}{7} \times 35$

= ₹ 200 Adv.

Fixed Overhead Efficiency Variance:

= (Standard production in actual hours – Actual production) × Standard overhead rate per unit

= (1,120 – 1,200) × ₹ 1

= ₹ 80 Fav.

OR

= (Standard hour for actual output – Actual hours) × Standard overhead rate per hour

$= \left(\frac{240 - 224}{7}\right) \times$ ₹ 35

$= \frac{16}{7} \times 35$

= ₹ 80 Fav.

Fixed Overhead Capacity variance:

= (Standard production in actual hours – Budgeted production) × Standard overhead rate per unit

= (1,120 – 1,400) × ₹ 1 = ₹ 280 Adv.

OR

= (Budgeted hours – Actual hours) × Standard overhead rate per hour

= (40 – 32) × ₹ 35

= ₹ 280 Adv.

Example 26

Shilka Company Ltd. manufactures a product for which the following information is available:

(1) Normal O.H. rate ₹ 3; (2) Actual hours operated 20,000; (3) Actual hours allowed for actual production 21,000; (4) Allowed O.H. for budgeted hours ₹ 70,000; (5) Actual O.H. ₹ 72,000.

You are to calculate: (i) Overhead Budget or Expenditure Variance, (ii) Volume Variance, (iii) Efficiency Variance, (iv) Capacity Variance, (v) Total O.H. Cost Variance.

Solution

(a) Budgeted O.H. ₹ 70,000.

(b) Recovered O.H. = Std. Rate per hour × Std. hours for actual output

= ₹ 3 × 20,000 = ₹ 60,000

(c) Standard O.H. = Std. Rate per hour × Actual hours
= ₹ 3 × 20,000 = ₹ 60,000

(d) Actual O.H. = ₹ 72,000

Notes: The difference between Standard and Budgeted overheads.

(i) O.H. Budget Variance Expenditure = Budget O.H. – Actual O.H.
= ₹ 70,000 – 72,000 = ₹ 2,000 (A)

(ii) O.H. Volume Variance = Recovered O.H. – Budget O.H.
= ₹ 63,000 – ₹ 70,000
= ₹ 7,000 (A)

(iii) O.H. Efficiency Variance = Recovered O.H. – Std. O.H.
= ₹ 63,000 – 60,000 = ₹ 3,000 (F)

(iv) O.H. Capacity Variance = Std. O.H. – Budgeted O.H.
= ₹ 60,000 – ₹ 70,000
= ₹ 10,000 (A)

(v) O.H. Cost Variance = Recovered O.H. – Actual O.H.
= ₹ 63,000 – 72,000 = ₹ 9,000 (A)

Notes: (a) Two variance method means Budget plus volume variance (capacity + efficiency).

(b) Three variance method means Budget plus capacity plus efficiency variances.

Example 27

The Sun Rise Company manufactures one product, Atlas. The standards for one unit of product Atlas are as follows:

	₹
10 1b. of material X at ₹ 1 per 1b.	10
3 hours of direct labour at ₹ 3 per hour	9
Overhead Burden	
Fixed ₹ 2 per direct labour hour	6
Variable ₹ 1 per direct labour hour	3
Total Standard cost for one unit of Atlas	28

Material X is added at the beginning of the manufacturing process. Burden is budgeted on the basis of direct labour hours. The inventory of work-in-process on February 1, consisted of 900 units of Atlas, 66.66% complete with regard to labour and burden. A purchase of 92,000 pounds of material X was made during February at a cost of ₹ 1.05 per pound. During the month, 26,000 hours of direct labour were worked at an average wage of ₹ 3.10 per hour. February plant capacity was 30,000 direct labour hours. Actual fixed burden costs amounted to ₹ 63,000 during February, and actual variable burden costs amounted to ₹ 26,000 during the month.

During February, 8,900 units on 'Atlas' were completed. The inventory of work-in-process as of February 28, consisted of 1,000 units of 'Atlas' 80% complete with regard to labour and burden. 92,000 pounds of X were used.

Required

Compute labour, material and overhead variances for the month of February.

Solution

Computation of Standard Pounds of Material

Ending inventory 1,000 + finished 8,900 – beginning inventory – 9,000 units × 10 lbs.
= 90,000 pounds standard material.

Computation of Standard Hours Worked

Units computed 8,900 + ending inventory
(1,000 × .8) – beginning inventory (900 × 2/3) 600
= 9,100 units × 3 = 27,300 Standard hours.

Labour wage rate variance	= 26,000 (3.10 – 3.00) = ₹ 2,600 (U)
Labour efficiency variance	= ₹ 3.00 – (27,300 – 26,000) = ₹ 3,900 (F)
Total labour cost variance	= {₹ 2,600 (U) + ₹ 3,900 (F)} = ₹ 1,300 (F)
Material price variance	= 92,000 (1.05 – 1,000) = ₹ 4,600 (U)
Material usage variance	= ₹ 1 (92,000 – 90,000) = ₹ 2,000 (U)
Total material cost variance	= {₹ 4,600 (U) + ₹ 2,000 (U)} = ₹ 6,000 (U)
Variable overhead spending variance	= ₹ 1 × 26,000 – ₹ 26,000 = 0
Variable overhead efficiency variance	= ₹ 1 (27,300 – 26,000) = ₹ 1,300 (F)
Fixed overhead efficiency variance	= ₹ 2 (27,300 – 26,000) ₹ 2,600 (F)
Fixed overhead budget variance	= ₹ 63,000 – (₹ 2 × 30,000) = ₹ 3,000 (U)
Fixed idle capacity variance	= ₹ 2 (30,000 – 26,000) = ₹ 8,000 (U).

Example 28

An Engineering Works has a standard costing system for its single output. Their standard was as follows:

Standard direct labour cost per unit: 20 hours at ₹ 1.50 per hour

Standard material cost per unit: 20 1bs. at ₹ 2 per lb.

Standard overhead rate: ₹ 3 per standard labour hour.

The following operating data were taken for November 2005:

In process at 1st November: Nil

Completed during the month: 1,000 units

In process at 30th November: 100 units on which 50% work is completed and for which all materials were issued.

Direct labour cost was ₹ 32,000 at ₹ 1.60 per hour.

21,000 1bs. of material were issued at ₹ 1.90 per lb.

Actual overhead: ₹ 64,000.

You are required to prepare a statement comparing Actual and Standard cost of production for November 2005, analysing variances on materials, labour and overhead costs.

Work-in-process at 30th November may be valued at standard cost.

Solution

Analysis of Variances

(i) Materials Cost Variance = (Actual Cost) – (Standard Cost)
= (21,000 × 1.90) – (22,000 × 2)
= ₹ 39,900 – ₹ 44,000
= ₹ 4,100 (F)

Materials Price Variance
= (Actual Price – Standard Price) × Actual Quantity
= (₹ 1.90 – ₹ 2) × 21,000
= ₹ 2,100 (F)

Materials Usage Variance
= (Actual Quantity – Standard Quantity) × Standard Price
= (21,000 – 22,000) × ₹ 2
= ₹ 2,000 (F)

Note: Materials Price Variance + Materials Usage Variance
= Materials Cost Variance
₹ 2,100 (F) + ₹ 2,000 (F) = ₹ 4,100 (F)

(ii) Labour Cost Variance
= (Actual Labour Cost) – (Standard Labour Cost)
= ₹ 32,000 – (21,000 × ₹ 1.50)
= ₹ 32,000 – ₹ 31,500
= ₹ 500 (U)

Labour Rate Variance

= (Actual Rate – Standard Rate) × Actual Time
= (₹ 1.60 – ₹ 1.50) × 20,000
= ₹ 2,000 (U)

Labour Efficiency Variance

= (Actual Time – Standard Time) × Standard Rate
= (20,000 – 21,000) × ₹ 1.50
= ₹ 1,500 (F)

Note: Rate Variance + Efficiency Variance = Labour Cost Variance
₹ 2,000 (U) + ₹ 1,500 (F) = ₹ 500 (U)

(iii) Overhead Cost Variance

= Actual Overhead – Standard Overhead
= ₹ 64,000 – (21,000 × ₹ 3)
= 64,000 – ₹ 63,000
= ₹ 1,000 (U)

Overhead Expenditure (Budget) Variance

= Actual Variable Overhead – (Standard Rate × Actual hours)
= 64,000 – (₹ 3 × 20,000)
= ₹ 64,000 – ₹ 60,000
= ₹ 4,000 (U)

Overhead Efficiency Variance

= (Actual Time – Standard Time) × Standard Rate
= (20,000 – 21,000) × ₹ 3
= ₹ 3,000 (F).

Note: Expenditure Variance + Efficiency Variance
= Overhead Cost Variance
₹ 4,000 (U) + ₹ 3,000 (F) = ₹ 1,000 (U).

QUESTIONS

1. Identify similarities and differences between budgets and standards. What are the uses of standard costing? Does it increase cost and efforts?
2. Should standard cost be incorporated in financial accounting entries or be shown separately? Explain the meaning of variances. Why overhead variances be treated as periodic costs. In account books should variances be treated as deferred item in balance sheet or income statement or be allocated between cost of goods sold and inventories?
3. Learning curves are relatively easy to estimate, however, their influence tends to be of very marginal value. Evaluate this statement. What is the most significant feature about the learning curves that makes it useful? Can they be used in setting standards for control?

4. Is there any difference between estimated cost and a standard cost. What are the limitations of perfect standard. How tight standards should be set?
5. What are the causes for each type of variances? How variances should be calculated and analysed?
6. Can the term "budgeted performance" and "standard performance" be used interchangeably? Is the title "flexible budget" a misnomer?
7. The standard cost sheet for a product shows the following unit cost for material and labour:

   Material – 2 kilos @ ₹ 1.50 ₹ 3.00

   Direct labour – 1 hr. @ ₹ 5.00 ₹ 5.00

   Standard capacity is 10,000 units per month overhead manufacturing costs are budgeted at standard capacity as follows:

	₹
Fixed	15,000
Variable	20,000
	35,000

   During August, 8,000 units were completed with following costs:

Material purchased	– 20,000 kilos @ ₹ 1.60
Material issued	– 16,200 kilos
Direct labour	– 8,100 hours @ ₹ 5.50

   Overhead manufacturing costs:

	₹
Fixed	15,000
Variable	17,000
	32,000

   Find: (a) standard overhead manufacturing cost per unit (b) material usage and price variance @ overhead costs variances under two variance analysis and under three variance analysis.
8. A company uses standard cost system. It is based on budgeted monthly production of 100 units per day for the usual 22 work days per month. Standard cost per unit for direct labour is 16 hours at ₹ 2.00 per hour. Standard cost for overhead was set as follows:

	₹
Fixed overhead cost per month	35,200
Variable overhead cost for standard	35,200
	70,400
Expected direct labour hour	35,200

Rate per direct labour hour	2
Overhead per unit	32

During the month of September, the plant operated for only 20 days. Costs for the 2,080 units produced were:

	₹
Direct labour 1/*N* 32,860 hours @ ₹ 2.10 =	69,006
Fixed overhead	35,400
Variable overhead	33,860

Calculate the net variance from the standard for direct labour cost and overhead. Analyse the cause using three variance analysis.

9. The following information relates to a given department of Tata's for the fourth quarter of 2015.

   Actual total overhead (fixed plus variable) – ₹ 1,78,500
   Budget formula – ₹ 1,10,000 + ₹ 0.50 per hour
   Total overhead application rate ₹ 1.50 per hour

	₹
Spending variance	8,000 (U)
Volume variance	5,000 (F)

   (A) Determine the actual hours worked in this department during the quarter.
   (B) What were the standard hours allowed for good output in this department during the quarter.
   (C) What overhead variance analysis has been made? Which analysis is better for internal reporting?

10. Bose & William Co. Ltd. produces a product called "BW", a fluid used in the operation of machines. Each month it manufactures and bottles 6,000 litres of this product to fill the needs of customers. The production being in five separate runs of 1,200 litres each. The standard product mix of making 1,200 litres of "BW" is:

    Material A : 700 litres @ ₹ 0.25 per litre
    B : 600 litres @ ₹ 0.20 per litre
    C : 200 litres @ ₹ 0.45 per litre

    June production of 6,000 litres was as follows:

Material	Actually used	Actual price ₹
A	3,400 litres	0.26 per litre
B	2,900 litres	0.22 per litre
C	1,300 litres	0.40 per litre

    Calculate materials price, mix and yield variances for June.

11. The production manager of a company tells you that he exercises management by exception in controlling operations. He examines a performance report like the one shown below and calls for further analysis and investigation if the variance in greater than 10% of total standard cost of more than ₹ 1,000. He is not responsible for any rate or price variances, and is therefore, concerned with efficiency variances.

    During April, the following occurred:

    1. Materials used 4,200 gallons
    2. Direct labour hours 6,100
    3. Production 1,500 units.

    The standard cost of unit of product is as follows:

	₹
Materials (3 gallons @ ₹ 40)	12
Direct labour (4 hours @ ₹ 6)	24
Variable overhead (₹ per DLH)	32
Total standard variable cost	68

    Compute the variances for which the production manager is held responsible. Determine which variances should be investigated according to his criteria.

12. Consider the following situations independently. Data refer to operations for a assume the use of a flexible budget for control of variable and fixed overhead based on standard direct labour hours. Fill in the blanks in each case.

	A ₹	B ₹	C ₹
1. Actual fixed overhead	—	9,900	12,550
2. Actual variable overhead	7,500	12,000	9,500
3. Denominator activity in hours	10,000	–	6,000
4. Standard hrs. allowed for good output	11,000	12,000	–
Flexible budget data:			
5. Fixed factory overhead	5,000	–	–
6. Variable factory overhead (per standard hour)	0.70	–	0.75
7. Budgeted fixed factory overhead	5,000	–	–
8. Budgeted variable factory overhead	–	–	–
9. Total budgeted factory overhead	(a)	(b)	21,000
10. Standard variable overhead applied	–	–	9,000
11. Standard fixed overhead applied	–	–	–
12. Denominator variance	–	600 F	–

	A ₹	B ₹	C ₹
13. Variable overhead spending variance	–	–	100 F
14. Variable overhead efficiency variance	–	–	–
15. Fixed overhead budget variance	300 U	–	–
16. Actual hours of input	12,200	11,700	–

(a) = ₹ 21,200 at 10,000 hours for standard hours allowed.
(b) = ₹ 27,800 at 16,000 hours for output achieved.

13. Bajaj International uses a standard cost system, using flexible budgets. All indirect costs are assigned on the basis of standard D.L.H. The following standard cost per unit was determined on the basis of a projected monthly denominator activity for 2015:

	₹
Direct materials: 3 Lbs @ ₹ 6	18.00
Direct labour: hours @ ₹ 6	12.00
Variable indirect cost: 2 hrs @ ₹ 1.50	3.00
Fixed indirect cost: 2 hrs. @ ₹ 1	2.00
	35.00

The following is the summarized report for February, 2016:

Variance Analysis

	Standard cost Applied ₹	Price or Rate ₹	Efficiency ₹	Denominator
Direct material used	1,62,000	14,000 F	6,000 U	–
Direct labour cost	1,08,000	18,200 U	1,200 U	–
Variable indirect cost	27,000	5,250 U	300 U	–
Fixed indirect costs	18,000	1,500 U	–	4,000 U

Find the following:

1. Number of units produced
2. Actual number of direct labour hours of input
3. Actual wage rate
4. Actual fixed indirect costs
5. Denominator activity (monthly) in units
6. Actual price per pound of direct material
7. Actual pounds of direct material used.

Note: 1,500 U is entire flexible budget variance for fixed indirect costs.

14. A firm uses a predetermined total overhead rate of ₹ 4.00 per unit based on a denominator capacity of 6,00,000 units a year or 50,000 units a month.

    During October, the firm produced 5,200 units and following combined overhead variances are found:

	₹
Overhead budget variance	1,500 U
Overhead denominator variance	5,000 F

    During November, unit production was 4,900 units and the actual overhead incurred was ₹ 2,000 less than October's overhead.

    Find the overhead budget and denominator variances for the month of November.

13

Decision-making—Short Term

DECISION-MAKING

Before a firm can embark on the decision-making process, there is a need for some attempt to be made to specify the objectives of that business. The traditional view was that the objective of a firm is to promote interests of owners of a firm. But nowadays one of the main objectives of a firm is not to maximise profit but to maximise the wealth of the shareholders, i.e. minimisation of corporate cost flows. Organisational objectives were seen to be the result, as Cyert, and March (1963) point out of negotiations and conflicts between various interested coalitions. Short-term decisions can be assumed to have no direct effect on cash flows after the current decision period. The process of decision-making can be stated thus:

(a) Specification of the objectives of the firm.

(b) Search for projects available to the firm and available resources.

(c) Construction of models expressing relationship between fundamental variables and the values reflected in the objectives.

(d) Test the model i.e. its efficiency.

(e) Use the model to identify the best set of projects judged in terms of objectives.

The following expression is a mathematical model for a firm manufacturing two products. $CF = 16a + 25b - 16{,}000$ (assumed figures). In this model, a and b represent the volume (both manufactured and sold) of two products. CF is the cash flow. The parameter 16 and 25 measure the contribution margin of both products (sales – variable costs) and 16,000 are fixed costs. This is only one expression of one possible relationship between cash flows and the fundamental variable of volume.

Variable Costing and Absorption Costing

Variable costing is also called direct costing or marginal costing. According to this concept the cost of products manufactured is considered to be composed only of those manufacturing cost that increase or decrease as the volume of production rises or falls. According to this point of view, the cost of finished goods includes, in addition to direct materials and direct labour, only those factory overhead costs which vary with the rate of production. The remaining factory overhead costs, which are fixed items, do not become part of the costs of finished goods but is considered to be an expense of the period.

On the other hand, under absorption or full or conventional costing, all costs are absorbed into finished goods. This concept is indispensable in the determination of historical cost and taxable income, but is not very useful to management in making decision. "Historical costs in themselves are irrelevant to the decisions, although they may be the best available basis for predicting future costs. Relevant costs for decisions are expected future costs that will differ under alternatives. Historical costs, although helpful in predicting relevant costs, are always irrelevant *per se*."

Variable Costing and Income Statement

The difference between two forms of costing may be illustrated by the following:

Example 1

We assume following data:

Total sales and production	2,000 units
Direct material cost per unit	₹ 1
Direct labour cost per unit	₹ 1
Variable overhead cost per unit	50 paisa
Fixed overhead costs	₹ 4,000
Sales price per unit	₹ 6
Opening stock	40 units
Closing stock	40 units

Solution

Variable costing		₹	Absorption costing		₹
Sales		12,000	Sales		12,000
Less Cost of			Cost of goods produced	9,000	
Goods produced	5,000		*Add* Opening stock	180	
Add Opening stock	100			9,180	
	5,100		*Less* Closing stock	180	
Less Closing stock	100	5,000	Cost of goods sold		9,000
Contribution margin		7,000	Net Profit		3,000
Less Fixed overhead		4,000			
Net Profit		3,000			

The income shown above is same because there is no change in inventory and we assume that sales and production do not change. Note that income shown under absorption casting will be more than as shown by direct costing if production exceeds sales.

The absorption costing method does not differentiate between variable and fixed costs and expenses. The difference between the two amounts of income from operations will be due to the treatment of fixed manufacturing costs under the two methods. Also observe the valuation of ending inventory, one takes the variable cost and the other total cost. In variable costing it is the contribution margin approach that helps in decision-making in the short run than absorption costing approach.

Impact on Profits

The two different methods of costing have the following effect on profits:

1. Where sales and production levels are constant through time profit is the same under two methods.
2. Where production remains constant but sales fluctuate, profit rises or falls with the level of sales, assuming that costs and prices remain constant, but fluctuations in net profits figure are greater with variable costing than with absorption costing.
3. Where sales are constant but production fluctuates, variable costing provides for constant profit, whereas under absorption costing profit fluctuates.
4. Where production exceeds sales, profit is higher under absorption costing than under variable costing for the absorption of fixed overheads into closing stock increases their value thereby reducing the cost of goods sold.
5. Where sales exceeds production, profit is higher under variable costing. The fixed costs which previously were part of stock values are now charged against revenue under absorption costing. Therefore, under absorption costing, the value of fixed costs charged against revenue is greater than that incurred for the period.

The difference between net income (profits) under both methods can be shown as:

$$\begin{pmatrix}\text{Profit}\\\text{computed}\\\text{by}\\\text{absorption}\\\text{costing}\end{pmatrix} - \begin{pmatrix}\text{Profit}\\\text{computed}\\\text{by}\\\text{marginal}\\\text{costing}\end{pmatrix} = \begin{pmatrix}\text{Fixed}\\\text{factory}\\\text{overhead}\\\text{per unit}\end{pmatrix} \times \begin{pmatrix}\text{Change}\\\text{in}\\\text{inventory}\\\text{units}\end{pmatrix}$$

Or

$$\text{Difference in units} = \begin{pmatrix}\text{Difference in}\\\text{sales and}\\\text{production}\end{pmatrix} \times \begin{pmatrix}\text{Predetermined}\\\text{overhead}\\\text{rate}\end{pmatrix}$$

USES OF VARIABLE COSTING

Variable costing focuses attention on the product and its costs. This is in two directions (1) to internal uses, (2) to external uses.

The Internal Uses

(a) *As a managerial aid*: Variable costing is one such concept that is acceptable for published financial statements in which the results of operations and financial conditions are reported. It is useful to management in making decisions relating to cost control, product pricing, production planning and other management functions. The classification of costs as either fixed or variable provides a basis for study of contemplated changes in production levels or proposed actions concerning new markets, plant expansion or special promotional activities. It helps the management to trace changes in sales to their consequence in net income.

(b) *As an aid in cost control*: All costs are controllable by someone within a business enterprise, but they are not controllable at the same level of management. For a specific level of management controllable costs are cost that it controls directly and uncontrollable costs are costs that another level of management controls. For example, plant supervisor can control direct materials cost and not the insurance premium on building variable manufacturing costs are responsive to the control by the operating level of management because the amount of such costs vary with changes in the volume of production. The fixed factory overhead costs are ordinarily the responsibility of a higher level of management.

Variable expense actually incurred can be analyzed by comparing them with allowable budget figure for work performed. Reports prepared on the direct costing basis continuously reminds the management of the original profit objective for the period.

(c) *As a guide to product pricing*: The optimum price is that which gives the maximum excess of total revenue over total cost. This happens at the equilibrium point and a higher or lower price will affect the demand and thus the profits. The cost of producing one unit more or less than the equilibrium is the marginal cost. In multiproduct the management will price each product taking into account the contribution margin of each product.

In the short run an enterprise is committed to the existing capacity of its manufacturing facilities and pricing should be based upon making the best use of such capacity. The fixed costs cannot be avoided and variable expense can be eliminated if there is no production. So, the selling price should not be less than the variable cost. However, in the long run, the information provided by absorption costing is needed. There is no easy solution to pricing problems and the management accountant can prepare various pricing plans for both short run and long run.

(d) *As an aid in production planning*: Production planning also has both short run and long run implications. In the short run, production is limited to existing capacity, and operations decisions must be made promptly before opportunities are lost. An off season order received by seasonal demand industry will not interfere with production schedule. For short run decisions marginal costs are relevant. The order should be accepted if revenues are equal to marginal income.

(e) *As an aid to profit planning*: Direct costing is useful in planning for short periods. It facilitates cost-volume-profit relationship. It also aids the management in planning an evaluating profit resulting from a change in volume, a change in sales mix, make or buy decisions and sales territories. Two aspects of profit planning may be examined:

(i) *Sales mix studies*: It means the relative distribution of sales among various products manufactured. Some products are more profitable than other, the management should concentrate its sales efforts on that product that will provide the maximum total operating income. Two important considerations are there (a) the production facilities required for its manufacture and (b) the amount of marginal income to be derived from its manufacture.

Take an example. Two products are made and the company is operating at full capacity. The amount of production facilities to each product is equal. Product B provides more contribution margin and it is desirable to increase the sales of product B.

	Product A ₹	Product B ₹
Sales price	6.00	8.50
Variable cost	4.50	6.50
Contribution margin	1.50	2.00

Suppose B requires twice the amount of production facilities than A. In that case the production of one unit of product B would require decrease of two units of A. The effect on C/M will be an increase of ₹ 2 for B and decrease of ₹ 3 for A i.e. net decrease of ₹ 1. So, sales mix must be changed in that case that will increase sales of A and not B. Sales mix is based on assumption such as ability to sell one product in place of another and using production facilities for one product than another.

(ii) *Contribution of sales territories*: An income statement presenting contribution margin by sales territories is often useful to management in appraising past performance and in directing future efforts. See the following income statement:

	Territory A ₹	Territory B ₹	Total ₹
Sales	3,15,000	5,02,500	8,17,500
Less Variable costs	1,89,000	2,51,250	4,40,250
Contribution margin	1,26,000	2,51,250	3,77,250
Less Fixed costs			2,42,750
Income from operations			1,34,500

The sales volume, contribution margin and C/M ratio to sales for each territory is useful in comparing sales territories, evaluation performance and directing operations towards more profitable activities. The ratio of C/M to sales is 40% for A and 50% for B territory.

Thus, variable costing helps to know how much to produce, what to produce, whether to produce and at what cost to produce.

External Uses of Variable Costing

The variable costing method simplifies the understanding of both the income statement and the assignment of costs to inventories.

The amount of fixed cost charged to inventory is affected by the quantities produced and by the inventory valuation method used. If production is more than sales, absorption costing will show more profit than direct costing and *vice versa.* But this is true only when LIFO and standard costing methods are used and is not valid if FIFO and average costing method of inventory valuation are used.

There is difference between C/M under direct costing and gross profit under absorption costing. The operating income will be the same under both the methods if there no stocks exists or when no change in the total cost assigned to inventory occurs from the beginning to the end of the period. However, the use of direct costing for financial reporting is not accepted. Companies use it for internal responsibility reporting, profit planning, management control and short-range price setting.

RELEVANT COSTS

Not all costs are relevant in decision-making. The ability to distinguish relevant cost and use of contribution, marginal approach is the foundation for many decisions. The salary of a factory manager is relevant if the factory performance is measured, but is not relevant for measuring the product profitability. A cost is relevant if (a) it is an expected future cost and (b) that it will differ among alternatives. The main question is "What difference does it make?" If the objective of the decision-maker is to maximize long run net income all past (historical) costs are irrelevant to any decision about future. It is the variable costs that are relevant. But do not conclude that all variable costs are relevant and all fixed costs are irrelevant. Historical costs (also called sunk costs, coverable or committed or past costs) are relevant because they provide data that helps to sharpen predictions of future relevant costs. But they are irrelevant for decision about the future. The book value of an old equipment is always irrelevant in replacement decisions. Disposal value is relevant. It is always advisable to use total costs and not unit costs. For a given set of facilities for resource, the key to maximising net income is to obtain the largest possible contribution per unit of constraint (limiting) factor. Incremental or differential costs are also relevant. We shall examine now each situation (a) relevant cost and contribution margin (b) the case of key or limiting factor (c) differential or incremental costs.

Example 2

Mr. A's scooter runs for 3,00,000 miles in a year and operating costs are:

	₹
Gasoline—15,000 gallons @ ₹ 20	30,000
Oil changes and lubrication—@ ₹ 210	2,100
Tyre wear (based on life of 2,00,000 miles, a new tyre set of four costs ₹ 3,000)	4,500
Regular maintenance and repair	5,400
Insurance	5,000
Washing and Servicing	2,000
Licenses	2,000
Garage rent and parking charges	8,000
Depreciation ₹ 88,000 – ₹ 44,000 ÷ 2 year life	22,000
Unit cost = ₹ 81,000 ÷ 3,00,000 miles or 270 Paisa per mile	81,000

Find:

1. If A drives 2,00,000 miles per year or if he drove 4,00,000 miles, find the average cost per mile.
2. How must a friend of A should pay for 2,000 miles?
3. A's wife wants a similar scooter, which will be driven, 4,000 miles per year; but suppose the total mileage of two scooters is still 30,000 miles. What will be the operating cost of the second scooter? Find out average unit cost and what are relevant costs here?
4. What costs are relevant to the question of selling the scooter at the end of one year (market value ₹ 60,000) and using other means of transportation.
5. What are the relevant costs by buying a scooter (if A does not have any) and using other transport?

Solution

Rent and parking fees are regarded as fixed, while tyre were is treated as variable cost.

		2,00,000 miles ₹	4,00,000 miles ₹
1.	Gasoline	20,000	40,000
	Oil changes and lubrication	1,400	2,800
	Tyre wear	3,000	6,000
	Regular maintenance and repair	3,600	7,200
	Total variable cost	28,000	56,000
	Insurance and other fixed cost	39,000	39,000
	Total costs	67,000	95,000
	Cost per mile	3.30 Paisa	23750 Paisa
	Variable cost per mile	1.40 Paisa	140 Paisa

2. The minimum price the friend should pay 140 Paisa × 2,000 = ₹ 280.
3. Note here the variable costs are unaffected by the decision to buy the second and fixed costs are relevant. A situation exception to general rule.

	Scooter II ₹	Scooter I ₹	Total ₹
Miles	40,000	26,000	3,00,000
Fixed costs	39,000	39,000	78,000
Variable costs @ 1.40 Paisa	5,600	36,400	42,000
Total costs	44,600	75,400	1,20,000
Cost per mile	1.1150	29.0	4.00

4. The original cost of ₹ 88,000 is irrelevant here. Can A afford to continue to run a scooter representing an investment of ₹ 60,000, its current realizable value? The cost of continuing the scooter will be the same, except interest on ₹ 16,000 per year (₹ 60,000 – ₹ 44,000 ÷ 1 year).
5. All of the costs would be relevant (plus interest on investment) because all could be avoided by not buying.

Example 3

A company had the following data of standard cost:

	₹
Direct materials per unit	1.30
Direct labour per unit	1.50
Variable overhead per unit	0.20
Fixed overhead (₹ 1,50,000 ÷ 1,50,000 unit)	1.00
Factory cost	4.00

Sales price ₹ 5 per unit. Selling and administrative expenses are fixed at ₹ 65,000 yearly, except sales commission @ 5% of sales. If 1,000 units offer is received from a customer @ ₹ 3.80 per unit, should the company sell at this price?

Solution

	₹	₹
Sales @ ₹ 3.80		3,800
Variable costs: 1,000 units @ ₹ 3	3,000	
Selling commission @ 5%	190	3,190
Contribution margin		610

So the offer should be accepted because short run profit will be lost of ₹ 610. The absorption cost is ₹ 4, but is irrelevant in this decision.

The decision to adopt contribution margin approach as a regular part of an accounting system depends on prospective costs and benefits. It is not a question of absorption cost or variable cost.

Example 4

Relevant Cost of Raw Materials

Relevant cost of raw materials is given by their casual replacement cost (or current resale value or value applied to other product).

A company has been asked to do a special job by a customer who offers ₹ 22,000 for it. The job requirements are as under:

Material	Units required ₹	Units in stock ₹	Book value of units in stock ₹	Realizable value ₹	Replacement cost ₹
A	1,000	0	nil	nil	6
B	1,000	600	2	2.50	5
C	1,000	700	3	2.50	4
D	200	200	4	6	9

Further Information

(1) Material B is used regularly by the company and if stocks are required for this job, they would need by replaced to meet other production demand.

(2) Materials C and D are in stock as a result of over buying and have restricted use. No other use of C is possible, but D could be used as a substitute for 300 units of E, which is costing ₹ 5 per unit. (No stock of it at present).

Decide: Should the job be accepted?

Solution

(1) Material A must be bought in full at the replacement cost of ₹ 6 per unit = ₹ 6,000.

(2) B is used regularly. 600 units further would be needed to replace them. Relevant cost are = 1,000 units × ₹ 5 = ₹ 5,000.

(3) Material C should be bought 300 units more @ ₹ 4 per unit. The existing stock of 700 units would be required. Which means they can be sold at ₹ 2.50 each so relevant cost is (300 × ₹ 4) plus (700 × 2.5) = ₹ 2,950.

(4) Material D since substitute for E is useful, so ₹ 1,500 is opportunity cost i.e. ₹ 5 × 300. Hence total relevant cost from 1 to 4 is = ₹ 15,450, the job should be accepted.

Relevant Cost of Labour and Overhead

Continuing above example, suppose the work requires two types of labour *x* and *y*.

(1) Grade *x* labour is at present has no work. They are paid a normal wage of ₹ 3 per hour. This job will need 500 hours of *x* labour.

(2) Grade *y* labour is busy and men will be diverted from other work. They are earning a contribution to fixed overhead of ₹ 4 per hour. This job need 200 hours of labour *y*, which is @ ₹ 3.50 per hour.

(3) Variable overhead is @ ₹ 1 per active hour.

(4) Fixed overheads are absorbed as 25% of direct labour cost. This job needs a consultant for ₹ 300.

Find relevant costs of labour and overheads.

Solution

	₹
Grade *x* labour – Wages	nil
Variable overhead (500 hours × ₹ 1) =	500
Grade *y* (200 Hours × ₹ 3.50) =	700
Variable overhead (200 × ₹ 1) =	200
Contribution foregone (200 hours @ ₹ 4 per hour) =	800
Constancy	300
Relevant costs	2,500

Here fixed overheads are irrelevant.

Relevant Cost of Machinery

Continuing the above example, this job needs a special machine for three months. Its hire charges are ₹ 75 per month, with a minimum of ₹ 300. The other machines, is used for this job, will loose ₹ 200 in their eventual sales value after the contract.

Relevant costs

	₹
Incremental cost of hire	300
User cost of other machines	200
	500

Total relevant cost of material, labour and machine = ₹ 18,450. The job should be undertaken.

KEY OR LIMITING OF CRITICAL OR CONSTRAINT FACTOR SCARE RESOURCE AND DECISION-MAKING

Relevant costs may be expressed sometimes as opportunity cost, which may be internal or external opportunity cost. Opportunity cost is the benefit foregone by choosing one opportunity instead of next best alternative. Internal opportunity costs arise where there are mutually exclusive opportunities to choose between, but they are more significantly involved in decision effecting scarce resources i.e. constraint on production and sales activity. It is the maximum contribution that is foregone by using limited resources for a particular purpose. An external opportunity cost is the difference between total net cash out flows if the opportunity is accepted and those if it is rejected. When there is a budget limiting factor other than sales demand, profits will be maximised by producing those items which earn the greatest contribution per unit of limiting factor. Opportunity costs are not recorded in accounting system because they are related to actions not being taken.

By scarce resource or factor here we mean the circumstances due to which there is restriction on the availability of one or more resources. The firm then is unable to accept all opportunities where revenues exceed external opportunity cost. As a result, it may be necessary to impute additional costs to the use of these resources and these additional costs are called internal opportunity costs. There may be one resource constraint and many resource constraint. Here we take the first situation. The problem of many resource constraint will be dealt within the chapter of 'Linear programming'. This mathematical model deals with that.

If only one resource is in limited supply, the firm should produce the product with the highest contribution of the limiting resource. By using all available supply of resource in the production of this product, the firm will maximise the total contribution—assuming all the units produced can be sold.

Another expression for internal opportunity cost is dual price or shadow price. It is the amount by which contribution could be increased if one additional units of the resource was made available. Suppose labour hours is scarce factor, then any other resources used in production will have dual prices equal to zero. Extra units of these other resources could not be applied to increase contribution, since production is limited by the available labour hours. In general, if the available supply of resources is not fully utilized in the optimal production plan, the dual price of the resource is zero. Dual price can be useful only when optimal plan has been established.

Example 5

A firm has only 2,000 hours of labour time available, the budgeted sales demand and unit production costs are as follows. The cost of labour is ₹ 3 per hour.

	Product		
Sales	*A* 2,000 units ₹	*B* 1,000 units ₹	*C* 666 units ₹
Unit variable cost:			
Materials	22.50	12	9
Labour	3.00	6	9
	25.50	18	18
Selling price	30.00	30	30
Contribution	4.50	12	12

Which product be given priority?

Solution

It is product B that should be given priority product:

	A ₹	*B* ₹	*C* ₹
Selling price	30	30	30
External opportunity cost	25.50	18	18
Internal opportunity cost	4.50	9	13.50
(₹ 4.50 per hour)	30.00	27	31.50
Surplus (deficit)	nil	3	1.50

A earn ₹ 4.50 per hour, *B* ₹ 6 per hour and *C* ₹ 4 per hour. *B* requires 2,000 hours to make, so *A* and *C* cannot be made in that case. Contribution of *A*, net profitable product must be foregone in order to make *B*. Therefore, ₹ 4.50 per hour is internal opportunity cost. *A* takes one hour, *B* two hours and *C* three hours.

Had we known the internal opportunity cost in advance of decision, we could have determined the optimal production plan without the ranking by charging each product with the full opportunity cost of labour. We would then select the products whose selling prices exceeded their full opportunity costs. A revised cost structure would be shown as below:

	Product		
Labour Hours	*A* 1 Hour ₹	*B* 2 Hours ₹	*C* 3 Hours ₹
Labour @ ₹ 7.50 (opportunity cost)	7.50	15	22.50
Other variable costs	22.50	12	9.00
	30	27	31.50
Selling price	30	30	30.00
Surplus (deficit)	nil	3	1.50

The calculations show the product *B* shows surplus, and therefore, should be produced up to its demanded limits i.e. 1,000 units. *C* shows deficit and should not be produced. *A* shows neither surplus nor deficit, therefore, should be produced in so far as labour hours are available after producing *B*.

These results tell the general rule that where resources are valued at full opportunity cost (a) the product of which we wish to make as we can sell have surpluses, (b) there is a marginal product that will neither show surplus not deficit, (c) products excluded from the optimal plan have deficits.

Example 6

A Company gets an offer for ₹ 21,000 to make a machine. The machine involves an extra cost of materials ₹ 3,000.

Labour 2,000 hours @ ₹ 4 per hour

Variable overhead ₹ 2 per hour

Fixed overhead ₹ 4 per hour

Labour is in limited supply. If the offer is accepted, it will require some labour to be diverted that earns a contribution of ₹ 5 per hour towards fixed overheads and profit. Should the offer be accepted?

Solution

External opportunity cost:	₹	
Materials	3,000	
Labour	8,000	
Variable overhead	4,000	
Internal opportunity	15,000	
Cost (contribution foregone)	10,000	
Total cost	25,000	– 21,000 = Loss 4,000

The offer should not be accepted.

Suppose the contribution of ₹ 5 break up is as under:

	₹
Revenue per hour	12
Material per hour = 1	
Labour per hour = 4	
Variable overhead per hour = 2	7
	5

Suppose further in 2,000 hours the labour that is directed to this job earns ₹ 10,000, then normal work will contribute ₹ 4,000 more than this offer.

(a) Contribution of the job = ₹ 21,000 – Variable cost ₹ 15,000
= ₹ 6,000

(b) Normal earning of labour ₹ 10,000 and contribution difference (b – a) is ₹ 4,000.

Example 7

A firm manufactures three spare part *x, y* and *z* and same machine is used for them. The variable cost of each is as under:

	Machine hours	Variable cost ₹
1 unit of *x*	3	20
1 unit of *y*	2	36
1 unit of *z*	4	24
	Assembling per unit	20
		100

Next year 4,000 each spare part will be produced. But 24,000 hours of machine time will be available next year. A sub-contractor agrees to supply *x* at ₹ 29, *y* at ₹ 40 and *z* at ₹ 34. Advise the priority of making the spare parts or to buy.

Here the assembling cost in irrelevant.

(a)	*x* ₹	*y* ₹	*z* ₹
Variable cost of making	20	36	24
Variable cost of buying	29	40	34
Extra cost of buying	9	4	10
Machine hour saved by buying	3 hours	2 hours	4 hours
Saving of extra variable cost of buying per hour	3	2	2.50

(b)	Hours per unit	Total hours needed
x	3	12,000
y	2	8,000
z	4	16,000
		36,000
	Hours available	24,000
	Capacity short fall	12,000

There are enough machine hours to make all 4,000 units of *x* and 3,000 units of *z*.

(c) Production of 1,000 units of *z* and 4,000 units of *y* can be given to sub-contractor. This is the cheapest production policy available.

Make	Machine hours	No. of units	Unit ₹	Total V.C. ₹
x	12,000	4,000	20	80,000
z	12,000	3,000	24	72,000
	24,000			1,52,000
Buy:	Hours saved			
z	4,000	1,000	34	34,000
y	8,000	4,000	40	1,60,000
	12,000	Total V.C. of components		3,46,000
		Assembling cost		80,000
		Total variable cost		4,26,000

Example 8

A company has two products, each of which is processed in the same two production departments:

Product	Contribution per unit ₹	Machine hours required per unit Deptt. *x*	Deptt. *y*	Units
A	10	4	2	1,000
B	6	1	3	2,500

Capacity is 4,500 hours in department *x* and 7,500 in department *y*. How many units of *A* and *B* be produced to give maximum profit?

Solution

Product *A* is more profitable of the two, one probability would be to produce, 1,000 units of *A* and 500 units of *B*. But in the case *y*'s capacity will remain idle. Alternatively if 2,500 units of *B* are produced, Deptt. *x* will have idle capacity. The opportunity cost will help to find solution. One way is to use the substitution ratio in department *y*. Cutting one unit of *B* will release capacity for 1½ unit for *A*. It means net increase in use of department *x* will be five hours ($A\ 1\frac{1}{2} \times 4 - B\ 1 \times 1$). *x* has an idle capacity of 2,000 hours if *B*'s all units are produced and none of *A*. This means if *B*'s 400 units are released, which is equal to 600 units of *A*, then capacity of both departments can be utilized fully. So produce *A* 600 units. *B* 2,100 units.

This problem can be solved by algebraic equation.

For *A*: $4\ A + 1\ B = 4500$

For *B*: $2\ A + 5\ B = 7500$

Solving it we get the same results. For this kind of problem linear programming is best solution, when algebraic solution is not available.

DIFFERENTIAL OR INCREMENTAL COST OR MARGINAL COST

A differential or incremental (or sometimes decremental) cost is the difference in cost of alternative choices i.e. the difference between incremental (or decremental) costs of each option. They are future costs. The two terms are interchangeable. These costs can be used for short-term decisions such as:

(1) Accepting or refusing a certain order of reducing price for a special order in the market.
(2) Make or buy the product (Lease or sell).
(3) Process further or sell the materials.
(4) Product combinations (Sales mix).
(5) Stop or curtail production/department.
(6) Adding or deleting a product.
(7) Selecting new territories.

Some of these may be explained with examples.

(1) Accepting or Refusing a Special Order

In the short run a firm can increase total profits by accepting orders at prices which exceed the differential costs. These costs of the order usually are composed of only variable costs. Using a short run decision, rule of accepting orders which cover variable costs and contribute something to fixed overhead is called "contribution pricing".

Example 9

P & Sons build boats. The price quoted of a boat is as follows:

	₹
Direct materials	5,000
Direct labour	8,000
Overhead	2,000
	15,000
Plus 20% mark up	3,000
	18,000

The overhead cost is determined by estimating total overheads for the year and allocating them at 25% of direct labour. Total overheads were estimated at ₹ 1,50,000 of which ₹ 90,000 is fixed and the remainder is variable in direct proportion to direct labour. A customer offers ₹ 15,000. Should this offer be accepted?

Solution

	₹	₹
Differential revenue		15,000
Less: Differential costs:		
Direct Material	5,000	
Direct Labour[1]	8,000	
Variable overhead	800	
		13,800
Differential net margin		1,200

The offer should be accepted because any selling price offered or reduced equal to differential costs of ₹ 13,800 would leave net income unchanged.

The contribution margin approach shows short run and long run effects of pricing decision. In actual words price discrimination is possible if markets can be separated and the different markets have different price elasticities. In this example, incremental costs were manufacturing costs and in other these costs may be variable selling, general or administrative. Both quantifiable and non-quantifiable factors generally exist when deciding about such an order. The order will be rejected if the firm is operating at full capacity or could not be met within required time.

(2) Make or Buy the Product

Many manufactured products are the results of assembling several parts into a unit of final product. Most parts can be either bought from an outside or made by the assembling firm using its own facilities. Several qualitative factors are to be considered e.g. reliability of suppliers and quality of goods supplied with own made goods. The quantitative factors to be considered are incremental costs and opportunity costs of the alternatives. The committee of Management Accounting of N.A.A. of U.S.A. takes the position that make or buy evaluations should include indirect costs assignable on a long-term basis except where future costs of a short run decision can be predicted with certainty. Uncertainty suggests the practice of recognizing full costs including allocation of fixed costs.

1. ₹ 1,50,000 is 25% of labour, so direct labour is ₹ 6,00,000 and variable overhead rate is $\frac{60,000 \text{ (v. overhead)}}{6,00,000 \text{ (D.L.)}}$ = 10% of direct labour cost.

Example 10

Lakeme Corporation is selling face cream. They introduce Afgan Snow, a new product, to be sold in boxes of 24 tubes for ₹ 8 per box. Because of available capacity no additional fixed charge will be incurred to produce the product. However, a ₹ 1,00,000 fixed charge will be absorbed by the product to allocate a fair share of the Corporation's present fixed costs to the new product. Using the estimated sales and production of 1,00,000 boxes, the following costs were developed:

Direct material	2.00 per box
Direct labour	3.00 per box
Total overhead	1.50 per box
Total	6.50 per box

A cosmetic manufacturer offers to supply empty tubes @ ₹ 0.90 per 24 tubes. If this offer is accepted, the Corporation's direct labour and variable overhead costs would be reduced by 10% and direct material costs by 20%.

Required:

(1) Should the Corporation make or buy the tubes?

(2) What would be the maximum purchase price acceptable to the Corporation for the tubes?

(3) Instead of sales of 1,00,000 boxes, revised estimates show sales volume at 1,25,000 boxes. For this new sales volume additional equipment, at an annual rent of ₹ 10,000 must be acquired to manufacture the tubes. This incremental cost would be the only additional fixed cost required even if the sales increased to future goal of 3,00,000 tubes. Should the firm buy or make the tubes?

(4) The firm has the option of making and buying at the same time. What would your answer be to No. 3 if this alternative was considered?

Solution

	Total cost to make ₹	Total cost to buy ₹	Total savings cost of buying ₹	Unit savings (cost) of buying ₹
Direct materials	2,00,000	1,80,000	20,000	0.20
Direct labour	3,00,000	2,40,000	60,000	0.60
Total overhead	1,50,000	1,45,000	5,000	0.05
Purchased parts	0	90,000	(90,000)	(0.90)
Total	6,50,000	6,55,000	(5,000)	(.05)

(1) The differential savings in production costs from buying are only ₹ 0.85 per box (0.20 + 0.60 + 0.05) while the costs of buying are ₹ 0.90 per box. Therefore, the cost to make results in saving of ₹ 0.05 per box for ₹ 5,000 total cost savings.

(2) The firm would not pay more than ₹ 0.85 per box.

(3) Cost of making:

	₹
Variable cost (0.85 × 1,25,000) =	1,06,250
Fixed cost	10,000
Total cost to make	1,16,250
Less: Cost of buying (0.90 × 1,25,000)	1,12,500
Differential savings of buying the firm should buy	3,750

(4) The firm should make 1,00,000 boxes ₹ 0.85 per unit and additional units should buy @ ₹ 0.90 per unit.

	₹
1,00,000 units @ ₹ 0.85 =	85,000
25,000 units @ ₹ 0.90 =	22,500
	1,07,500

This is cheaper than either alternative in No. 3.

(3) Process Further or Sell the Materials—Joint Products

When a manufacturing process invariably produces two or more products, the output is called joint product and the process is called joint process. The refining of crude petroleum is an example. Some of these joint products are valuable; some have little value. Some can be sold as they emerge from the joint process i.e. split off point or processed further. The decision to sell as such or process further cannot be based on total cost or even total variable cost. The cost prior to split off are irrelevant. All costs before split off are *sunk costs*. The costs of joint process or processes are relevant only in determining whether process should be carried at all.

Example 11

From a particular joint process a company produces three products *x*, *y* and *z*. Each product can be sold at the split off point or processed further. Production costs of further processing are variable and requires no additional facilities. The total joint production costs are ₹ 60,000 sales values and costs for a year were as follows:

Product	Unit produced ₹	Sales value at split off ₹	If Processed Further: Total sales value ₹	If Processed Further: Added costs ₹
x	6,000	25,000	42,000	9,000
y	4,000	41,000	45,000	7,000
z	2,000	24,000	32,000	8,000

Joint costs are allocated to the products to the relative physical volume of output.

Required:

(a) For units of *z*, the unit production cost must be relevant to sell or process further decision is ₹ 5, ₹ 12, ₹ 4 or ₹ 9.

(b) To maximize profits which product should be processed further (1) *x* only or (2) *x, y* and *z* or (3) *y* and *z* only (4) or *z* only.

Solution

(1) In the absence of facts about relative physical volume, it is not possible to know allocation of joint costs. However, allocation of joint costs are not relevant for decision because they are not sunk costs for this purpose. The relevant units costs for a sell or process further decision are:

Product ₹	Added cost ₹	Unit produced ₹	Differential unit cost
x	9,000	6,000	1.50
y	7,000	4,000	1.75
z	8,000	2,000	4.00 (Answer)

(2) Comparing differential revenue and differential cost, only *x* should be processed further:

	X ₹	*Y* ₹	*Z* ₹
Differential revenue from further processing	17,000	4,000	8,000
Differential cost from further processing	9,000	7,000	8,000
Differential profit from further processing	8,000	(3,000)	0

The joint processing costs are irrelevant.

(4) Decision to Continue or Discontinue a Department/Segment/Product

The most recent income statement of different departments of a firm is given below. Further income statements are expected to show about the same results.

	Deptt. P ₹	Deptt. M ₹	Deptt. G ₹	Total ₹
Sales	10,000	20,000	20,000	50,000
Variable cost	6,000	8,000	12,000	26,000
Contribution margin	4,000	12,000	8,000	24,000
Fixed costs:				
Separable, discretionary	3,500	6,000	2,000	11,500
Joint, allocated on the basis of sales amount	2,000	4,000	4,000	10,000
Net Income (loss)	(1,500)	2,000	2,000	2,500

One may say that department *P* should be dropped because it is on loss. The correct answer can be found by preparing an income statement assuming that this department is closed.

	Deptt. *M* ₹	Deptt. *G* ₹	Total ₹
Sales	20,000	20,000	40,000
Variable costs	8,000	12,000	20,000
Contribution	12,000	8,000	20,000
Less Fixed costs:			
Separable	6,000	2,000	8,000
Joint	5,000	5,000	10,000
Net income	1,000	1,000	2,000

The total net income is ₹ 500 less than before because of reallocation of joint costs. So the department should be retained. This reduction in net income is often called incremental loss.

Suppose if the space of department *P* can be rented to somebody on ₹ 600 per month. The rental income ₹ 600 foregone, if the firm continues with department *P*, is the opportunity cost of department *P*, *if the opportunity cost exceeds incremental profit, the opportunity should be taken; if not the firm should continue on its present course of action.*

The relevance of the various combinations of fixed costs to short run decisions affecting segments/department/product of business is shown below:

	Separable	*Joint*
Discretionary	Relevant	Not relevant
Committed	Not relevant	Not relevant

Only variable and separable discretionary fixed costs are relevant to short-term decisions. Committed costs are those that cannot be avoided in the short run, whereas discretionary costs can be incurred or not, depending upon managerial decision.

Suppose instead of renting a new department can be started. Its sales are estimated ₹ 15,000, variable costs ₹ 9,000 and separable fixed costs ₹ 3,000. The situation will appear like this:

	Deptt. *M* ₹	Deptt. *G* ₹	Deptt. New ₹	Total ₹
Sales	20,000	20,000	15,000	55,000
Variable costs	8,000	12,000	9,000	29,000
Contribution margin	12,000	8,000	6,000	26,000
Separable fixed costs	6,000	2,000	3,000	11,000
Incremental profit	6,000	6,000	3,000	15,000
Joint costs	—	—	—	10,000
Net Income	—	—	—	5,000

Note: Joint costs can be allocated and shown separately for each department.

The incremental profit of new department of ₹ 3,000 is opportunity cost of continuing department *P*.

Following two terms may be explained that are often used:

(1) *Imputed cost*: It is a type of *opportunity cost*. They are hypothetical costs representing cost or value of a resource measured by its use value e.g. interest on invested capital, salaries to the owner. They do not involve cash outlay and are not considered in company's regular cost or profit calculations. For decision-making inclusion of such costs is important.

(2) *Out of pocket cost*: They are differential costs. It is a short-term concept. They are current near future outlays for the decision at hand e.g. the acceptance of an order so that otherwise idle capacities may be used would entail a compilation of out of pocket costs that would be avoided by not accepting the order. They are of two types (a) escapable (b) non-escapable. Depreciation is not out of pocket costs.

Example 12

A company now, operating below 50% of its capacity, expects the sales to drop below the present level of 5,000 units per month. The selling price is ₹ 3, variable cost ₹ 2 per unit. Fixed costs ₹ 5,000. If the sales drop there will be a loss. The management decides to shut down the factory. The shut down costs are ₹ 2,000 per month. What is your decision?

Solution

Marginal contribution = ₹ 3 – ₹ 2 = ₹ 1 per unit. Fixed cost ₹ 5,000 (if operates) minus ₹ 2,000 (if shut down). Additional cost of operation is ₹ 3,000.

So, $\frac{\text{Cost ₹ 3,000}}{\text{₹ 1}}$ = 3,000 units is the minimum sales below which the factory should be shut down.

Apply formula (SALES – V.C.) – F.C. and one can find loss or profit at different levels of production e.g. at 1,000 units, 2,000 units and 5,000 units.

(5) Pricing Decision

It can be explained by an example:

Example 13

A firm has a standard cost of ₹ 5 per unit, break up as follows:

	₹
Variable cost:	0.50
Material	2.00
Labour	0.50
Indirect manufacturing cost	3.00
Fixed cost (based on 1,000 units standard cost ₹ 2,000)	2.00
Total	5.00

The firm will produced and sell 900 units during coming period at 90% capacity at a price of ₹ 6.25. A customer will supply 100 units of material and agrees to buy at ₹ 4.50 per unit, should this price be accepted?

Solution

	₹	₹
Income from sub-contract 100 units @ ₹ 4.50		450
Less Differential costs:		
(a) Labour 100 units @ ₹ 2	200	
(b) Variable indirect expenses @ 0.50	50	250
Excess of revenue		200

₹ 2,000 will be incurred whether to produce 900 or 1,000 units.

	₹	Not accepted 900 units ₹		Accepted 1,000 units ₹
Sales		5,625		5,625 + 450
Material	450		450	
Labour	18,000		2,000	
Variable cost	450		500	
Fixed cost	2,000	4,700	2,000	4,950
		925		1,125

It should be accepted.

PRICING AND OUTPUT DECISIONS

At a starting point in many decisions, it is necessary to see the demand of the product and potential prices. Under conditions of uncertainty the demand curve slopes down if price increases and *vice versa*. The marginal revenue is a change in the total revenue associated with a change in the volume of sales. Marginal revenue can be negative. However, in some cases it could be assumed that over a small range of sales quantity change, prices do not need to be changed and so the marginal revenue is:

Change is sales volume × price. The principle of price elasticity of demand is a link between the response of changes in volume of sales to changes in prices. It is expressed as a positive number. Formula:

$$\frac{\text{Percentage change in quantity of } x \text{ demanded}}{\text{Percentage change in the price of } x}$$

In price this may be used, but is decision-making one can always says "a small increase in price will affect sales volume minimally". The majority of decisions in business affect the costs, revenues and operating volume. One must know the relationship of these elements.

The cost are classified into fixed and variable costs. Their relationship has already been discussed in Chapter 7.

In pricing and output decisions information about demand and cost is combined.

A simple way to present is the profit volume chart (*see* Chapter 4). It is necessary to concentrate on a small range of activities and to produce different versions of this chart. This may be because of lack of information about whole range of price—volume data or cost data production capacity constraints.

In determining the price of a firm's products an analysis of the market structure is also important like cost analysis. Market structure helps together information about the size of the total product market i.e. market sales at various prices, the number of firms selling that product, barriers to enter market, if any, and any substitute available (market independence). On the basis of these four characteristics, the scale of a firm may be monopoly or oligopoly or competition.

In pricing and output decisions the firm has to see whether it is a price setter or price taken. The firm has to take into account long-term considerations into account for setting price. Cost plus pricing describes an approach to pricing which relies for its information on data provided within the firm about forecast product costs, rather than relying on a major input of market demand. There are limitations of this method, e.g. it may over price or under price the product. There is a problem of absorption costing generating different rates of overhead absorption. It does not distinguish between relevant incremental fixed costs and committed costs that are irrelevant.

QUESTIONS

1. What are the relevant costs in decision-making?
   Distinguish between avoidable and unavoidable costs.
2. What is the use of "opportunity costs"? Can one cost not serve all purposes?
   Define "imputed costs", "Sunk costs" and "out-of-pocket cost".
3. How incremental costs help in decision-making?
   An advertisement reads as follows:
   "Wanted—Ride to Agra from Delhi.
   All increment costs involved will be paid.
   Phone 27184063.
   Agra is 130 miles from Delhi:" Is there any mistake in the advertisement.
4. The Lucas Company has a production facility which can be used to produce three products in any combination.
   The following is the detailed information:

	Products		
	1	2	3
	₹	₹	₹
Selling price	10	30	6
Variable cost	9	15	2
Unit capacity required per unit	1	10	2
Units of capacity available	2,00,000		
Fixed costs	1,80,000		
Market limitation	nil	4,000	40,000

   Required:
   (1) Find the best combination of products.
   (2) What is the profit?
   (3) Will an increase in fixed costs affect the choice of products and profit?
   Assume ₹ 2,80,000?
5. Nubo Manufacturing, Inc., is presently operating at 50% of practical capacity, producing about 50,000 units annually of an electronic component. The company received an offer from a customer to purchase 30,000 components at ₹ 6 per unit, FOB Nubo plant.
   The company has not previously sold components to that customer. Budgeted production costs for 50,000 and 80,000 units follows:

Number of units	50,000	80,000
	₹	₹
Costs: Direct material	75,000	1,20,000
Variable direct labour	75,000	1,20,000
Factory overhead	2,00,000	2,60,000
	3,50,000	5,00,000
Cost per unit	7	6.25

Required:

Explain what apparently causes the drop in cost from ₹ 7 to ₹ 6.25 per unit when production increases from 50,000 to 80,000 units. Show the effect on profit if order is accepted.

6. A company makes three products in the same factory. Determine whether product C should be dropped.

	A ₹	B ₹	C ₹
Sales	5,00,000	4,00,000	1,00,000
Variable cost	2,95,000	2,80,000	75,000
Contribution margin	2,05,000	1,20,000	25,000
Fixed costs	1,65,000	90,000	45,000
Net Income	40,000	30,000	(20,000)

7. The Oatman Company uses a certain part in its final product. The part is not being manufactured by the company, and the cost data related to its manufacture are given below. A total of 10,000 units are used each year:

	Per unit ₹	10,000 units ₹
Variable manufacturing costs	13	1,30,000
Fixed overhead : Separate	2	20,000
Joint	3	30,000
	18	1,80,000

One firm has offered this particular part to Oatman Company at ₹ 16 per unit.

8. H & W products have 36,000 hours of plant capacity for the manufacture of two products.

	H ₹	W ₹
Sales price per unit	40	30
Variable cost per unit	30	15
Units that can be manufactured in one hour	8 units	4 units

Determine which product should be produced.

9. The Anuprav International (P) Ltd. makes all its products in batches. It costs ₹ 42,000 to set up the production facilities to make a batch which can run from 10,000 to 60,000 units. The size of a batch depends on the expected for the product in the coming year because only one batch of each product is made during a year. Any units not sold during the year in which they are made become worthless. The variable cost of "Pancharisht" one of the firms products, is ₹ 4 per unit. Sales last year were 40,000 units of ₹ 7 per unit. It has been decided to make 45,000 units this year.

   Find:

   1. If 30,000 "PANCHARISHT" are sold, what is the incremental profit.
   2. Assume that all 45,000 units made are sold, but 60,000 units could have been sold.

      What was the opportunity cost of not making the additional 15,000?
   3. Calculate break-even if 35,000 units are sold.

10. In 2020 X Company produced for joint products at a joint cost of ₹ 50,000. These products were processed further and sold as follows:

Product	Sales ₹	Additional processing costs after split off ₹
A	2,30,000	1,90,000
B	50,000	40,000
C	80,000	30,000
D	15,000	17,000

X Company has the opportunity to sell A, B and C at split off for ₹ 30,000, ₹ 12,000 and ₹ 50,000 respectively. There is no market for D at split off. Find out the net income of the company in 2020. Could 2020 net income have been larger? If so, how much larger?

11. The Vicco Company sells to both wholesalers and retailers. The firm has 20 salesmen and cannot easily increase the size of the sales force. An analysis has shown that a salesman's call on a wholesale customer yields an average order of ₹ 90, on a retailer ₹ 50. However, prices to a whole sales are 20% less than to retail ₹ Cost of goods sold (all variable) is 60% of prices charged to retailers. A salesman can call on seven wholesalers or 12 retailers per day. The greater number of retailers reduces travel time between calls.

Advise:

1. Should salesmen concentrate on wholesalers or retailers? Provide an analysis based on one salesman for one week showing the difference.
2. What other factors required consideration?

Variable costs	45% of sales
Fixed costs	₹ 75,000

As a division head, would you accept or reject the proposal? Why? How may a company avoid similar kinds of problems in the future?

12. Standard costs and other data for two component parts used by Griffon Electronics are presented below:

	Part A 4 ₹	Part B 5 ₹
Direct material	0.40	8.00
Direct labour (variable)	1.00	4.70
Factory overhead	4.00	2.00
Unit standard cost	5.40	14.70
Units needed per year	6,000	8,000
Machine hours per unit	4	2
Unit cost if purchased	5	15

In past years, Griffon has manufactured all of its required components; however, in 19 A only 30,000 hours of otherwise idle machine time can be devoted to the production of components. Accordingly, some of the parts must be purchased from outside suppliers. In producing parts, factory overhead is applied at ₹ 1 per standard machine hour. Fixed capacity costs, which will not be affected by any make-buy decisions, represent 60% of applied overhead.

The 30,000 hours of available machine time are to be scheduled such that Griffon realizes maximum potential cost savings. What relevant production costs for part A 4 and B 5 should be considered in the decision to schedule machine time. The allocation of machine hours is to be based upon potential cost savings per machine hour. How many units of part A 4 and B 5 should be produced.

13. The Officers of Bradshaw Company are reviewing the profitability of the company's four products and the potential effect of several proposals for varying the product mix. An excerpt from the income statement prepared under a full cost approach and other data follow. No significant changes in inventory levels are expected.

	Products			
	P ₹	*Q* ₹	*R* ₹	*S* ₹
Sale	10,000	18,000	12,600	22,000
Cost of goods sold	4,750	7,056	13,968	18,500
Gross profit	5,250	10,944	(1,368)	3,500
Operating expenses	1,990	2,976	2,826	4,220
Income before tax	3,260	7,976	4,194	(720)
No. of units sold	1,000	1,200	1,800	2,000
Selling price per unit	10	15	7	11
Variable cost of goods sold	2.50	3	6.50	6
Variable operating expenses per unit	1.17	1.25	1	1.20

Determine the effect on income of each of the following independent proposals, assuming that the activity of other remain the same.

(a) Product *R* is discontinued.

(b) Product *R* is discontinued and a consequent loss of customers causes a decrease of 200 units in sales of product *Q*.

(c) The sales price of product *R* is increased to ₹ 8, with a decrease in the number of units sold to ₹ 1,500.

(d) The plant in which product *R* is produced can be utilized to produce a new product *T*. The total variable costs and expenses per unit of product *T* are ₹ 8.05 and 1,600 units can be sold at ₹ 9.50 each. Product *R* is discontinued and product *T* is introduced.

(e) Part of the plant in which product *P* is produced can easily be adapted to the production of product *S*, but changes in quantities may make changes in sales price advisable. If production of product *P* is reduced to 500 units (to be sold at ₹ 12 each), production of product *S* will be increased to 2,500 units (to be sold at ₹ 10.50 each).

14. A company makes two products and the data for the two products are as follows:

Per unit	A ₹	B ₹
Selling price	10	15
Variable cost	7	9
Contribution margin	3	6

You have, 1,000 machine hours of capacity available and know that you can turn out three units of *A* per hour or one unit of *B* per hour, determine which product should be sold.

14

Divisional Performance Measurement and Transfer Pricing

DECENTRALISATION

The total centralisation of a business means that maximum constraints are imposed by central management and minimum freedom in decision-making enjoyed by divisional managers. A decentralised firm makes extensive use of investment centres. Individual managers are responsible for and control of revenues, expenses and investment. The horizontal organisational structure is decentralised and a vertical organisational structure is centralised. In a highly decentralised firm, operating units, usually called divisions, are almost autonomous. Division managers are responsible for both production and marketing, as well as functions like personnel and accounting. They do not have control over long-term financing organisations are seldom totally centralised or decentralised. There may be a limited decentralisation, i.e. the divisions have limited powers. In either case, control may be achieved through goal setting and performance evaluation.

Arguments for Decentralisation

In the present context, a division refers to a profit or investment centre. The essence of divisionalisation in profit responsibility. Decentralised decision-making is likely to result in better decisions because the people who make them are closer to the scene of action and have a smaller area of responsibility to worry about. Secondly, greater efficiency result from the sense the divisional managers have that they are running "their" businesses. Thirdly, giving a person a responsibility for running a division is perhaps the best way of providing preparation for a top management role at the corporate level. The performance of divisional managers can be judged by their success in attaining the divisional goals. It is the profit, as a measure of performance in a division, that plays important role for it keeps the firm going and is reflection of firm's growth.

The managerial performance and the performance of a division are different. The former is limited as to how the manager controls the activities of a division.

Fourthly, as the business grows in size of activities and personnel the ability of an organisation to make decisions effectively and quickly is reduced by its chain of command. By decentralisation the quality of decision-making and management can be improved. Fifthly, when a business operates in uncertainty and turbulent environment, the local management will be better able to make correct, responsive decision than central management lastly. Decentralisation results in responsibility which leads to better performance. This accords with behavioural theory of Hertzberg in which 'responsibility' is viewed as a motivator.

Preconditions for Effective Decentralisation

The following conditions must exist to avail the above advantages (a) operational independence, (b) identification and separation of costs and revenues, (c) access to source of supply and markets, (d) a revenue creating mechanism by reference to external sales or inter company transfer prices, (e) central policies to co-ordinate divisional operations.

Arguments against Decentralisation

Decentralisation is not favoured for number of reasons. Numerous interdependencies exist between parts of a business and at different levels. These may be in relation to product, technology and production, cash flow, profitability and corporate strategy and portfolio. The degree of interdependency determines the decision-making freedom, divisionalisation and divisional structure. Secondly, through economies of scale costs are reduced. Thirdly, goal congruence problem is little because decisions are taken in keeping corporate objectives. There is no autonomy-control conflict. Fourthly, the problems of design of divisional profit measures and costs of operating the system need not to be considered. Lastly, management of family companies may not like to loose control.

DIVISIONAL PERFORMANCE

Divisional performance is concerned with everything relevant to a division. If divisional performance is to be judged by profitability, then a distinction must be drawn between controllable profit, by which division's manager should be judged and divisional net profit. Probably no single measure of performance, used exclusively, is free from the danger that it may lead to misdirected effort on the part of management. All the problems of profit measurement that are found in a non-divisionalised company are present in the divisionalised company. There is danger in seeking one best measure of performance. The measures of performance used should be influenced materially by the nature of the responsibilities of the division whose performance is being measured.

There are two methods of measuring performance and controlling activities (a) Financial measures (b) non-financial measures. Controllability and measurement of financial performance is (1) through standard costing, (2) through internal resource allocation, (3) through profitability measures,

(4) through responsibility accounting. Here we shall examine the control and performance evaluation through profitability measures first and responsibility accounting in next chapter. Profitability can be measured through net income and various ratios related to profitability. They are:

(A) Net Income, (B) Investment turnover, (C) Operating rate, (D) Return on investment, (E) Residual Income.

Measures of Performance through Profitability

(A) *Net Income*: The most commonly used measure is net income of a division. The net income that is used should be the net result of all revenues and expense items controllable by division manager. This amount may be called divisional or controllable profit. It is this profit for which he is responsible. If a division is a profit centre, divisional profit is the most comprehensive measure for evaluation. If it is an investment centre, divisional profit is not comprehensive because it does not indicate the investment required to produce a particular profit. A division earning more profit than another division may not be better in that case. Divisional profit fails to consider the size of the investment committed to a division. Hence, the concept is not used to measure the performance of investment centre.

(B) *Investment Turnover*: It can be calculated by the formula:

$$\text{Investment turnover} = \frac{\text{Sales}}{\text{Investment (average)}}$$

If sales increases, turnover increases. But this is not a measure of manager's performance because sales can be increased by lowering the price or increased sales advertisement. It may be used with other ratios and it will help to know the cause of decreased profits.

(C) *Operating Rate*: It can be calculated by the following formula:

$$\text{Operating rate} = \frac{\text{Operating profit}}{\text{Sales}}$$

This rate merely gives an indication of efficiency of operations. The profit per rupee of sales is affected, in addition to efficiency of operations, by factors like changes in the level of sales, product mix sold, price of products sold or cost of materials and services used to produce the product sold. If the effect of these factors is computed and isolated, then this rate is useful. Moreover, the effects of factors responsible for change in operating rate should also be examined for their long run effects. This is because operating may have increased due to increase in sales. Or a change in the composition of sales from low margin item to high margin item may increase income.

This will reflect efficiency of sales division and not of production division or may be fortuitous market phenomenon.

(D) *Return on Investment*: (Or return on capital employed/invested). It is also called "Dupont System" of financial analysis. It was introduced around World War I by Dupont Company. This is a measure that take into account the relative sizes of divisions. It is an investment centre measure. The general form of R.O.C.E. formula is described as follows:

$$\text{R.O.I.} = \frac{\text{Profit}}{\text{Sales}} \times \frac{\text{Sales}}{\text{Capital employed}} \text{ or } \frac{\text{Net income}}{\text{Capital employed}}$$

The first ratio is percentage of profit to sales and second is capital employed turnover. The second ratio is expressed as times. The expanded form helps to focus attention on the two components of ROI. It is an average return on division investment. This ratio is used to measure managerial effectiveness and to determine investment policy. Profit is a reward of capital and capital must earn more than its costs before there is any profit.

Consider the following example:

Percentage of net income to sales (return on sales ratio)	Capital turnover (times)	ROCE
10%	2	20%
8%	2.50	20%
6%	3.333	20%
4%	5.00	20%
2%	10.00	20%

If company wants to increase ROI from 20% to 25%, sales increase by itself will not increase ROI because sales cancels out. It can do it by any action that (a) boosts sales which increase income, (b) reduced capital employed (total assets), (c) reduces costs, while holding the other two factors constant. In other words, an improvement in capital turnover or profit will increase ROI. ROI objectives are more commonly set equal to the firm's cost of capital, the average corporate rate of return or the corporate rate of return plus *x* per cent, than to some specific rate for investment centre.

Examine the following case of Company *A* and Company *B*. If *A* reduces assets to half and *B* increase net income to double the ROI of both will be same i.e., 20%.

	Company *A* ₹	Company *B* ₹
Net sales	4,00,000	40,00,000
Total assets	4,00,000	4,00,000
Net income	40,000	40,000
Return on sales ratio	10%	1%
Assets turnover	1 time	10 time
ROCE	10%	10%

Company *A* produces a higher return on sales but obtains a lower sales volume for the money invested.

It should be noted that opinions differ as to the methods to be used in determining the net income and capital employed.[1]

There are two basic problems associated with use of ROI for company divisional activities. (a) Investment base, and (b) the factors used in calculation of the ratio. Unless all factors are identical, this ratio is of little use. Suppose a company is using modern plant and ROCE is calculated on the basis of profits after depreciation before tax and the figures are profit ₹ 2,50,000. Investment i.e., net fixed assets less depreciation plus net current assets = ₹ 15,00,000. ROCE will be 16.6%. If another company in the same industry uses old equipment and its profits are ₹ 1,80,000 and investment ₹ 6,00,000, the ROI is 30%. It seems this company is better performing as its ROI is more. But company is better as it is using modern equipment.

Example 1

Following is the data of a company:	₹
Average assets available	10,00,000
Fixed costs	2,25,000
Variable costs	5 per unit
Desired ROCE	27.5%
Expected sales	2,00,000 units

(a) Find out the average unit sale price to obtain desired ROCE.
(b) What rate of return would be earned if sales is 3,00,000 units.

Solution

(a) 27.5% of ₹ 1,00,000 = ₹ 2,75,000 (Desired net income)

Sales = Variable costs + Fixed costs + Net income

2,00,000 units = 2,00,000 (5) + ₹ 2,25,000 + 2,75,000

One unit = ₹ 15,00,000 ÷ 2,00,000 units = ₹ 7.50 per unit

$$\text{Capital employed turnover} = \frac{2,00,000 \times ₹\ 7.50}{₹\ 10,00,000} = 1.5 \text{ times}$$

$$\text{Percentage of profit to sales} = \frac{2,75,000}{15,00,000} = 18.33\%$$

1. Some management accountants calculate it as net fixed assets plus working capital (or net current assets).

(b) Rate of return on 3,00,000 units:

	₹
Sales	22,50,000
Variable cost	15,00,000
Contribution margin	7,50,000
Fixed costs	2,25,000
Net Income	5,25,000
ROCE	52.5%

(E) *Residual Income*: Several companies use this method. This method has the advantage that (1) it is feasible to have different rates of return for different assets, (2) similar investment is required to earn the same return, (3) there is no problem in acquisition or disposition of assets regardless the level of ROCE, provided that residual income is increased.

Residual is the net income of an investment centre, less "imputed" interest on capital employed. It can also be defined as the amount of income that a divisional produces in excess of the minimum desired rate of return (which is always greater than or equal to the cost of capital).

Example 2

There are two divisions of a company *A* and *B*. Each has net income after tax ₹ 25,000. The imputed interest (minimum desired rate of return) is 16%, calculate ROI for *A* and RI for *B*:

	Division *A* ₹	Division *B* ₹
(1) Net income (after tax)	25,000	25,000
(2) Imputed interest or desired rate of return 16%	Nil	16,000
(3) Capital Employed	1,00,000	1,00,000
ROCE	25%	—
R.I. (1-2)	—	9,000

Some managers prefer RI as it concentrates on maximizing number (in amount) rather than a percentage.

The use of this method shows that a division with highest ROCE might be less valuable to the firm as a whole than a division with a lower rating using the ROCE. Observe the following:

	1			2		
	Division I ₹	Imputed Interest	Division II ₹	Division I ₹	Imputed Interest	Division II ₹
Investment	10,00,000	10%	1,00,00,000	10,00,000	18%	1,00,00,000
Net income	2,00,000		15,00,000	2,00,000		15,00,000
Imputed interest or Desired minimum Return	1,00,000		10,00,000	1,80,000		18,00,000
R.I.	1,00,000		5,00,000	20,000		(3,00,000)

Situation I is favourable to Division *B* from the viewpoint of the firm and in situation 2, Division *A* is more valuable.

The following situation of another problem may be examined:

Division	Capital Invested	ROCE	Net Income target	Actual Income	R.I.[1]	Residual Rate
A	20,00,000	10%	2,00,000	3,00,000	1,00,000	5%
B	40,00,000	15%	6,00,000	3,00,000	1,00,000	2.5%
C	10,00,000	25%	2,50,000	3,00,000	50,000	5%

Problem with this, as seen from above example is to arrive at the minimum ROCE related to capital cost. In addition, achievement of income target is subjective to a variety of factors other than the efficient use of resources. Effective use of this method requires two things: (a) ROCE and income target, (b) operation of the following concepts of valuation of accounting, namely, measuring RI within divisional accounts, valuing fixed assets at replacement value, and using annuity method of depreciation to compensate for inflation.

PROBLEMS IN EVALUATION

One author suggests that if the following factors are controlled ROCE will take care itself (1) Do not raise funds which you cannot use, (2) Use legitimate credit to the full, (3) Collect cash promptly, (4) Control stock level, (5) Control plant utilisation.

Whether ROCE or RI is used as a criterion for evaluation, we have to determine what revenues, costs, and investments are to be included or excluded in the calculation. For calculation of income of a division, it is necessary to identify variable costs and fixed costs that are separable. Fixed costs that are joint to several divisions should not be used in the computation because division has no control over them. Following are the problems, because of difference of opinion or otherwise, in the calculation of ROI (1) Investment Base, (2) Profit, (3) Valuation of fixed assets and inventory.

1. Difference between actual net income and target net income.

(1) *Investment base.* (A) What assets are to be included for calculating divisional investment? Obviously those assets that can be readily identified with a particular divisions. When calculating the capital employed base of a division, a portion of such assets of the firm be included to find investment base. Same is the case with costs are revenues. There may be some unallocated costs and unassigned assets. Because of them a division will show more ROCE than of the firm. So as much cost as possible is to be allocated to divisions and virtually all assets are assigned to divisions. Care should be taken that costs and assets that are joint should not be arbitrarily allocated.

Example 3

The following data is imaginary of a company having three divisions. It is assumed that the imputed interest (minimum desired ROI) is 10%.

	Divisions			Unassigned	
	A ₹	B ₹	C ₹	Costs ₹	Total ₹
Investment in Assets:					
Cash	2,000	3,000	6,000	3,000	14,000
Accounts receivable	6,000	8,000	9,000	—	23,000
Inventory	10,000	18,000	24,000	—	52,000
Prepaid exp.	1,000	1,500	2,000	2,000	6,500
Plant & equipment (net)	20,000	32,000	44,000	6,000	1,02,000
Investments	1,000	—	—	10,000	11,000
Total assets	40,000	62,500	85,000	21,000	2,08,500
Element of Income:					
Sales	10,000	40,000	70,000		1,20,000
Variable cost	3,000	22,000	40,000		65,000
C/M	7,000	18,000	30,000		55,000
Fixed costs (separable)	3,000	9,000	14,000		26,000
Divisional profit	4,000	9,000	16,000		29,000
Fixed costs (joint)	—	—	—		8,000
Net Income					21,000

	A	B	C	Firm
ROI	10%	14.4%	18.8%	10.1%
RI	Nil	2,750	7,500	1.50

In the above example, divisions earn more than the firm and their combined RI is consumed by unallocated costs and unassigned assets that brings firm's RI down. The assets that are not available for productive used should be excluded both in divisions and firm for investment base.

(B) *Liabilities*: If liabilities are included in the computation of return on assets, both ROCE and RI for all divisions and for the firm as a whole will be higher. It should be noted that it is difficult to assign all liabilities to divisions. Moreover, the management may sometimes decide about the methods of financing in a large firm. If we deduct liabilities that are definitely related to divisions, then we take investment as controlled assets minus divisional liabilities. The effect can be illustrated by continuing example three. Suppose the assumed liabilities are as follows:

	Divisions			Firm
	A ₹	B ₹	C ₹	₹
Total assets	40,000	62,500	85,000	2,08,500
Divisional liabilities	6,000	17,000	31,000	54,000
Divisional investment	34,000	45,500	54,000	1,54,500
Unassigned liabilities	—	—	—	73,000
Total investment	34,000	45,500	54,000	81,500
ROI	11.8%	19.8%	29.6%	25.8%
RI	600	4,450	10,600	12,850

In Example 3, we have seen that there may be common investment by the firm for several divisions (e.g. building furniture). They should be allocated to division on some sound basis. Moore and Jaedicke observe "Traceable investment should be best measure of divisional investment rather than traceable investment plus some allocated share of common investment."

(2) *Income determination*: There may be a difference of opinion as to whether operating profit or net profit (after tax and/or interest) figure should be taken. The profit figure may be divisional controlled profit, or its direct profit or its net profit.

Following calculations show these computations:

	Divisional Controllable Profit ₹	Direct profit or traceable ₹	Net profit ₹
Revenues	1,000	1,000	1,000
Direct costs:			
Variable cost	700	700	700
Fixed controllable costs	100	100	100
	200		
Non-Controllable fixed costs		50	50
		150	
Indirect costs:			
Allocated firm's overhead		—	60
			90

Carefully observe what items constitute each type of profit. Controllable costs are costs for which a specific manager is held responsible. It is suggested by some authors that divisional controllable profit is best figure. But there are some problems with this figure. This figure cannot be used for intra-division comparison unless inventory, depreciation procedure are similar. There is problem of revenue recognition and definition of controllable costs. Fixed costs here refer to costs fixed not in amount, but with respect to volume.

Harold Bierman and Thomas R. Dyckman[1] list the following problems of income measurement that are particularly relevant to ROI. They are (1) Revenue recognition and matching of expenses with revenues, (2) Treatment of repairs and maintenance costs, (3) Accounting for inventory, (4) Treatment of non-productive supplies, (5) Choice of depreciation method, (6) Adjustment for changes in price level, (7) Allocation of common costs, (8) The effect of changes in level of production on income. Examples can be presented showing two divisions that will have different ROI due to different accounting methods and not by variations in efficiency.

(3) *Valuation of fixed assets and inventory*: Many of the problems of measuring investment base are related to problems of income measurement. But three are more important—(1) valuation of fixed assets, (2) valuing inventories and (3) allocation of assets administered directly from central office.

The valuation of fixed assets has following problems (A) What items should be capitalized and what items charged to expense e.g. repairs, maintenance charges and may huge expenditure for developing new products. (B) The second problem is inflation. What should be done about the fact that one unit used to measure the investment in the fixed assets is the money when the value of that unit of money has different meanings in different years. The purchasing power of money changes. (C) The third problem is to decide about depreciation. Whether the ROCE should be calculated with assets valued at gross book value or net value? The arguments in favour of using original cost of fixed asset are: Assets of manufacturing companies, unlike mining companies, are considered to be continuing rather than on depleted and abandoned basis. Gross assets of one plant can be compared better with those of another plant where depreciation practices may be different. Accumulated depreciation not deducted from gross assets since it represents the retention in business of funds required to keep intact the shareholders original investment. Method of depreciation has nothing to do with efficiency of operations. The arguments in favour of next fixed assets are: while invested capital is conventionally understated at the present time, the wrong method of

1. *Managerial Cost Accounting*, p. 393.

increasing it cannot be relied on to furnish the right results. Cash built up *via* depreciation allowance, if added to gross assets, amounts to overstating the investment. Gross fixed assets value fails to consider the ages of assets in use and changes in prices may render comparisons invalid.

(3a) *Depreciation*: The more important problem arises because of different depreciation methods in use. They are straight line approach or some type of accumulated or accelerated method. The later are sum of year's digits, annuity (or compound interest) Internal rate of return method, and diminishing balance method. Some firms may use current replacement cost method. Each depreciation has some desirable and some undesirable features. These different depreciation methods produce different depreciation amounts, which lead to different income amounts and also different net book values for fixed assets. The effect of different methods on calculation of ROI over a period is following, assuming cash operating income and other expenses are constant.

Method of depreciation used:	ROI
Straight line method	Increases at double rate
Sum of year's digit method	Increases at very fast rate
Diminishing balance method	Increases at very fast rate
Compound interest or annuity method	Remains constant.

The following example shows this.

Example 4

A firm's cash operating income is ₹ 2,000 for three years. Its fixed assets consist of a machine only costing ₹ 4,212 and has a useful life of three years. The residual value is nil. The internal rate of return is 20%. Calculate the depreciation by different methods and ROI on that basis. For purposes of fixed percentage on declining balance method assume 50% depreciation.

Solution

Year	Compound interest or Annuity method			Straight line method			Sum of year's digit method		
	1	2	3	1	2	3	1	2	3
Cash operating Income (₹)	2,000	2,000	2,000	2,000	2,000	2,000	2,000	2,000	2,000
Less Depreciation	1,157	1,389	1,667	1,404	1,404	1,405	2,107	1,404	702
Net Income	843	611	333	596	596	596	107	596	1,298
Investment base	4,213	3,056	1,666	4,213	2,809	1,405	4,213	2,106	702
ROI	20%	20%	20%	14%	21%	42%	–3%	28%	185%

Note:

Depreciation on C.I. method calculated as follows:

Cash in flow – (Internal rate of return × Assets net book value at the beginning)

Year 1 ₹ 2,000 – (20% of 4,213) = 1,157
Year 2 ₹ 2,000 – (20% of 3,056) = 1,389
Year 3 ₹ 2,000 – (20% of 1,667) = 1,667

Year	Investment at the beginning	Depreciation[1]	Imputed interest @ 20% on Col. I	Accumulated Depreciation
1	4,213	2,000	843	1,157
2	3,056	2,000	611	1,389
3	1,667	2,000	333	1,667

Residual income under annuity method is nil in all years, i.e. net income minus imputed interest:

Diminishing Balance Method

	I year	II year	III year
Depreciation	2,106	1,053	526
Net Income after depreciation	–106	947	1,474
Investment base	4,213	2,106	1,053
ROI	(–3%)	45%	139%

Some writers[2] suggest that time adjusted net revenues be used rather than cash proceeds revenue to compute depreciation as is done in annuity method. The time adjusted net revenues means revenues less the expenses exclusive of depreciation, all adjusted for the timing of the receipt and disbursement of cash, i.e. in above example if income is not cash but say by credit sale and accrual system of accounting is followed.

The present value of cash proceed and present value of time adjusted revenues and expenses. It is only when the analysis shifts from overall profitability of the investment to a period-by-period profitability analysis that the difference between cash flow depreciation and time adjusted revenue and expense depreciations makes a difference. If the yield is greater than time value of money, i.e. net present value of investment is not zero, then they suggest that for purposes of performance evaluation the firms time value of money and not investment yield rate be used. This method of depreciation is not followed in practice and is out of the purview of the book.

Annuity method of depreciation is an attempt to overcome limitations of ROI. This method makes ROI reconcilable with IRR. This is an exante

1. The present value of ₹ 1 annuity @ 20% for 3 years = 2.1065

$$\text{Depreciation} = \frac{₹\ 4,213}{21,065} = ₹\ 2,000.$$

2. Harold Bierman Jr. and Thomson R. Dyckman, *Managerial Cost Accounting*, Collier Macmillan, 2nd Ed., pp. 411-16.

reconciliation, when achieved cash flow differ from expected cash flow, ROI calculation no longer equals IRR and argument is favour of annuity method disappears. ROI measure using the annuity method is equally irrelevant for appraisal of current period performance.

Of all these methods, current replacement cost is favoured by majority of writers. This is the cost of attaining similar assets in a condition similar to those now in use. The basis for this valuation is that this method eliminates the problem posed by different depreciation methods and allows for changes in prices. But practical difficulties of determining replacement cost explain their infrequent use.

(3b) *Inventory*: Lastly, the problem of inventory valuation. LIFO is accepted as a method of inventory valuation for accounting purposes. If it is used, the inventory value represents goods dating back to the moment of introducing LIFO. It rarely gives an actual cost of inventory or an indication of its present value. Second problem with this method is about writing down obsolete or spoiled items, taking a meaningful physical inventory. In the case manufacturing firms, problem is of deciding what costs are inventoriable.

BEHAVIOUR PROBLEMS OF ROI AND RI

Residual income is calculated after a charge for depreciation on fixed assets controlled by the division, whereas it is not in controllable profit. Amey, L.R. and Solomon, D. give the following Formula to calculate RI.

Revenue — From external sales and internal transfers *less* variable cost.

Variable profit — *Less* controllable divisional overheads.

Controllable profit — *Less* depreciation and expenses on divisional fixed assets.

Less: Interest on controllable investment, non-operating losses (add gains) fixed 'subsidy' charges by other (Add charges to), division for internal transfers.

Controllable Residual Income

Less interest on non-controllable divisional investment, non-controllable divisional overheads, incremental central expense chargeable to division.

Net Residual Income

Less tax on divisional income.

Costs and revenues which are variable with decisions of divisional manager are included in controllable profit. The controllable items means that items which is the responsibility of the division.

There are two difficulties with the procedure of charging interest (1) If the asset purchased is promising returns after some years, the interest should be capitalized or regarded as expense. It can be solved by allocating interest cost between the assets and expenses of the period. (2) The second difficulty follows from the first. Suppose asset costs ₹ 10,000, interest @ 5% promises return after two years ₹ 11,025. The cost in first year is adjusted to ₹ 10,500 (500 interest one year), then no operating income is reported when the expected revenue of ₹ 11,025 are earned i.e., there is no income above the implicit interest cost of ₹ 1,025 and ₹ 10,000 explicit cost of the asset. However, the other side of implicit interest cost of ₹ 1,025 is implicit interest revenue. This revenue should be recognized during some period if implicit cost is recognized. Suppose the ROI are 5% for both years. The Income statement for both periods will appear as under:

Other expenses are nil and revenues assumed.

	Period 1 ₹	Period 2 ₹
Revenues	5,378	5,378
Less Expenses and depreciation[1] (by annuity method)	4,878	5,122
Operating income	500	256
Less implicit interest cost[2]	500	256
Income after interest	0	
Plus implicit interest revenue	500	256
Change in shareholders equity	500	256

It is possible to obtain constant ROI 5% for both periods. But be careful wrong combination of interest calculations and depreciation method will result in meaningless income measures. Both must be consistent with each other.

Residual Income Concept Better

The use of RI as a criterion for divisional performance may prove better than ROCE. Consider the following situations:

(1) *Firm Vs. Division's ROCE*: Sometimes divisional managers are encouraged by ROCE to pass up projects that are worthwhile to the firm as a whole. They will be encouraged to reject projects and promise returns in excess of cost of capital, if the promised return is lower than the ROCE currently being earned by division.

Example 5

The current ROCE of a division is 30%. The firms cost of capital is 20%. The divisional manager is confronted with an investment of

1. ₹ 10,000 ÷ by present value 1.8594 multiplied by P.V. for one year of ₹ one @ 5% is 0.9070 = ₹ 4,878, Balance ₹ 10,000 – 4,878 = ₹ 5,122. Annuity method.
2. 5% on ₹ 10,000 and 5% on 5,122.

₹ 3,00,000 that will give increased profit of ₹ 75,000 (i.e., 25% ROCE). The present investment is ₹ 10,00,000 in the division. Advise should the new investment be rejected?

Solution

	₹
Investment current	10,00,000
Additional investment	3,00,000
Total	13,00,000
Divisional Profit:	
Present	3,00,000
From new investment	75,000
	3,75,000

ROCE after new investment 28.8%. RI will be present ₹ 1,00,000 (3,00,000 – 20% of ₹ 10,00,000).

After new investment ₹ 1,15,000 (3,75,000 – 20% of 13,00,000)

If RI is applied the project is accepted and on the basis of ROCE, manager is likely to reject it.

(2) *Comparison of various divisional projects*: Solomon, D. suggests the use of RI concept for assessing (i) profitability of divisional capital investment and (ii) the profitability of total capital investments where capital, although not controllable by the division, is nevertheless identifiable with it.

Example 6

An autonomous division invests capital ₹ 2,00,000, ₹ 4,00,000 and ₹ 5,00,000 respectively in three projects *x, y* and *z*. The cost of capital is 14%. The operating profits are ₹ 40,000, ₹ 70,000 and ₹ 75,000 respectively. The ROCE and RI be computed.

Solution

	Project		
	x	*y*	*z*
Investment	2,00,000	4,00,000	5,00,000
Operating profit	40,000	70,000	7,500
ROCE	20%	17.5%	15%
Less Interest 14%	28,000	56,000	70,000
RI	12,000	14,000	5,000
Residual return on capital	6%	3.5%	1%
Incremental yield	—	$\frac{30,000}{2,00,000} = 15\%$	$\frac{5,000}{1,00,000} = 5\%$

ROCE favour *x* and RI favours *y*, although *z* displays highest absolute profit. The figure of RI recognizes that *y*'s incremental investment of ₹ 2,00,000 yields additional revenue of 30,000 which is equivalent to 15% (10% above the cost of borrowing), whereas at the margin *z* earns only 5%. If controllable costs of capital had been 15%, project *z* would still show an average gross return of 15% but RI will fall to zero.

(3) *Increase in interest rate*: The sensitivity of divisional profitability to changes in interest rates may be seen in the above example, if the cost of capital now moves to 18%.

	Project		
	x	*y*	*z*
Operating profit	40,000	70,000	75,000
ROCE	20%	17.5%	15%
Less Interest	36,000	72,000	90,000
RI	4,000	(2,000)	(15,000)
Residual return on capital	2%	(0.5%)	(3%)
Incremental yield	—	15%	5%

Absolute operating profit still favours investment in *z*, while a gross return measure favours *x* as before. But the soundness of RI is again revealed by comparison of incremental yield on capital employed. Both *y* and *z* fall short of their borrowing costs.

CRITICISM AND POPULARITY

L.R. Amey (1969) comes down heavily against Solomon, D., argument for charging interest to divisions when assessing their performance. J.J. Mauriel and R.N. Anthony (1966) in an American survey of 1378 companies discovered that among nearly 100 companies more than 25% utilized RI concept. J.M. Samuel 1969, to Mepham (1980) noted the incongruities of Amey's criticism. If divisional capital is fixed, maximizing the ROI on divisional capital employed would be equivalent to maximizing controllable net profits in absolute terms. If divisional capital is variable, imputing a charge for interest on capital and utilizing RI as a performance criteria achieves something. Capital will now entail a cost to be borne by both the division and the central office. The RI criteria would alert both the division and the central office which they wish to avoid such as losses sustained investment of *y* and *z* in Example 6.

Amey would no doubt prefer to avoid 'sub-optimal' use of resources resulting from the pursuit of project *x* alone and advocate expansion of absolute controllable operating profit by more capital as long as any return at all can be secured. But such a policy is only rational if the marginal return on capital employed exceeds it incremental cost. In other words, RI before tax in absolute terms is positive.

J.J. Mauriel and R.N. Anthony survey suggested 60% companies use ROCE and 7% RI and 20% both. A survey by Allen Hill (1982

U.K.) showed that 38% companies followed overall objective of return on capital for their division and 12% absolute profits and 20% growth in sales. He found performance is ganged by controllable ROCE, which fails to account for an interest charge, rather than any notion of RI, in absolute terms or otherwise. He found that significant investment autonomy for larger divisions. There is divergence between fact and theory and hoped that divisional performance measurement becomes a matter of wide debate.

USES AND LIMITATIONS OF ROCE

ROCE serves as a measures of management's efficiency. It affords comparison of managerial results both internally and externally. It develops a sense of responsibility in divisional managers.

But there is a lack of agreement on the optimum ROI. The valuation of assets, partly these used jointly, give rise to problems. As a single measure of performance it gives misleading results. The divisional managers may overlook the long-term interest of the firm for the sake of current good looking ROCE.

However, there are some questionable use of ROCE in certain cases, e.g. capital budgeting decisions, pricing decisions and inter firm comparisons. Following example may be examined.

ROI analysis is sometimes criticised because of the amount of time and resources it takes to develop a credible model. However, organisations that have taken the time to build good ROI models recognise the objectivity that financial analyses can provide to justify investments in large projects. This is especially valid when multiple projects are being evaluated. The ROI process provides a level playing field to compare benefits and choose those projects with the highest corporate value. Analyzing the costs and benefits of a specific project can also eliminate unplanned costs and project overruns, driving more efficient project completion. IBM has carried out case studies of Whirlpool Corporation, Staples Inc. and Honeywell AirCraft landing systems to demonstrate the value that ROI analysis provided in the project planning stages. Measuring and proving the return for these integration projects enabled each enterprise to accomplish its major integration objectives. More importantly, the returns have resulted in better business decisions, higher customer satisfaction, and business efficiencies that affect the bottom line. Staples has increased its customer base, Honeywell is making more efficient decisions, and Whirlpool has revamped its integration strategy and architecture, saving money and effort in the process. Given below is Whirlpool Corporation case study carried out by Gartner consulting on behalf of IBM.

Case Study: Whirlpool*

Background

Whirlpool Corporation (Whirlpool) is the world's leading manufacturer and marketer of major home appliances, with over 60,000 employees and annual sales in excess of $10 billion. The company manufactures its products in 13 countries and markets them in more than 170 countries under major brand names such as Whirlpool, Kitchen Aid, Roper, Estate, Bauknecht, Ignis, Laden, Inglis, Brastemp and Consul. Whirlpool Corporation is also the principal supplier to Sears, Roebuck and Co. of many major home appliances marketed under the Kenmore brand name.

Problem

Jim Haney, Whirlpool's chief technologist and architect whose team is responsible for evaluating new technologies, determined that over two-thirds of the budget for a recent project was being spent on integration. This prompted him to initiate an evaluation of Whirlpool's business integration strategy to understand and improve the company's integration environment. The analysis revealed that Whirlpool was relying on point-to-point integration solutions, using over eight types of integration products, which resulted in a costly and inefficient integration environment. In addition, Whirlpool did not have a centralized competency center to make informed and cost-effective decisions regarding integration initiatives.

Solution

In an effort to reduce costs, improve quality and increase speed-to-market with regard to integration initiatives, Whirlpool embarked on the following initiatives:

- Instituted a governance committee to design and oversee Whirlpool's integration strategy.
- Established standards around integration products and processes.
- Focused on a hub-and-spoke architecture to extract time and cost savings from related integration projects.
- Analyzed the ROI for its new integration strategy.

These efforts resulted in a comprehensive business integration strategy that was supported by an ROI analysis. From a purely labour standpoint, savings were realized within three quarters; when comprehensive infrastructure investments were included to accommodate architectural changes related to the new strategy, positive ROI was realized within six quarters. Whirlpool believes that the cost savings, quality of work, and labour efficiencies associated with its application integration strategy will increase over time. Whirlpool uses IBM's WebSphere Business Integration software products for application integration projects.

ROI Analysis

Whirlpool focused on the IT hard-cost savings associated with integration when developing its ROI assessment. The analysis was intentionally conservative. In addition, while business benefits were understood, they remained qualitative in nature. The two areas of focus included labour effort savings and overall cost savings.

Labour Effort

"Labour effort savings" is defined as the amount of resource hours that were reduced through employing the new integration strategy and tools. The majority of the savings result from increased reusability of business objects and connectors. Whirlpool estimated its own savings which were more conservative than those estimated by the application integration software vendor and an independent third-party services provider. Whirlpool's scenario assumes a six- to eight-month ramp up period during which projects are subject to increased overhead and training costs. Over a 2.5-year time horizon, Whirlpool estimated that it would begin seeing labour effort savings in the third quarter of integration deployment. The table below illustrates Whirlpool's estimates on labour effort savings using their new application integration strategy.

Table A: Whirlpool Labour Estimates

Whirlpool Labour Estimates	2001		2002				2003				Total
	Q3	Q4	Q1	Q2	Q3	Q4	Q1	Q2	Q3	Q4	10 Qtrs.
Proposed Application Integration Strategy (hrs)	8,648	8,835	6,278	7,756	6,931	5,874	10,464	9,834	4,186	4,186	72,990
Current Method (hrs)	8,256	8,039	10,614	13,572	13,097	12,147	14,464	12,589	7,144	7,144	107,065
Savings @ $60/hour*	$(23,480)	$(47,750)	$260,175	$348,975	$369,975	$376,425	$240,000	$165,300	$177,450	$177,450	$2,044,520

* Average fully loaded rate. *Source*: Whirlpool Corporation.

Overall Savings

Overall savings included numerous metrics associated with infrastructure costs such as software licensing, hardware investments needed to support integration and high-availability (fail-over) assurance, as well as ongoing maintenance/upgrades. Whirlpool estimated that savings could be realized in the sixth quarter (approximately the mid-point of the 2.5-year time horizon). The following table illustrates Whirlpool's overall estimated cost savings.

Table B: Whirlpool's Overall Estimated Cost Savings

Quarterly	2001		2002				2003			
	Q3	Q4	Q1	Q2	Q3	Q4	Q1	Q2	Q3	Q4
Savings	191,610	169,170	486,565	555,159	567,879	563,739	540,511	434,870	391,862	391,448
Cost	(459,248)	(206,748)	(1,256,172)	(30,000)	(292,496)	(59,562)	(1,460,200)	(125,500)	0	(39,500)
Net Benefit (Cost)	(267,638)	(37,578)	(769,607)	525,159	275,383	504,177	(919,690)	309,370	391,862	351,948
Cumulative										
Savings	191,610	360,780	847,345	1,402,504	1,970,383	2,534,122	3,074,633	3,509,502	3,901,364	4,292,812
Cost	(459,248)	(665,996)	(1,922,168)	(1,952,168)	(2,244,664)	(2,304,226)	(3,764,426)	(3,889,926)	(3,889,926)	(3,929,426)
Net Benefit (Cost)	(267,638)	(305,216)	(1,074,823)	(549,664)	(274,281)	229,896	(689,794)	(380,424)	11,438	363,386

Source: Whirlpool Corporation.

Note: While cumulative savings were projected to be positive in Q4 2002, additional scalability investments were projected for the first half of 2003.

Business Benefits

The business benefits of the Whirlpool integration initiative were understood but kept at a qualitative level, similar to how one would measure them in a VOI framework. The business-related value creation of the business integration strategy included bring products to market faster, reacting to market changes in a more timely manner, upgrading business applications more quickly, and improving efficiencies around R&D and general business processes. These benefits in turn were thought to improve competitiveness, decrease costs, and increase sales, customer satisfaction and retention.

While the business units viewed these benefits positively, IT needed to educate the enterprise on the long-term aspect of the integration strategy. The first few projects would not be cheaper or faster due to the ramp-up time and new architecture investments. But once the hub-and-spoke infrastructure and procedures were in place and the first sets of integration objects were created, savings would be realized quickly.

CAPITAL BUDGETING DECISIONS

Example 7

A divisional manager has net book assets of ₹ 5,00,000 and wants to make a profit of ₹ 80,000, i.e. ROI 16%. He wants to replace an asset. The existing asset has a net book value of ₹ 4,000 and could be sold for that amount. It is earning a profit after tax and depreciation of ₹ 2,000 P.A. The new asset costs ₹ 1,04,000 and would earn a profit before depreciation of ₹ 24,000. Taxes 50%. Depreciation on straight line method @ 10%. What would be effect on ROI by replacement? Will the decision be affected by N.P.V. method? Assume life of asset 10 years and internal rate 10%.

Solution

	Profit ₹		Capital employed ₹
Current	80,000	Current	5,00,000
Less Profit of old machines	2,000	Deduct old asset	4,000
	78,000		4,96,000
Add Net profit of New machine (₹ 24,000 – 10,400)	13,600	*Add* New asset	1,04,000
	91,600		6,00,000

$$\text{ROCE} = \frac{91,600}{6,00,000} \times 100 = 15.3\%.$$

The asset should not be replaced because ROCE is down.

	₹
Net cash outlay on new machine = ₹ 1,04,000 – 4,000	1,00,000
Depreciation on new machine	10,400
Depreciation on old machine	400
Differential depreciation	10,000
Cash inflows of new machine	24,000
Less Depreciation	10,000
Savings	14,000
Less Tax	7,000
	7,000
Add Back depreciation	10,000
	17,000
P.V. @ 10% = 6.145 × 17,000	1,04,465
N.P.V.	4,465

The asset according to NPV method should be replaced. This difficulty arises with RI and ROCE because the book rate of return is different from IRR.

NON-PROFIT PERFORMANCE MEASURES

The criticisms of accounting measures of performance has led to consideration of alternative indices of performance. The following problems arise with such indices:

(a) Choice of indices must relate to the objectives assigned to the areas of responsibility being controlled. Two areas which have been increasing in importance are responsibility to the community and responsibility to employees. If a division's objective, for example includes profit targets and sales growth targets, an index of sales growth must be included.

(b) Indices may be designed to compensate for the short-term nature of profit measures. They fail to include intangibles which affect future cash flows and profit.

(c) Indices may try to reflect performance of areas where outputs are non-financial or difficult to express financially like quality control.

Three non-financial measures of performance these days are common (a) Quality control, (b) Control of cycle time and (c) Control of productivity.

Quality control is the effort to ensure that products and services perform to the customer requirement. For knowing the cost of quality control, a "Cost of Quality Report" is prepared which shows the financial impact of quality. It shows costs incurred to prevent the defective products, cost incurred to identify defective products and services, cost of defective components and cost of delivery caused by defective products or services e.g. repairs or returns in. The concept of "Total Quality Management" (TQM) is the application of quality principles to all organisation's endeavours to satisfy customer. To implement TQM, quality control charts are prepared, i.e. a statistical plot of measures of various product dimensions or attributes.

One key to improving quality is to reduce cycle time. It is the time taken to complete a product or service or any of the components of a product or service.

Managing productivity is the third effort to improve competitiveness. Productivity is a measure of outputs divided by inputs. Don't compare productivity measures over time. The measures of productivity relate to labour, materials, equipment, capital and physical capacity.

One of the management control principle is "value chain" of the company. The Value Chain is the sequence of functions that adds value to the company's products or services. These functions include R&D, product process design, production, marketing, distribution and customer service.

Example 8

Anurag Ltd. is a small division of Tyagi group which specializes in manufacturing of medical instruments. Anurag's performance over the last three years is shown below:

	2018 ₹	2019 ₹	2020 ₹
Sales	3,50,000	4,25,000	4,50,000
Less:			
Instrument costs	1,40,000	2,12,500	1,85,000
Direct labour	60,000	76,500	80,000
Overheads	50,000	60,000	75,000
Depreciation	30,000	30,000	30,000
Finance charges	25,000	32,000	35,000
Head office costs	20,000	35,000	40,000
Net profit	25,000	(21,000)	5,000

Following directions are followed by the division:

(1) (a) The transfer price shall be at marginal cost plus a 50% make-up.

(b) All overheads are paid for by the division but controlled by the head office. The overheads controlled by the division have been as follows:

2018	2019	2020
₹ 30,000	₹ 45,000	₹ 55,000

(c) Depreciation is provided on straight line basis and the amount of depreciation ₹ 30,000 comprises plant and machinery ₹ 8,000, Building ₹ 12,000, fixtures and furniture ₹ 6,000 and others ₹ 4,000. The head office handles all buildings and other assets by the division.

(d) Finance charges mainly represent costs of divisional working capital, although head office adds a 5% premium to the actual rates incurred before drawing up divisional profit reports. Actual average annual rate paid by for the last three years have been 2018 (15%); 2019 (20%); 2020 (18%).

(e) Head office costs are allocated to divisions on the basis to turnover and include charges for management services, central advertising and financing. The head office controls the allocation system of these costs.

The following additional information is available:

(f) In 2020, the divisional director submitted following statement to the head office:

	2018 ₹	2019 ₹	2020 ₹
Distribution costs:			
Charged by the head office	8,000	7,000	9,000
Current local market price for divisional requirements	6,000	5,000	7,500
Selling costs:			
Charged by head office	5,000	4,000	6,000
Current local market price for divisional requirements	4,000	3,000	4,500
Head office charges:			
Estimated value to the division	2,000	3,000	4,500

(2) During the three years the division is operating at full capacity. The internal transfers have been:

2018	2019	2020
₹ 1,20,000	₹ 1,50,000	₹ 1,65,000

(3) The market value of fixed assets estimated as follows:

	2018 ₹	2019 ₹	2020 ₹
Plant & Machinery	70,000	60,000	40,000
Buildings	6,00,000	7,50,000	10,00,000
Fixture & Furniture	30,000	25,000	22,000
Others	20,000	10,000	5,000

(4) The average weighted cost of capital for past period has been 12% and this rates has been used for investment appraisal purposes.

Draw a statement which could be used by the head office to assess whether the division is viable or should be closed.

Solution

	2018 ₹	2019 ₹	2020 ₹
Revenues			
(a) External sales	2,30,000	2,75,000	2,85,000
(b) Internal transfer	1,53,280	1,45,500	2,02,290
	3,83,280	4,20,500	4,87,290
Less:			
Component costs	1,40,000	2,12,500	1,85,000
Direct labour	60,000	76,500	80,000
Controllable contribution	1,83,280	1,31,500	2,22,290
Less:			
Controllable divisions overhead	30,000	45,000	55,000
Controllable profit	1,53,280	86,500	1,67,290
Less:			
(a) Depreciation on controllable assets (Machinery, furniture and others)	18,000	18,000	18,000
(b) Interest on controllable division's Investment			
(i) controllable assets	14,400	11,400	8,040
(ii) working capital	18,750	25,600	27,391
	51,150	55,000	43,431
Controllable Residual income	1,02,130	31,500	1,13,859
Deduct:			
(a) Depreciation on Buildings (uncontrollable assets)	12,000	12,000	12,000
(b) Other overheads (uncontrollable)			
(i) At charged rates	7,000	4,000	5,000
(ii) At adjusted market rates	10,000	8,000	12,000
(iii) Head office allocation	2,000	3,000	5,000
(iv) Interest on Buildings	72,000	90,000	1,20,000
Net Residual income	1,03,000	1,17,000	1,54,000
	(870)	(85,500)	(40,141)

Notes: Internal transfer price is direct cost + 50% mark up.

(a) The mark up on external sales are:

$$2018 = \frac{110}{120} = 91.6\%$$

$$2019 = \frac{86}{189} = 45.5\%$$

$$2020 = \frac{130}{155} = 83.9\%$$

Only the figure for 2020 approximates the internally constructed market price. Therefore, the internally transferred production should be adjusted to the mark up of the goods sold on the outside market. Thus:

Year	Direct cost of internally transferred production ₹		Equivalent market value ₹
2018	80,000	× 1.916	1,53,280
2019	1,00,000	× 1.455	1,45,500
2020	1,10,000	× 1.839	2,02,290

(b) Interest of fixed assets calculated @ 12%

(c) The opportunity cost of holding working measured as under:

$$2018 \text{ ₹ } 25{,}000 \times \frac{15}{20} = \text{₹ } 18{,}750$$

$$2019 \text{ ₹ } 32{,}000 \times \frac{20}{25} = \text{₹ } 25{,}600$$

$$2020 \text{ ₹ } 35{,}000 \times \frac{18}{23} = \text{₹ } 27{,}391.$$

Head office premium is artificial charge and it is assumed that working capital level is controllable at division level. Uncontrollable overheads have been adjusted to the market values at which the division could have purchased the services or their estimated values to the division.

Example 9

Praveen Ltd. consists of four divisions, each of which is autonomous. The cost of capital is 10%.

The following is the position in the year beginning on 1-1-2021, if no investment is proposed.

Division	Capital employed on 1-1-2021 ₹	Budgeted net profit 2021 ₹	Budgeted sales 2021 ₹
A	3,20,000	80,000	8,00,000
B	4,50,000	1,50,000	14,00,000
C	2,80,000	84,000	7,00,000
D	2,00,000	26,000	2,00,000

It is proposed that:

Division A: Investment of ₹ 1,00,000 be made to yield sales of ₹ 1,50,000 P.A. and net profit of ₹ 20,000 P.A. for 10 years.

Division B: To sell a project for ₹ 75,000 (original cost 6,00,000 seven years ago with expected life of eight years). The projects, budgeted net profit in 2021 is ₹ 15,000.

Division C: (i) Sales of a product line at book value. The equipment cost ₹ 60,000 two years ago with an expected life of three years. This line is budgeted to yield a net profit of ₹ 20,000 in 2021 along with.

(ii) Replacement of (1) above by investing ₹ 1,00,000 in a new product to yield per annum net.

Division D: Investment of ₹ 80,000 in a project to yield sales of ₹ 36,000 P.A. and net profit of ₹ 11,200 P.A. over the next five years.

It is assumed that sale or investment would be completed by 1-1-2021 so as to include in ROCE. Ignore tax.

Required:

(i) Calculate the new ROCE for each division as on 31-12-2021.

(ii) State whether the interest of the company as a whole will be favourably or adversely affected by the proposed transactions.

(iii) Calculate the lowest price at which the equipment should be sold by B if the transaction is to break even financially for the group.

(iv) Calculate the residual income for each division that transactions go ahead.

Solution

(i) Division	*A* ₹	*B* ₹	*C* ₹	*D* ₹
Profit original 2021 budget	80,000	1,50,000	84,000	26,000
Proposed:				
Additions of profit	20,000	—	30,000	11,200
Reductions to profit		15,000	20,000	
Revised profit	1,00,000	1,35,000	94,000	37,200
Capital employed				

Original 2021 budget	3,20,000	4,50,000	2,80,000	2,00,000
Proposals:				
Additions to capital	1,00,000	—	1,00,000	80,000
Employed/Reductions to C.E.	—	75,000	20,000	—
Revised C.E.	4,20,000	3,75,000	3,60,000	2,80,000
ROCE	23.8%	36.0%	26%	13%
ROCE on original budget	25%	33%	30%	13%

(ii) If we calculate NPV of all proposals for each division @ 10%, the overall cost of capital for the period in each case, we get,

Division A = NPV ₹ 84,200, proposal accepted.

Division B = NPV ₹ 81,900, proposal rejected.

Division C = assume that new product line is renewed every three years at the same investment outlay. Annual cash flow ₹ 63,333 with no residual value.

NPV of one replacement cycle = ₹ 2,51,730

so replacement should not take place.

Division D = NPV ₹ 23,088, proposal accepted.

Result

	A	B	C	D
ROCE	Reject	Accept	Reject	Accept
NPV	Accept	Reject	Reject	Accept

so only R and S get consistent advice.

(iii) The minimum price must be the value which equates to ₹ 90,000 (0.91) = ₹ 81,900.

(iv) Assume that profits and capital employed are controllable.

	A ₹	B ₹	C ₹	D ₹
Profit forecast	1,00,000	1,35,000	94,000	37,000
Interest charge (10%)	42,000	37,000	36,000	28,000
R.I.	58,000	98,000	58,000	9,000

TRANSFER PRICING

Introduction

A transfer price is a price charged by one segment of an organisation for a product or service that it supplies to another. It measures exchange of products and services between responsibility centres within a company. They could cover the pricing of:

1. Service rendered by service departments to user departments like computer services, debt collection and warehousing.
2. Transactions between legally independent organisations but under the same management.

3. Transactions between divisions entrusted with profit responsibility.
4. Under bilateral monopolistic conditions.

A determination of transfer price is of critical importance is divisional performance evaluation because price influence both revenues of the selling division and costs of the buying division. When profit are used as a measure of divisional performance, the concept of transfer pricing is conductive to the promotion of goal congruence. If the corporate management can establish profit centre concept by assignment of responsibility for cost and revenue, and a transfer price can be established which, given a volume of sales, would cause a divisional manager to make the same decision that would be made by the top management, it can delegate unlimited authority to divisional managers whether they purchase or sell, within or outside the organisation.

If both units are organised as profit centre, a price must be placed on such transfer, otherwise a conflict arises because managers would like to buy low and sell high. Transfer prices serves two roles, which give rise to such unfortunate conflict.

(a) As a price, it is a guide to the local decision-making. For producing divisions how much to produce and for buying division how much to purchase.

(b) The prices and subsequent profit measurement help the top management to evaluate the profit centres as separate entities. But as set of transfer price providing motivations that produce maximum profits to the primary cause one division to operate at a loss. Conversely, a set of transfer price that may be satisfactory for evaluating divisional performance may lead the divisions to make sub-optional decisions. This conflict between decision-making and evaluation of performance is essence of transfer pricing. Sometimes legal aspect of transfer price may be relevant, e.g. in case of oppression of minority or when multinational companies use different transfer pricing systems to reduce their tax liabilities.

METHODS OF TRANSFER PRICING

The transfer prices may be based on:

(a) cost, (b) market selling price, (c) negotiation, (d) arbitrary transfer price, (e) dual pricing.

(a) *Transfer prices related to costs*: They appear to be fair and logical. The concept of cost is subject to varied interpretations. In the process, the basic assumptions and sometimes, even the arithmetic of it get challenged. The various types of alternatives are:

(A) *Actual cost*: It may be (i) Full cost or (ii) Full cost plus a mark up (iii) Marginal cost (called direct costs as well) (iv) Incremental cost plus fixed fee. The fixed fee is a reservation price calculated on the budgeted fixed cost plus a percentage return on capital employed.

(B) *Standard cost*: It may be (i) Standard full cost with or without mark up or (ii) Marginal cost or (iii) Standard variable cost to manufacture plus lumps sum stare of fixed manufacturing cost with or without a charge to cover return on capital employed.

Example 10

The two departments of a firm *A* and *B*, have the following information:

	Department A ₹	Department B ₹	Total ₹
Sales	8,000	24,000	32,000
Cost of production	12,000	10,000	22,000
Profit	—	—	10,000

Department *A* sells half product to *B*. You are required to calculate transfer price at cost, at cost plus profit of 25%, and at assumed standard cost plus.

Solution

Transfer price at cost

If the transfer price is at cost, *A* would have sold to *B* of ₹ 6,000. This would cost *B* as follows:

	Deptt. A ₹	Deptt. B ₹	Total ₹
Open market sales	8,000	24,000	32,000
Transfer sales	6,000	Nil	Nil
Total sales	14,000	24,000	
Transfer costs	Nil	6,000	
Own costs	12,000	10,000	22,000
Profit	2,000	8,000	10,000

A would prefer to sell in the market to earn more profit.

Transfer price at cost plus 25%

	Deptt. A ₹	Deptt. B ₹	Total ₹
Open market sales	8,000	24,000	32,000
Transfer sales	7,500	—	—
	15,500	24,000	
Transfer cost	Nil	7,500	
Own costs	12,000	10,000	22,000
Profit	3,500	6,500	10,000

Transfer price at standard cost plus 25%

We assume that department *A*'s standard costs are ₹ 12,000 and actual costs ₹ 16,000 and transfer as usual is half.

	Deptt. *A* ₹	Deptt. *B* ₹	Total ₹
Open market sales	8,000	24,000	32,000
Transfer sales	7,500	—	—
	15,500	24,000	
Transfer costs	Nil	7,500	
Own costs	16,000	10,000	26,000
Profit (loss)	(500)	6,500	6,000

In the above case if transfer is at cost plus 25%, then department *A*'s total sales would be ₹ 18,000 (₹ 8,000 + ₹ 10,000) and costs will be ₹ 16,000. It would earn profit of ₹ 2,000. For Department *B* the total costs will be ₹ 20,000 (₹ 10,000 + ₹ 10,000) and its profit will be ₹ 4,000. The total profit of the firm will be the same as ₹ 6,000.

The drawback of standard price plus is that where market price exists manager would compare standard price and market price. Standard price plus can be used in the absence of market price. Then it will motivate managers to increase output and reduce expenditure level.

Marginal costs: The transfer price should equal the division's marginal costs (often, approximately the variable) directly associated with production and transfer, plus any opportunity costs to the total organisation. The rule is easier to state than apply. The marginal costs are essentially the easily established prime costs of materials and direct labour for which reasonable recent cash payments have been made. It is more difficult to establish the indirect costs directly associated with the goods or service transferred which should be included.

If there is no intermediate market for the product of the supply division, the opportunity cost is zero. The transfer price in that case will be equal to marginal (variable cost) cost of the transferring division. But managers are reluctant to transfer goods and services at marginal cost, since it will reduce the division's performance measure. Consider the following example:

Example 11[1]

Division *A* is the only producer for an intermediate product used by Division *B* and all transfers of *A* are made internally. The cost break up is a follows:

Division *A* = Fixed costs ₹ 500 variables costs ₹ 0.10 per units.

Division *B* = Fixed cost of ₹ 1,250 and if it processes more than 1,000 units.

1. Adapted from Kaplan, *Advance Management Accounting*.

Additional cost per unit it incurs of ₹ 0.25 currently *B* is purchasing 2,000 units from *A*. At this level *A* has calculated Fixed cost per unit 0.25 P. and variable cost 0.10 P. per unit. *A* wants to sell to *B* at 0.40 P. Should *B* accept this transfer price? Will it make any difference for *A* if marginal cost of 0.10 P. be the transfer price? The forecast for revenue for *B* is given below:

Sales in units	Net Revenue per 1,000 units ₹
1,000	1,750
2,000	1,350
3,000	1,100
4,000	925
5,000	800
6,000	666

Solution

B's output	*B*'s own cost	Transfer cost	*B*'s Total cost	*B*'s Revenue total	Profit or (loss)
1,000	1,250	400	1,650	1,750	100
2,000	1,500	800	2,300	2,700	400
3,000	1,750	1,200	2,950	3,300	350

B may buy @ ₹ 0.40, 2,000 units and not more, otherwise *B* profit goes down. The total profit for the firm at 2,000 units is ₹ 500 and this profit for the firm will increase if *A* sells 4,000 units to *B* and not more. Observe the following:

Output units	*A*'s cost ₹	*B*'s cost ₹	Total cost ₹	Total Revenue ₹	Combined profit or ₹
1,000	600	1,250	1,850	1,750	(100)
2,000	700	1,500	2,200	2,700	500
3,000	800	1,750	2,550	3,300	750
4,000	900	2,000	2,900	3,700	800
5,000	1,000	2,250	3,600	4,000	750

So, keeping the firm's goal in view, *B* should buy up to 4,000 units. If *A* charges 10 P., the marginal cost, it will cause loss to *A* of ₹ 500 and gain to *B* of ₹ 1,300 for sale of 4,000 units.

This example tells us the conflict between transfer price to motivate optimal local decision-making and its role to evaluate divisional performance.

If the competitive market for intermediate product does not exist, marginal cost will be motivating as transfer price. The unifying concept for obtaining an appropriate transfer price is to recognize opportunity cost to the firm as a whole for making the transfer. The only opportunity cost of transfer from *A* to *B* is the variable cost of 10 P. per unit, which represents incremental cost of *A* incurred for producing additional unit for the intermediate product. The rule is that transfer price should be equal to incremental cost so long as there is unutilized capacity. This incremental cost rule is theoretical. One problem is supply division will record a loss. While large profits are shown for buying division. Secondly, marginal cost rule also starts break down when the supply division is operating near a capacity constraint because opportunity cost shifts from variable cost. Moreover, marginal cost transfer price will also misrepresent the cost function of producing intermediate product.

(b) *Market price*: It is the most desirable transfer price because it generally leads to optimal decisions. It may be actual market price or modifiable market price. There are three problems that conflict each other in transfer pricing, i.e. goal congruence, incentive and autonomy.

They are not present in market price. R.N. Anthony says that in market transfer price three guidelines are to be followed (i) a market price should be used, (ii) the seller should have the option of not selling internally, (iii) an arbitration procedure should be available to settling disputes in the firm. The third should not be frequently used. The market price may be reduced if buying division purchases in large quantities. Moreover, the quality, dependable delivery and assurance of supply must be assured to the buying division.

In a competitive situation transfer prices are more likely to be related to selling, i.e. market price. But complications set in because a perfectly competitive situation is largely a theoretical assumption of economists. The problem areas arising from the use of market prices for transfer prices are, fluctuations in prices, different markets, product differentiation, varying level of quality and service and extra features. The service consist of credit terms, grade and delivery terms etc.

If there is idle capacity, rigid adherence to market price may lead to incongruent decisions. Idle capacity here means that the market will not purchase all the maximum possible output at a price exceeding the incremental cost of production. See the following example:

Example 12

Strong Mills Ltd., manufactures a special chemical in Department *A*, which is operating at 80% capacity i.e. 8,000 kilos per week. Its variable costs are ₹ 7 per kilo and fixed costs are ₹ 15,000 per week. The chemical is transferred to Department *B* or *C*, which uses it to produce perfumes. The details of these departments are given below:

Department *B*	Department *C*
Production 2,000 kilos	6,000 kilos
Fixed costs ₹ 1,000 per week	₹ 1,600 per week
Variable cost ₹ 2 per kilo	₹ 4 per kilo
Selling price ₹ 15 per kilo	₹ 18 per kilo

The transfer price is ₹ 10 per kilo, which is current market price. The current position is as under:

	Deptt. *A* ₹	Deptt. *B* ₹	Deptt. *C* ₹	Total ₹
Sales to outsider	0	30,000	1,08,000	1,38,000
Transfer sales	80,000	—	—	—
	80,000	30,000	1,08,000	—
Less Costs:				
Transfer price	0	20,000	60,000	
Variable cost	56,000	4,000	24,000	84,000
Fixed costs	15,000	1,000	16,000	32,000
Profit	9,000	5,000	8,000	22,000

The company wants to increase to capacity of *A* because there is no opportunity to sell outside. *B* and *C* can produce up to 1,000 kilos extra per week. Suppose, if *B* produces extra 1,000 kilos the selling price falls to ₹ 13.80 and if *C* produces 1,000 kilos the selling price falls to ₹ 17. Should the capacity be increased?

Solution

At 100% capacity the profitability will be as follows. Note that *A* gains, but *B*'s and *C*'s profit falls and hence they will oppose to increase their capacity. The solution is that market price should not be used. The transfer price may be marginal cost of ₹ 7 plus profit margin sufficient to cover fixed costs of *A* and earn profit, i.e. to apply opportunity concept.

	A ₹	*B* ₹	*C* ₹	Total ₹
Sales to outsider	0	41,400	1,19,000	1,60,400
Transfer sales	1,00,000	—	—	
	1,00,000	41,400	1,19,000	
Less Costs:				
Transfer price	0	30,000	70,000	—
Variable cost	70,000	6,000	28,000	1,04,000
Fixed costs	15,000	1,000	16,000	32,000
Profit	15,000	4,400	5,000	24,400

The market price, therefore, is not suitable in all cases, particularly in case of non-existence of an intermediate market.

If the intermediate market is imperfectly competitive, additional volume can be obtained only if selling price is lowered. This means that the existing market price at a particular volume level is no longer applicable for the decision how much to produce and sell. Thus, market price should be a special case rather than a universal guide.

Advantages of Market Price

1. Divisional managers are assured of independence in respect of sourcing decisions.
2. They represent true opportunity costs.
3. They provide incentive for efficient production because excessive cost cannot be passed on the buyers.

Disadvantages

1. It can be applied only to fairly standard products under stable market conditions.
2. It breaks down where there is excess capacity.
3. Low initial prices are often quoted to get a foothold in the market.
4. There are problems of quality differential between outsiders; products and the companies own standards.

(c) *Negotiated transfer price*: In theory a transfer price based on negotiations between buying and selling divisions would be more acceptable. This presupposes that the divisional managers and those who are involved in determining prices have adequate information of market situation and product costs. This will enable them to arrive a transfer prices, which are fair to both parties. In practice, negotiations do not always result in harmonious relations as they should, because of varying positions of strengths, unresolved conflicts and cases going by default for either lack of information or bad presentation of one's case.

Usually, this price is used in the absence of a competitive outside market or may be sometimes based on cost. The negotiation becomes time consuming, it needs frequent revision of prices and leads to a greater degree of authority and control over the profit of the divisions.

(d) *Arbitrary transfer price*: This price was used in the past and is set arbitrarily by the executive management at a level which is best in the interest of the firm as a whole. This system defeats the very purpose of decentralizing profit responsibility.

(e) *Dual pricing*: There is no single best transfer price method for all situations. The method selected should be based on the purpose which the transfer price is to serve. There is no necessity of having a single transfer price. One transfer price may be used for one purpose and another for a second purpose. For example, the supply division may use market based, negotiated or arbitrary transfer price for intra company sales. It may use marginal cost for internal transfers, if there is one product and no market for intermediate product. The marginal cost may be variable cost of supply division plus an equitable portion of fixed costs. But the major weakness of dual price because of which is it not used widely in practice. The trouble is that all managers in the "sub-units win, but the organisation as a whole may lose". The supply division gets a high price, and buying division gets a low price. Both managers of these divisions get too sloppy regarding cost controls within their sub-units.

Transfer Price and External Markets

The analysis of transfer pricing problem can be simplified by distinguishing between situations:

(a) Where no external market exists for purchases or sales. It means the product is unsaleable on eternal market or not purchasable on external market. It may be due to many reasons e.g. no external demand or partly processed product or qualitative difference.

(b) Where an external market exists. This means that the intermediate product could be sold on the external market or purchased on the open market. It is a matter of judgement, in practice, to sell or buy an "equivalent" product.

The transfer pricing bases in each case are:

(a) *Where no external markets exist:*

(1) full cost pricing, (2) variable cost pricing, (3) marginal cost pricing, (4) dual transfer price, (5) standard cost.

(b) *Where external markets exist:*

(1) The basic formula applied in most cases is:
Transfer price = Cost to the point of transfer plus opportunity cost for the organisation as a whole.

(2) Sometimes full cost plus mark up is regarded as a good approximation of the market price.

(3) Quoted or negotiated market price.

COST PROBLEM AREAS

Problem areas when using costs as a basis for transfer pricing could be broadly covered under materials labour and overheads.

Materials: (1) Purchase costs could vary from consignment to consignment. (2) One could dispute the percentage to be added on account of manufacturing losses. (3) One has to decide if abnormal losses have to be provided. (4) Control process *vs.* market prices. (5) FIFO, LIFO, average or derived from specific consignment.

Labour and overheads: The following areas may lead to conflict:

1. Level of activity to be adopted. 2. Efficiency variables. 3. Abnormal items. 4. Basis of overhead allocations. 5. Expenditure incurred to derive

long term benefits. 6. Varying capacity utilization each year and impact thereof on overhead allocation. 7. Share of Research and Development corporate office expenses.

ADVANTAGES AND DISADVANTAGES

The concept of transfer pricing could be used to: (1) identify unit contribution to total profit. (2) encourage profit consciousness. (3) measure management performance. (4) maximize operating profitability. (5) locate profits to minimize tax. (6) facilitate decentralized and local decision-making. (7) motivate divisional managers towards goal congruence. (8) serve as a tool for control.

(a) *Measuring performance*: The best method of intra company pricing for purposes of evaluating the divisional management of the supply division market price. In the absence of market price, the negotiated or arbitrary price may be used. If the objective is to measure performance the transfer price should not be based on cost. The use of full cost with or without a reasonable profit, would be better. For the supply division, it is suggest market price be used to compute its revenues, the marginal costs of the selling division, should be used to determine the cost to the buying division.

(b) *Decision-making*: Four general types of decision may be considered (i) make or buy, (ii) pricing of an end product, (iii) level of output, (iv) capital budgeting decision and decision to drop products. All these decisions should be made on the basis of marginal or differential cost techniques from the point of view of the firm. But for the division, market price and marginal cost should be compared before a final decision. For some decision-making purposes like make or buy, capital budgeting and abandoning a product the differential costs of the goods transferred from the division to division should be known. For decision as pricing or output, the marginal costs of the product must be used to determine optimal solutions.

(c) *General financial accounting*: They include determination of income and financial position of a firm. The inventories should be recorded at cost to conform to generally accepted accounting principles. This cost is full cost. This requires that the head office should know the unit cost of product by the selling division. The element of divisional profit (loss) must then be eliminated from the inventory of purchasing division and income of selling division in preparing consolidated financial statements. Harold Bierman and Thomas R. Dyckman suggest.[1] The following transfer pricing methods for each of the above use.

1. Measuring Performance – Market price (negotiated if market price is unavailable) and marginal cost.

1. *Managerial Cost Accounting,* Collier Macmillan Int., 2nd Ed., p. 441.

2. Decision-making	–	Marginal cost, variable cost (as a substitute for marginal cost) and differential cost.
3. Generally accepted Financial Accounting	–	Full cost of product (excluding intra company profits).

The transfer pricing has disadvantages too, namely (1) unit managers tend to prefer divisional profits over corporate profits. (2) lengthy disagreement on prices. (3) extra administrative costs. (4) need for conventions, if no market prices are available. (5) argument over disposition of cost variances. (6) prices to minimize tax liabilities. (7) task of eliminating book profits arising from inter-divisional profits. (8) Inter-division conflict increases when transferor division has space capacity.

ORGANISATIONAL FRAMEWORK

There is no one method of arriving at transfer prices which could be considered as ideal in all circumstances. As a matter of fact a form of transfer pricing suitable under one situation may cause difficulties under another. A study of nature of industry, organisation structure, its culture, degree of centralisation, etc. would be helpful before an attempt is made to arrive at a suitable basis for determining transfer prices. When evolving procedures for determining transfer prices, factors which could be considered are:

1. The role of the corporate office and if the prices will be centrally administrated.
2. The extent of inter-unit negotiations.
3. Accounts role.
4. Whether the prices will belated to costs or derived from selling price.

The company's organisational structure would be quite relevant. When considering the same, the following will have to be considered:

(a) nature of industry and size of operations,
(b) extent of vertical and lateral integration,
(c) extent of decentralisation, and
(d) objectives before the management.

Other significant aspects that need to be considered are:

(1) *Sourcing decisions*: Both the divisions, viz. buying and selling, can take sourcing decisions independently on their own; they cannot take such decision, and only some of the divisions can take such decision.

(2) *Manufacturing processes*: (i) Mass, batch, or unit, (ii) for stock or against specific orders, and (iii) whether raw material, intermediate or end products.

(3) *Market situation*: (i) Buyers' *vs.* sellers' market, (ii) if market price is readily available, (iii) extent and nature of competition, (iv) control exercised by the centre would cover areas such as

(i) sourcing, (ii) pricing, (iii) profitability, (iv) return on investment, (v) cost performance, (vi) approval unit budget, (vii) cash flow, (viii) approval of capital expenditure, (ix) turnover, and (x) market share.

TRANSFER PRICES AND PUBLIC SECTOR

Of late, public sector industries are also charged with the task of earning adequate return on capital. There is renewed emphasis on decentralisation setting targets and management by objectives. Transfer price will, therefore, be not unique to industries in the private sector. However, there are some problems peculiar to the public sector such as (i) social objective *vs.* profits objectives, (ii) divisional managers do not have full control over his resources and (iii) large turnover of divisional managers.

International trade: With liberal cash incentives available on exports and complicated tax laws, transfer pricing has special relevance in the export trade. Some of the areas that need to be booked into are utilization of spare capacity, tax implications and taking full advantage of various government concessions.

The problems associated with transfer prices have out grown the field of accountants. Management specialists and behavioural scientists are now equally interested in the subject. Problem situation arise from weak leadership, lack or relevant information and cost data and lack of confidence. There could be no formal or informal agency to resolve conflict situations and where it is in existence their intervention could be irregular and extent of their effectiveness doubtful. There could also be no regular review of existing transfer price and systematic revision. For this issue such as how often, to what and timings have to be decided.

Transfer prices is a management tool besides being an instrument of accountants. Its effectiveness depends upon how well it is structural and used. It calls for clear divisional objectives, an operational manual which is revised regularly, institutionalized mechanism to resolve conflict situations, and regular review of transfer prices.

MAXIMISATION PROBLEM

Where cost behaviour pattern changes there is a problem to produce more than 'optimum' among as it would cause reduction in profitability. Under such circumstances transfer price should be such that motivates the profit centre manager to produce at the optimum level of output, neither below nor above this level. We have considered this in Example 9.

Example 13

A firm has two divisions, *S* and *T*. The division *S* transfers all its output to *T*, which finishes the work. The costs and revenues at various levels of capacity are as follows:

Output Units	Cost '*S*' ₹	Net Revenues '*T*' Revenue minus cost Incurred in *T* ₹	Profit ₹
600	600	2,950	2,350
700	700	3,250	2,550
800	840	3,530	2,690
900	1,000	3,780	2,780
1,000	1,200	4,000	2,800
1,100	1,450	4,200	2,750
1,200	1,800	4,350	2,550

The profits of the firm are maximized at output of 1,000 units. What transfer price would motivate managers of '*S*' and '*T*' together to produce 1,000 units, no more no less.

Solution

The transfer price will be notional revenue to '*S*' and a notional costs to '*T*'.

(a) '*S*' will continue to produce more output until the costs of further production exceed the transfer price revenues. (b) '*T*' will desire to receive more output from '*S*' until its net revenue from further processing is not sufficient to cover the incremental transfer price costs.

Output units	Division 'S' incremental costs ₹	Divisional 'T' incremental Revenue ₹
600	Nil	Nil
700	100	300
800	140	280
900	160	250
1,000	200	220
1,100	250	200
1,200	350	150

(A) Since '*S*' will continue to produce more output if the transfer price exceeds the incremental costs of production, a price of at least ₹ 200 per 100 units (₹ 2 per unit) is required to "persuade" the manager of '*S*' to produce as many as 1,000 units, but a price in excess of ₹ 250 per 100 units, would motivate the manager of '*S*' to produce 1,100 units (or more).

(B) By a similar argument '*T*' will continue to desire more output form '*S*' if the incremental revenues exceed the transfer costs from '*S*'. If

'*T*' wants 1,000 units, the transfer price must be less than ₹ 220 per 100 units. However, if the transfer price is lower than ₹ 200 per 100 units. '*T*' will ask for 1,100 units from '*S*' in order to improve its divisional profit further.

Hence:

(i) The total profit of the firm is maximized at 1,000 units of output.

(ii) Division '*S*' will wish to produce 1,000 units, no more and no less, if the transfer price is between ₹ 2 and ₹ 2.50 per 100 units.

(iii) Division '*T*' will wish to receive and process 1,000 units, no more and no less, if transfer price is between ₹ 2 and ₹ 2.20.

(iv) A transfer price must, therefore, be selected in the range of ₹ 2 to ₹ 2.20 per unit (exclusive).

Thus, if a price of ₹ 2.10 per unit is selected profit at 1,000 units of output would be:

	Division '*S*' ₹	Division '*T*' ₹	Total ₹
Sales/Net revenue	2,100	4,000	4,000
Costs	1,200	2,100	1,200
Profit	900	1,900	2,800

At a transfer price ₹ 2.10 any increase in output above 1,000 units or shortfall in output below this amount would reduce the profits of the firm as a whole, but also the divisional profits of '*S*' and '*T*'.

Decentralisation and Transfer Pricing

Example 14

Division *T* makes a component which is used by division *W*. For 1995 the details are:

	Division *T* ₹	Division *W* ₹
Units	50,000	50,000
Variable costs	2,50,000	6,00,000
Fixed costs	1,50,000	2,00,000

The above are the budgeted separate costs of each division, find transfer price in each of the following alternative cases:

(1) Division *T* can sell the component externally for ₹ 10 per unit, at which price *W* can buy it from outside suppliers.

(2) As in (1) but Division *W* at present buys from supplier *G* at ₹ 10 per unit and there is a reciprocal agreement between suppliers *G* and another Division *Z* within the organisation. Under this agreement,

G agrees to buy one product from division *Z*, at a profit of ₹ 4 per unit to that division for every component which *W* buys from *G*.

(3) There is no external market for the component and division *W* is selling in a very competitive market.

Solution

1. If external market exists for *T*'s product
   Transfer price = cost + opportunity cost
   = ₹ 8 + ₹ 2 = ₹ 10.
2. If external market exists with reciprocal sales agreement
   Transfer price = ₹ 8 + (₹ 2 + ₹ 4) = ₹ 14.

This price should result in the manager of division *W* continuing to buy from supplier *G*. This decision is to be taken from the point of view of the organisation as a whole, as if the component is transferred internally. Division *T* and Division *Z* are foregoing external profit of ₹ 2 and ₹ 4 respectively.

3. In case of intense competition and there is no external market, the transfer price should be ₹ 8.

If Division *T* transfer at full cost, then the marginal cost of *W* will be ₹ 20 and cannot sell less than this. Therefore, there is a strong case for fixing the transfer price at marginal cost of *T*, i.e. ₹ 5 per unit. Any selling price by *W* in excess of marginal cost of both *T* and *W*, i.e. ₹ 17 (₹ 5 + ₹ 12) will give a contribution to the fixed costs of the organisation as a whole.

But the transfer price of ₹ 5 by *T* will not motivate the manager of *T*. For this the overall profit earned by the organisation may be divided between *W* and *T* for purpose of evaluation of the performance and motivation. The transfer price could be agreed which divides this overall profit in an equitable manner between the two divisions.

ILLUSTRATIVE EXAMPLES

Example 15

A company has two divisions *A* and *B*. *A* manufactures a component which it sells to *B*. The component is not available elsewhere and is never sold outside the company. One component is used in each unit of product of *B*. Most of the cost are fixed and for any output up to 2,000 units its total costs are ₹ 1,200. Thereafter total costs increase at the rate of ₹ 200 for every additional 2,000 units made. *A* has fixed transfer price of ₹ 1 per unit.

B's costs in assembling the device in the finished product and selling it are, in addition to the transfer price ₹ 2,400 for any output up to 2,000 units and ₹ 400 for every 2,000 units thereafter. *B* finds that it can only increase its sales by spending more on promotion or reducing sales.

Sales in units	Net sales revenue per 1,000 units
2,000	3,800
4,000	3,400
6,000	3,000
8,000	2,500
10,000	1,920
12,000	1,540

All costs, output rates and sales are per working day.

Required:

(1) What level of sales maximizes *N*'s net income and calculate *A*'s net income and net income of the company at the level.

(2) What level of sales maximizes company's net income, assuming divisional structure is abandoned.

Solution

Division A

Sales, costs and net income at different levels:			
Units	6,000	8,000	10,000
Sales per 1,000 units (₹)	3,000	2,500	1,920
Total sales revenue	18,000	20,000	19,200
Direct costs:			
Transfer price	6,000	8,000	10,000
Assembling (variable)	1,200	1,600	2,000
	7,200	9,600	12,000
Contribution	10,800	10,400	7,200
Fixed costs	2,000	2,000	2,000
Profit	8,800	8,400	5,200

At 6,000 units *A* will have maximum net income.

At 6,000 units *B* will have maximum net income of ₹ 4,400 (₹ 6,000 – 600 – 1,000). Net income of the company at 6,000 units will be ₹ 8,800 + 4,400 = ₹ 13,200.

Level at which Company will have maximum net income

	₹	₹	₹
Sales (units)	6,000	8,000	10,000
Sales revenue (net) (₹)	18,000	20,000	19,200
Less:			
Cost of *A*	1,600	1,800	2,000
Assembling cost of *B*	3,200	3,600	4,000
	4,800	5,400	6,000
Net income	13,200	14,600	13,200

Maximum net income is at 8,000 units.

Example 16

Geeta Ltd. comprises of two divisions, the Engineering division and the Electronic division, each of which is an independent profit centre. The electronic division makes two components, one called Rama and the other called Rana. The following are details of costs:

	Rama		Rana
Material	Parts ₹ 2 = 2	Parts	₹ 1
Labour	2 hours @ ₹ 14 = 28	½ hour @ ₹ 14	₹ 7

Annual overheads for the electronic division are ₹ 4,00,000 all fixed. This division's capacity is set at 50,000 hours per year.

Only one outside customer orders Rama component maximum of 15,000 per year @ ₹ 60 per component. The rest of the capacity is devoted to Rana component, which has unlimited demand and @ ₹ 12 per component.

The engineering division produces only special battery, which requires a special component from Japan @ ₹ 60. Its costs are:

Battery

	₹
Special component	60
Other materials	8
Labour 5 hours @ ₹ 10	50

The overhead costs, all fixed, ₹ 80,000 and market price of this battery is ₹ 140 per battery. It is found that Rama could be used for this special component, with some modifications. These modifications require a new total of 6 hours per battery. Engineering division has, therefore, asked electronic department to declare a transfer price at which Rama component could be sold internally.

Required:

(a) To calculate how many Rama components should be transferred to engineering division to replace the special component, if 5,000 batteries are expected to be sold. If price of battery is uncertain what should be the transfer price of Rama.

(b) If batteries sold are 12,000 @ ₹ 140 per unit, how many of the 12,000 batteries should be built using Rama component.
All other data remains the same.

Solution

(A)	RAMA ₹	RANA ₹
Price	60	12
Material	(2)	(1)
Labour	(28)	(7)

Contribution per unit	30	4
Contribution per hour	15	8
Total hours now used	30,000	20,000
Engineering options	Using special component	Using Rama
Price	140	140
Parts (Total)	(68)	(10)
Labour Rama	(0)	(28)
Labour	(50)	(60)
Contribution per unit	22	42

Overall company's viewpoint:

	₹
(a) Transfer 5,000 RAMA	
Sell 15,000 RAMA @ ₹ 30 contribution	4,50,000
Transfer 5,000 RAMA	0
Sell 20,000 RANA @ ₹ 4 contribution	80,000
Sell 5,000 Battery @ 42 contribution	2,10,000
Total contribution	7,40,000
(b) No transfer	
Sell 15,000 RAMA @ ₹ 30 contribution	4,50,000
Transfer 0 RAMA	0
Sell 40,000 RANA @ ₹ 4 contribution	1,60,000
Sell 5,000 Battery @ 22 contribution	1,10,000
Total contribution	7,20,000

(B) For each Rama transferred, two hours of time (labour capacity) are given-up in electronic department and in those two hours, four Rana could be produced, each contributing ₹ 4.00.

Transfer price = ₹ 30 + ₹ 16 = ₹ 46 per unit
₹ 16 is opportunity cost.

If Engineering department selling price were fixed at ₹ 140, it could accept any transfer price up to ₹ 50 (₹ 60 of special component— ₹ 10 for labour for modification).

If transfer price is set at say ₹ 49, and the price of the battery drops to ₹ 116. From Engineering department's point of view, contribution will be ₹ 2 if special component is used [₹ 116 – (60 + 8 + 50)] and contribution will be ₹ 1 if Rama is used [116 – (49 + 8 + 60)].

Engineering division will not produce any battery from company's view the contribution margin on the battery is ₹ 18 [116 – (64 + 28 + 6)].

Alternative I: No transfer, and therefore, no Engineering sales	
	₹
Sell 15,000 RAMA @ ₹ 30 contribution	4,50,000
Sell 40,000 RANA @ ₹ 4 contribution	1,60,000
	6,10,000
Alternative II: Transfer 5,000 RAMA	
Sell 15,000 RAMA @ ₹ 30 contribution	4,50,000
Sell 20,000 RANA @ ₹ 4 contribution	80,000
Sell 5,000 Battery @ ₹ 18 contribution	90,000
	6,20,000

Therefore, if the price for battery is uncertain, the transfer price must be set at its minimum acceptable ₹ 46.

(C) For a transfer of any amount between 0 and 10,000 Rama the foregone opportunity cost is the production of Rana. In this range, the relevant costs are equal to transfer price of ₹ 46 established in (B) above. Now the relevant cost becomes.

Outlay + opportunity cost = ₹ 30 + 30 = ₹ 60
(₹ 60 – ₹ 30)

At this price, it is cheaper for Engineering division to buy special component for ₹ 60, since ₹ 10 of labour charges are saved.

Transfer 10,000 RAMA	Transfer Price
	₹
Internal demand 0 – 10,000	46
10,000 – 25,000	60

QUESTIONS

1. What are the possible methods of establishing transfer prices? Describe where each might be used to advantage.
2. The inclusion of inventories in the investment base of a division has been criticized, even though there is no question that division manager has control over the inventories because (i) the required rate of return on inventory motivates the manager to hold less inventory than normal, assuming that the rate of return required by the division greater than the average storage cost (ii) and fluctuations in inventory levels will be accentuated, since managers will avoid holding high level of inventory levels will be accentuated, since managers will avoid holding high level of inventory. Discuss the possible side effects on inventory policies brought about by the inclusion of inventories in rate of return calculations. Also discuss how various cost flow assumptions (LIFO, FIFO) could effect the measurement of R.O.I. for a division of a company.

3. Define "Residual income". What is the effect on "return on assets" of different depreciation methods?
4. The following data refer to the ABC division of a company that sells one product:

	₹
Selling price	10
Variable cost	6
Total fixed cost	1,00,000
Investment	4,00,000

Answer the following questions, considering each independently.
(a) If the manager of ABC desires a 20% ROI, how many units must he sell?
(b) If 40,000 units are sold, what will ROI be?
(c) The minimum desired ROI is 15%. If 45,000 units are sold, what will RI be?
(d) The manager desires a 25% ROI and wishes to sell 40,000 units. What price must he charge?
(e) The minimum desired ROI is 20% and RI is ₹ 30,000. What are sales in units?

5. The following budgeted income statement for a division of Sagar International. The division sells to both outsiders and another division within the firm.

	Income of super division	
	Inter company sales To subdivision ₹	Sales to outsiders ₹
Sales:		
100,000 units @ ₹ 10		10,00,000
50,000 units @ ₹ 8	4,00,000	
Variable costs (₹ 4 per unit)	2,00,000	4,00,000
Contribution margin	2,00,000	6,00,000
Fixed costs (₹ 3,00,000) allocated at ₹ 2 per unit)	1,00,000	2,00,000
Profit	1,00,000	4,00,000

Required:
(1) Subdivision has an opportunity to buy all of its units from an outside supplier for ₹ 7 per unit. Fixed costs will be unaffected. Sales to outsiders cannot be increased. Should the main division meet ₹ 7 price? Consider both the firm and the main division.

(2) The main division is offered the opportunity to sell 90,000 units to a consumer cooperative store at 6.50 per unit.

The price of 1,00,000 units now sold to outsiders would not be affected. However, the sales to subdivision at ₹ 7 per unit would be lost because capacity in main division is only 1,90,000 units. Subdivision would have to buy the component from the outside supplier at ₹ 7. Should the order be accepted? Consider both the firm and main division.

6. A Company has four operating divisions. One of these is called division Lal that makes plastics. The manager of this division is in first year service with the firm and wants to make good show. He has budgeted capital expenditure of ₹ 20,00,000 for the coming year and is trying to decide on a method of depreciation, straight line or sum of the year's digits. The assets have useful life of four years. Total assets currently employed in the division are ₹ 40,00,000 of which ₹ 20,00,000 is plant and equipment that is being depreciated at ₹ 4,00,000 per year; the other ₹ 20,00,000 consists of current assets. The manager experts to show profits, before any depreciation of ₹ 16,00,000 in each of the next four years.

Required:

(1) Prepare budgeted income statements for the next four years, assuming (a) the use of straight-line depreciation on the new assets and use of sum-of-the years' digits depreciation on the new assets.

(2) Determine the total assets employed in the division at the end of each four years under both depreciation methods. Plant and equipment are shown at net book value. Current assets will remain at ₹ 20,00,000 over the four years.

(3) Compare return on assets and residual income each year. Assume 155% minimum desired return.

(4) Which depreciation method you recommend?

7. (a) Accountants typically ignore implicit interest in break-even analysis. What is the effect and importance of this behaviour?

(b) An asset costs ₹ 25,619 and will earn proceeds of ₹ 10,000 in year 1 and ₹ 20,000 in year 2. The time value of money is 0.05. Calculate the yield of the investment, and depreciation, income and return on investment.

8. From the following information, you are required to find the inventory turnover ratio, ROCE ratio after tax and rate of return on book value of assets after tax.

Working capital position on 31-12-2020

Current liabilities ₹ 1,98,625, current assets ₹ 1,67,125 (of which inventory is ₹ 90,200). Working capital deficit ₹ 31,500.

Profit & Loss Account for the year

	₹
Sales (90,000 units)	7,51,150
Cost of goods sold	4,51,000
Gross profit	3,00,150
Marketing and general expenses including ₹ 22,980 depreciation	1,49,920
Net income before tax	1,50,230
Less: 50% Tax	75,115
Net income	75,115

Fixed assets of the company are at book value of ₹ 3,50,000 on 31-12-2015. Sales of 1,00,000 units are forecast for 2016. Within this relevant range of activity, costs are estimated as follows (excluding tax):

	Fixed costs ₹	V.C per unit ₹
Cost of goods sold		4.90
Marketing and general expenses, including ₹ 15,450 depreciation	1,25,750	1.10
Total	1,25,750	6.00

The income tax rate is 50% current assets vary in direct proportion to sales. The market is likely to support a sales price of ₹ 8.40 at a sales volume of 100,000 units.

9. A Brick Kiln Company buys coal from a mine, which is converted into coke in company owned ovens. 80% of the coke is used in furnace and 20% is sold to outsiders. Coke used is charged to the concerned profit centre. Coke used by furnace is charged at ₹ 6 a ton which approximately is current market price less cost of marketing and freight costs. Normal output of coke is 80,000 tons and to outsiders is sold at ₹ 7.50 per ton.

   Cost of coal and other variable costs of coke production is ₹ 4.50 a ton. Fixed costs of coke division are ₹ 40,000 a year. The furnace manager tells that an outside supplier is ready to sell coke at ₹ 5 per ton on a long-term basis.

   Assuming that the company cannot increase its sales of coke to outsiders above 20% of normal production, calculate to guide the coke division manager in making decision as to whether or not to accept the offer. The furnace manager has authority to buy from outside.

15

Responsibility Accounting

The importance of controlling expenses is an essential element of profit maximization. The value of (departmental) contribution margin approach to income reporting derives largely from its emphasis on the assignment of responsibility for control. Elements of accounting system that provides the means of such controls, such as departmental margin income statement, are referred to as responsibility accounting. Responsibility accounting is the name given to that aspect of managerial process dealing with reporting of information to facilitate control of operation and evaluation of performance.

One of the basic functions of management is to direct operations of performance, as to achieve as nearly as possible the predetermined objectives. The managers must work in harmony towards the objectives and goals of the firm, i.e. to ensure goal congruence. Effective control over operations requires the assignment of definite responsibilities to personnel at various managerial levels. "Who did it?" Is essence of responsibility accounting. The responsibilities are carried out or not are to be judged by any performance evaluation criteria. However, one single criterion for evaluation is not enough because the managers would focus their effort only on that.

Responsibility reporting is the term used to this process of reporting data by areas of responsibility. Responsibility accounting, in addition to the selection of performance criteria, requires responsibility reporting. It is difficult to determine exactly by what a manager can be all responsible for. In almost any firm the performance of a particular manager will depend to some extent on the performance of other managers. Therefore, responsibility reports should include only those factors which a manager can control. These reports must be designed in accordance with the plan of responsibility for each operating segment. The management accountant can assist management by providing revenue and expense data for use in measuring actual performance on the basis of responsibility assigned.

Reports prepared for top level of management should ordinarily be broad in scope, presenting summaries of data rather than minute detail. They should be departmentalized to the extent responsibility is necessary. On the other hand, reports for personnel at the lower end of the managerial range should ordinarily be narrow in scope and contain detailed data. Putting the concept in practically difficult. There may be personal reactions and resistance.

Management Control Systems

A MCS is a logical integration of management accounting tools like activity-based costing and budgeting and variance analysis to report data and to evaluate performance. A MCS may be a separate system or a part of large system. MCS focus on organisation goals, internal management decision-making, motivation of employees and performance evaluation. To design it the existing constraints be found, responsibility centres be identified, install internal controls, weigh cost and benefit and provide motivation to employees. The designers of MCS must consider the organisational structure and define responsibility centres.

Centres and Hierarchies of Responsibility

It is essential that the manager must have clearly defined areas of responsibility—activities over which they exercise control. Generally, responsibility centres are classified in three categories, viz. **(a) cost centre, (b) profit centre, and (c) investment centre**. A cost centre is the area where costs are incurred but no revenue is earned. A profit centre controls both costs and revenues. These centres help to know the net income, contribution margin or incremental profit (cost) for evaluating performance. A profit centre can be natural or artificial. The former sells output outside the firm and the later sells its output within the firm. Investment centre controls not only costs and revenue, but is responsible for investment as well. The performance evaluation of these centres can be based on comparisons between budgeted and actual results.

Besides the responsibility centres, responsibility accounting depends upon the hierarchies of manager. It can be vertical or horizontal hierarchy.

In a vertical structure, there are no profit centres. Only the Chairman or Managing Director has control over both revenues and costs. Costs would be accumulated for each cost centre at the lowest level. The costs of these several lowest level would be accumulated to a higher level until the highest level cost centre. In case of horizontal structure, there are several profit or investment centres.

Responsibilities differ under two structures and hence the reporting system. Which structure is better is a question that has no definite answer? To illustrate the responsibility for manufacturing operations of an enterprise as represented in organisational structure depicted below.

RESPONSIBILITY FOR MANUFACTURING OPERATIONS

Exhibit 15.1

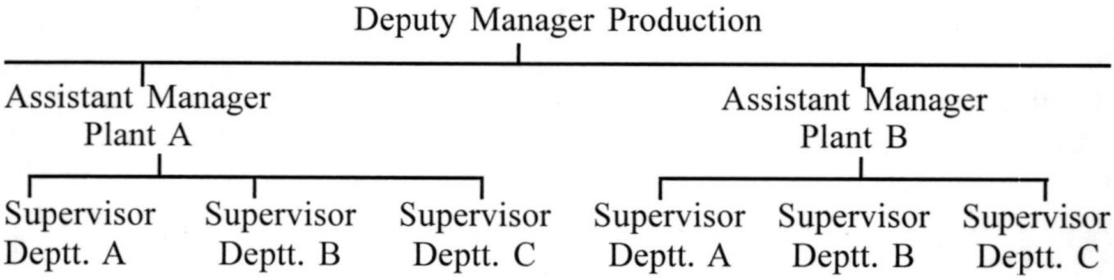

In the above example, there are three levels of management responsibility, e.g. Department Supervisor, Assistant Manager and Deputy Manager. Management reports assists each level of management in carrying out these assigned responsibilities. The budget performance below is an example of a part of a responsibility reporting system.

Exhibit 15.2
Budget Performance Report
Deputy Manager Production
For the month of July 2015

	Budget ₹	Actual ₹	Over ₹	Under ₹
Administration	9,500	9,600	100	—
Plant A	2,67,475	2,69,330	1,855	—
Plant B	1,95,225	1,94,700	—	525
	4,72,200	4,73,630	1,955	525

Budget Performance Report
Manager Plant A
For the month ended July 2015

	Budget ₹	Actual ₹	Over ₹	Under ₹
Administration	6,500	6,450	—	50
Department A	1,09,725	1,11,280	1,555	—
Department B	90,500	91,100	600	—
Department C	60,750	60,500	—	250
	2,67,475	2,69,330	2,155	300

Budget Performance Report
Department 'A'—Plant 'A'
For the month of July 2015

	Budget ₹	Actual ₹	Over ₹	Under ₹
Direct Material	30,000	31,700	1,700	—
Direct labour	48,000	47,750	—	250
Factory overheads:				
Indirect factory wages	10,100	10,250	150	—
Supervisors salaries	6,400	6,400	—	—
Power & light	5,750	5,690	—	60
Depreciation	4,000	4,000	—	—
Indirect material	2,500	2,525	25	—
Maintenance	2,000	1,990	—	10
Insurance and taxes	975	975	—	—
	1,09,725	1,11,280	1,875	320

The details presented in the budget depends upon the level of management to which report is directed. The report of supervisors presents details of budgeted and actual. He can concentrate on each item and find variance. A supplemental report can be prepared on the cause of variances to take constructive action. A scrap report is given below:

Material number	Units spoiled	Unit cost ₹	Loss ₹	Remarks
1	50	3.17	155	Machine Malfunction
2	76	0.80	60.80	Inexperienced worker
3	50	1.10	55.00	Sub-standard material

Other examples may include reports on direct labour rate variances, direct labour usage variance and cost of idle time.

Contribution Margin

Many organisations combine the contribution approach to measuring income with responsibility accounting. They report by cost behaviour and degree of controllability as well. Any cost that is influenced by manager's decision and action is called controllable. From the C/M, the fixed costs controllable by divisional managers are deducted, from that figure are deducted fixed costs controllable by others. The figure arrived is C/M by Divisional Managers. From this figure are deducted unallocated costs.

Transfer Pricing

The managers must be held responsible for only those costs over which they can exercise control. But in practice it is not so. In cost accounting, the costs are allocated to units of products and to the lowest level of cost centres as much as possible. The costs of service departments are allocated to the operating departments. The argument to allocate these costs is that the managers of operating departments receive benefits from the service departments and should be charged for those benefits. Such allocated charges can be viewed as transfer prices. But there is no method in which all costs of service department can be allocated without arbitrariness. Many methods may be used. They are:

(1) Allocate the cost-of-service departments on the basis of number of hours of service work performed in each department.

(2) Allocate a fixed amount regardless of use of service.

(3) Charge the cost of obtaining similar service from an outside service department.

(4) In the market charge each department a per hour rate based on budgeted variable costs predetermined for service costs.

All these methods have their respective merits and demerits. For example, under first method inefficiencies (high cost) of service department are passed on to the operating department. Method two produces a tendency to overuse the service. Under third method, service department is used as a profit centre. The fourth method is best of all. Actually, a manager should be charged with incremental cost associated with carrying out his function amounts allocated should be budgeted costs.

Measurement of Variance from Standard

The performance data may be structured around cost and profit centres. An evaluation of performance, however, assumes some benchmark. This benchmark may be previous period's performance, a set of vague expectations, or an explicit set of standards for inputs and outputs.

Once standards have been set and actual performance recorded, management develops data on how well the performance compared to standard. The nature of the problem depends on the number of factors that can be responsible for the observed deviation (or variance commonly called). It is based on management by exception principle. We describe here two possible models—the one factor model and two factor model.

One factor model: In this model, the entire variance is associated with one cause. Suppose the budgeted sales for marketing manager for the year are ₹ 10,00,000 and actual sales are ₹ 9,00,000. The variance of ₹ 1,00,000 is taken to be due to the marketing manager. While it is possible that others could have led to the unfavourable variance, one factor model does not investigate it further. This model is rarely used.

Two factor model: In this model there may be a (i) three way analysis or (ii) two way analysis.

In most cases, at least two factors are known to affect cost or revenue behaviour. Suppose the management has decided during the planning stage to cut prices and increase volume, thereby expecting to show a greater total profit than last year. The two factor model helps management to assess the various effects in price policy. Following example shows the three way analysis of the model. The management has raised its price from ₹ 1 to ₹ 1.25.

	Price ₹	Volume Units	Sales ₹
Present year	1.25	1,50,000	1,87,500
Last year	1.00	1,00,000	1,00,000
Change	0.25	50,000	87,500

		₹
(a) Change due to price = ₹ 0.25 × 1,00,000	=	25,000
(b) Change due to volume = ₹ 1 × 50,000	=	50,000
(c) Change due to price-volume = ₹ 0.25 × 50,000	=	12,500
		87,500

Formulas for the above:

(a) Last year volume × (difference in prices)
(b) Last year price × (difference in volumes)
(c) Difference in price × (difference in volumes)

Three way analysis is used when, sometimes, two way analysis may be misleading. This analysis helps to find out whether the cause of variance is one factor or the other factors, i.e. it apportions the entire variance between two factors. The three way analysis finds that the cause of variance is due to both factors jointly. Suppose the following data of a firm is available for a particular period.

Standard price	Standard quantity
₹ 100	1,000 units
Actual price	Actual quantity
₹ 110	1,000 units.

The two way analysis of variance will be as under:

Price variance = (Actual price – Standard price) × Actual quantity
₹ 11,000 = (₹ 110 – 100) × 1,100

Quantity variance = (Actual quantity – Standard quantity) × Standard price
₹ 10,000 = (1,100 – 1,000) × ₹ 100.

In responsibility accounting, the emphasis is laid upon the comparison of actual departmental expenses with budgeted or estimated costs, exclusive of service department. The two way analysis in that case may consist of (a) Spending variance and (b) Idle capacity variance. Both are calculated on departmental basis. Many accountants believe that only variable overhead should be compared and not the total overhead. So spending variance on departmental basis will be:

Actual variable departmental overhead minus Budgeted variable departmental overhead.

The idle capacity on departmental basis depends entirely on departmental costs without any allocation of service department costs. The formula is:

Idle capacity variance = Budgeted allowance for factory overhead (Actual hours worked) – (Actual hours) × Standard overhead rate.

Example 1

Actual departmental overheads ₹ 7,384
Standard hours allowed for actual production = 3,400 hours
Actual hours used = 3,475 hours
Variable overhead rate = ₹ 1.20 per hour
Fixed expenses budgeted = ₹ 3,200 (0.80 per hour)
Spending variance = ₹ 7,384 – (₹ 1.20 × 3,475 hours + ₹ 3,200) = 7,384 – 7,370 = ₹ 14 (U)
Idle capacity variance = Standard overhead rate

₹ 1.20 + 0.80 = ₹ 2 per hour	₹
Budgeted allowance based on actual hours worked	7,370
Actual hours × Standard overhead rate 3,475 × ₹ 2	6,950
	420 (U)

RESPONSIBILITY REPORTING

Responsibility accounting is based on a classification of managerial responsibilities at every level. Its stating point is responsibilities accounting information system, which rests on organisation chart. Each individual's budget should clearly identify the costs controllable by him. Lastly, there should be responsibility reporting. Reporting to various levels of management can be divided into responsibility performance reporting and information reporting. The responsibility performance reports are accountability reports which informs the concerned people how they have done in their areas and as well as motivates these people. Information reports are issued for the purpose of providing the manager with information relevant to his areas. They serve a different set of goals than the former reports.

The responsibility-performance reports should be based on certain basic principles. These reports should fit the organisation chart. They should be issued regularly, promptly and on time. They should be easy to follow and should have necessary details. These reports must not only give comparative data, but also should be analytical. Their number be kept at a minimum. Responsibility reports provide a basis for control. They should be kept under constant review. They should be tailored to the person who will use them, not to a function or job. They should be accurate. Reports should do more than communicate, they should motivate. Thus, they should be dept. of a minimum, simple, accurate timely P_y should motivate the employees.

Performance Reports and Responsibility Accounting

The performance targets set by the management involve a budget. Since budget is prepared in advance, uncertainty exists to forecast of future outcomes. An ex-ante budget is prepared before the reporting period and ex-post budget is prepared after reporting of figures based on actual output/sales. The emphasis of performance reports is on the short term. The common observation that budgets act as motivators where they are perceived "difficult but attainable" is of importance for the performance report and reinforces the proposition that the ex-post budget provides a better performance target than unattainable ex-ante budget.

The relationship between motivation and rewards is appealing for managers. But where performance is measured using accounting data and where interpretation of performance can lead to reassessment of targets, the link can become complicated.

Cost classification: For reasons relating to inventory valuation and income statement, the firm may have adopted an absorption costing system. The considerable cost of adapting the systems to a direct costing basis could be disincentive to constructing performance reports on a direct costing basis. Furthermore, managerial insistence on establishing "full cost", however irrational when viewed against the theory of relevant costs for decisions, is a powerful influence on system designers. In general, decision theory demands that only incremental costs are relevant to decisions. If, we assure that performance reports from a basis of short-term decisions, then the treatment of non-incremental costs as controllable costs or relevant costs or decisions is likely to stimulate adverse behavioural responses from the reportee and possibly also causing wrong decisions to be made.

The reasons for preparing contribution based reports in the short run apply equally to statements which include comparative information, such as operating statements and budgetary control statements. Again the emphasis would be on highlighting variances related to controllable variable items, and in particular to avoid complicating interpretation of the statement by excluding variances such as fixed overhead volume variance. This can be explained by following example:

Example 2

From the following data prepare variance report based on absorption costing and also based on direct costing.

Budgeted production/sales	50,000 units
Actual production/sales	53,000 units
Standard price per unit	₹ 12
Standard material cost per unit	₹ 3.90
Standard labour cost per unit	₹ 0.80
Standard variable overhead cost per unit	₹ 1.00
Budgeted fixed overhead	₹ 2,00,000

The Actual costs are:

Sales ₹ 6,08,700, material ₹ 2,06,700, labour 40,000, variable overheads ₹ 40,000 fixed overhead.

Solution

Absorption costing variance report

		₹	₹
(a)	Budgeted profit (Budgeted sales × standard profit per unit)	1,15,000	
(b)	Standard profit on actual sales	1,21,900	
	Volume variance (based on net profit)		6,900 (F)
(c)	Actual profit	1,32,000	
	Total net variance to be explained (b – c)		10,100 (F)
		Favourable ₹	Unfavourable ₹
(d)	Direct cost variance:		
	Material cost variance	Nil	Nil
	Labour cost variance	2,400	—
	Variable overhead variance	13,000	
(e)	Fixed overhead variance:		
	Expenditure variance	10,000	
	Volume variance (3,000 × ₹ 4)	12,000	
		37,400	
(f)	Sales price variance		27,300
	Net variance		10,100 (F)

Note: This format (i) disguises variations to the expected contribution. (ii) incorrectly measures volume variations in terms of net profit. (iii) mixes costs which in the short run would be controllable and non-controllable. Actual net profit is a combination of direct and indirect costs. Net variance is a combination of controllable and non-controllable costs. (iv) provides the link between the original budget and the profit which would have been expected based on actual output level.

Direct costing variance report

(a) Budgeted contribution	₹	₹
[₹ 50,000 × (₹ 12 – 5.70)]	3,15,000	
(b) Standard contribution on		
Actual sales (53,000 × 6.30)	3,33,900	
Volume variance		18,900 (F)
(c) Actual contribution	3,22,000	
(d) Total controllable variance to		
be explained		11,900 (U)
	Favourable	Unfavourable
(e) Direct cost variances:	₹	₹
Material cost variance	Nil	
Labour cost variance	2,400	
Variable overhead variance	13,000	
(f) Sales price variance		27,300
Net controllable variance		11,900
[to be reconciled with (d) above]		
(g) Actual contribution on actual sales		3,22,000
(h) *Less* Budgeted fixed costs	2,00,000	
(i) Adjustment for fixed overhead		
expenditure variance	(10,000)	
(j) Actual fixed costs		1,90,000
(k) Actual profit		1,32,000

Compare the items (a) to (k) of above format to that of absorption costing. This format provides most meaningful information for the management decision-making. It highlights the important features of a particular situation. This can be shown by following example.

Example 3

Following is the data of a mill:

Budget	₹	Actual	₹
Sales: 6,000 units @ ₹ 8	48,000	4,000 @ ₹ 8	32,000
Material: 6,000 @ ₹ 4	24,000	4,000 @ ₹ 5	20,000
Direct labour 5,000 hours @ 90 P.	4,500	5,000 @ ₹ 1	5,000
Contribution	19,500		7,000

Due to power shortage, the mill was able to manufacture during 60% of budgeted hours and Direct labour was paid in full. Analyse the contribution.

Solution

	₹	₹
(a) Budgeted contribution	19,500	
(b) Effect of power cut (60% means 3,600 units i.e. 2,400 less than budget @ 3.25 contribution)	(7,800) (U)	
(c) Volume efficiency variance (Actual production 4,000 – expected production 3,600 × 3.25)	1,300 (F)	
Standard contribution for production		13,000
(A) Material variance (Actual cost 20,000 – Standard cost 4,000 × ₹ 4)	4,000 (U)	
(B) Labour variance		
(i) Rate (500) (U)		
(ii) Efficiency 300 (F)		
(iii) Idle time (1,800) (V)	(2,000) U	(6,000)
Actual contribution		7,000

Note: Efficiency variance = (3,333 – 3,000) × 90P = ₹ 300 (F)
Idle time = 2,000 × 90 P = (1,800) (U)
Rate = 5,000 × 10 P = (500) (U)

PLANNING AND OPERATING VARIANCES

These variances are found to help the management to achieve maximum level of profitability. These variances are based on the evaluation of current prevailing conditions. The information used for planning decisions is different than the information used for operating decisions. Planning variances are helpful in finding managements planning abilities, provides a basis for identifying uncontrollable influences on performance, provides data for improving planning methods and reassesses original budgets and standards operating variance help to evaluate performance in the light of prevailing conditions rather than historic estimates. It reinforces responsibility accounting principles on the separation of controllable. Some writers subdivide the planning variances into prediction variances and model variances. Prediction variances are planning errors resulting from mistakes in estimating parameter values. Model variances are errors resulting from misassumption, deletions and other structural mistakes in the planning model. Similarly, operating variances are subdivided into implementation variances and measurement variances. Former represents a failure to reach achievable targets and the later indicates errors in measuring the actual cost of performances. Random variance is the variance that are divergences between actual costs and the statistically expected cost of random cost variable. Random variances are expected variances and should not lead to corrective action, whereas all above discussed variances give rises to corrective action if the potential benefits exceed correction costs.

The planning and operating variances depend on the source of information derived from "ex-ante" budget, "ex-post" budget and actual performance. The main problem in applying these variances is the determination of the "current" standard in the situation where original standard is no longer appropriate. Measurement of 'current' standard is subjective and likely to cause friction in the management.

Example 4

A firm's data is as follows:

Budgeted output and sales = 10,000 units
Actual output and sales = 9,000 units
Contribution per unit = ₹ 3
Standard material cost = 30 Paisa per unit
Actual price = 33 Paisa per unit
Standard labour hour = 4 hours
Standard rate per hour = ₹ 2
Actual hours = 38,000 hours.

Purchase manager is evaluated using material price variance and production manager by labour efficiency variance. It was expected to reduce average labour time by 10% and average material price to increase by 20%. By using the planning and operating variances, evaluate the firm.

Solution

Total variance		Planning variance	Responsibility	Appraisal variance	Responsibility
Sales volume	3,000 (U)	3,600 (U)	Uncontrollable	600 (F)	Sales Manager
Purchases price	270 (U)	540 (U)	Uncontrollable (or purchase manager)	270 (F)	Purchase Manager
Labour efficiency	4,000 (U)	7,200 (F)	Uncontrollable	11,200 (U)	Production Manager

In all cases planning and operating variances add up to the original variances, but the appraisal variance only agrees in interpretation with conventional variances in the case of labour efficiency. The planning variance for sales volume and labour efficiency may reflect only short-term adjustments. Price planning variance could be used to adjust standard for the next period.

Limitations: Responsibility accounting is an ideal system of cost control. But putting this system into actual practice is very difficult. It will face criticism, opposition and may defeat its own purpose. If personal reactions of people are not taken into account this system will fail. This system can be successful, like any other system, if individuals concerned co-operate each other. Co-operation is not a simple affair. Human relations play a very important role in its effective success.

Example 5

Practical capacity of a company is 12,500 units per month. Sales normally permit operations at 80% of practical capacity or 10,000 units per month. At normal capacity indirect manufacturing costs total ₹ 35,000 or ₹ 3.50 per unit. During January 2016, sales demand was above normal and 12,000 units were manufactured. Indirect manufacturing costs of ₹ 39,000 or ₹ 3.25 per units were recorded.

An argument has ensured between the plant superintendent and the foreman. The foreman says that he should be given credit for cutting the unit cost by one fourth. The superintendent says that the plant is inefficient and there is much waste. In spite of decrease in the unit cost, he insists that the foreman has let costs increase. You are required to prepare a report to be placed before the managing director of the company. The fixed indirect costs are ₹ 20,000 per month.

Solution

The superintendent is correct that the foreman has allowed costs to increase during January. The reason for decrease in unit cost of product is traceable to an increase in the volume of sales that permitted operations above normal capacity for which foreman cannot take any credit. The increase in volume of production brought a reduction of the one third in unit fixed cost.

Fixed cost per unit at normal capacity = ₹ 20,000 ÷ 10,000 = ₹ 2
Fixed cost per unit at attained capacity = ₹ 20,000 ÷ 12,000 = ₹ 1.67

Decrease in unit cost = $33\frac{1}{3}$ per cent
The foreman should be charged with unfavourable spending Variance of ₹ 1,000 as follows:

	₹
Indirect costs recorded	39,000
Indirect costs budgeted	38,000[1]
Unfavourable budget variance	1,000

Increase in variable cost brought an increase of $8\frac{1}{3}$ in variable cost per unit.

Variable cost per unit recorded = ₹ 19,000 + 12,000 =	1.58 ($\frac{1}{3}$)
Allowed = ₹ 18,000 + 12,000 =	1.50
Increase in unit cost	0.80 ($\frac{1}{3}$)

The decrease of ¼th or ¼th in unit cost is as follows:

Decrease from favourable increase in volume =	0.33 – ($\frac{1}{3}$)
Increase from unfavourable spending =	0.08 – ($\frac{1}{3}$)
	0.25

QUESTIONS

1. It is usually not possible to tell whether a cost is the responsibility of a specific manager simply by knowing the object classification

1. (Fixed cost + variable cost).

of the cost (rent, wages, salaries). For each of the following costs, indicate some circumstances under which it would or would not be the responsibility of the following:

(a) foreman, (b) department manager, (c) plant manager

1. Wages of factory workers.
2. Rent on equipment.
3. Electricity for machinery.
4. Cost of materials.

2. A company has two service departments: building services and administration. It has three operating departments and some of their data is as follows:

Operating Departments

	A ₹	B ₹	C ₹
Total separable Deptt. costs	3,60,000	4,40,000	12,00,000
Square feet of space occupied	6,000	9,000	15,000
Machine hours worked	42,000	70,000	88,000
Sales value of production	9,00,000	10,00,000	21,00,000

Costs for the service departments are as follows:

	₹
Building services	1,60,000
Administration	3,00,000

Allocated service department costs on three different basis and comment on them.

3. Prince Underwear Company wants to diversify the programme of production and started to produce woollen sweaters. About five months of the year given to produce sweaters and rest to underwears. Previously the production of underwear was over the entire year. Following is the income statement for the first year of production of sweaters.

Income Statement

	Underwear ₹	Sweaters ₹	Total ₹
Sales	58,00,000	30,00,000	88,00,000
Materials	5,50,000	4,50,000	10,00,000
Direct labour	4,00,000	1,50,000	5,50,000
Variable overhead	8,00,000	3,00,000	11,00,000
Total variable costs	17,50,000	9,00,000	26,50,000
Fixed production costs	7,00,000	5,00,000	12,00,000
General administrative costs (fixed)	14,00,000	10,00,000	24,00,000
Total costs	38,50,000	24,00,000	62,50,000
Net Income	19,50,000	6,00,000	25,50,000

Allocation was based on months of production. In the last year before woollen sweaters were introduced, the firm earned ₹ 9,00,000 on a sale of ₹ 59,00,000. Fixed production increased by ₹ 2,00,000 and general administrative costs rose ₹ 3,00,000 as a result of introducing woollen sweaters. The manager of the underwear section recently boasted that his profits have increased to more than double previous levels, with profit margin up even more.

Can you explain how the profits of the underwear section increased so substantially. Was the manager's skill or any other reason?

4. The standard variable costs per unit in mixing department are as follows:

Direct material:

Material A	—	5 kilo @ ₹ 2	₹ 10
Material B	—	5 kilo @ ₹ 1	₹ 5
Director labour	—	1 hour @ ₹ 4	₹ 4
Variable overhead	—	1 hour @ ₹ 1	₹ 1

During January 2016, 10,000 units were completed at the following variable costs:

		₹	₹
Material A	— 70,000 kilos @ ₹ 2.10	1,47,000	
Material B	— 30,000 kilos @ ₹ 1.00	30,000	
			1,77,000
Direct labour 12,000 hours @ ₹ 4			48,000
Variable overhead			10,000
			2,35,000

Using standard costs, the factory supervisor has charged the department head with an unfavourable variance of ₹ 35,000:

	₹	₹
Costs recorded	2,35,000	
Standard cost of 10,000 units	2,00,000	35,000

The head has complained that the charge for the unfavourable variance is unfair. On review, it was found that a slip up in the purchasing department caused a shortage of material *B*, which required as substitution of material *A*. There was a slow down strike for several days by the workers in the department. You have to prepare a report giving reasons for unfavourable variances in the mixing department.

5. At the end of each month, a company evaluates departmental costs performances by comparing budgets prepared for the period with costs recorded during the period. The January budget for the department *X* was used in the comparison. It was based on 1,000 units of equivalent production, the normal capacity used in applying overhead. The performance report for department *X* showed the following:

	Budget ₹	Actual ₹	Variance ₹
Variable costs:			
Direct material	20,000	23,100	3,100
Direct labour	10,000	10,070	70
Overhead	2,000	2,173	173
Fixed costs:			
Direct departmental	1,000	1,060	60
Service departmental allocations	2,000	2,226	226
	35,000	38,629	3,629

There were no units in process on 1st January, of the 1,100 new units started during the month, 900 were completed and 200 were in process on January 31, seventy-five per cent complete for labour and overhead. Material prices were 5 per cent higher than budget estimates, and direct labour was paid the budgeted rate of ₹ 5 per hour.

Calculate the cost per unit and prepare a report for fixing responsibility.

6. (a) Define responsibility accounting. Indicate the classification of revenues and expenses under this concept.
   (b) Find the correct answer of the following:
      (i) In deciding how or which cost should be assigned to responsibility centre or product, the important consideration is what avoidability, causability, controllability, variability or linearity.
      (ii) Periodic internal performance based on responsibility accounting system should distinguish between controllable and uncontrollable costs or be related to the organisation chart or include allocated fixed costs or include variances.
      (iii) The desirable measure of departmental performance is revenue less controllable departmental expenses or net income or contribution to indirect expenses or revenue less departmental expenses.

16

Cost Control and Cost Reduction

Introduction

The two terms, cost control and cost reduction, are used by some people interchangeably. Both are concerned with the efficient use of resources. Cost control is a static approach, which has the basic objective of containing costs within some predetermined target. In cost control, the objective is to ensure that costs of an organisation over a period are controlled within the parameters set. Whereas cost reduction can be considered as a dynamic concept which has the aim of reducing costs from some previously determined form, while maintaining the function 'value' of the product or service concerned. Thus, cost reduction has the objective of squeezing more from a given set of factors of production. Both cost control and cost reduction have something common, e.g., they both require a target to be set off after an initial cost analysis has been made. But both have distinct purposes and different techniques are used to achieve their objective.

Cost control can be used as a generic term in embracing all the methods of controlling cost of products or services through various stages. The standard costing and budgetary control, feedback systems are major methods of cost control. In both these methods first a target is set up. Then feedback information is received as to whether the processes are proceeding as per plan. Lastly, the variables are controlled when favourable or unfavourable variances appear. Then again a new target is set for next period.

Cost reduction aims to make real reduction in production costs or buying price of a good service without reducing suitability of these as far as the utility for its purpose is concerned. Cost reductions have effect of reducing the level of previous targets set in cost control system. Cost reduction is on ad hoc basis, whereas control system continue ongoing basis. Costs that require cost reduction are of two groups: (a) Engineered costs. Engineered costs technically necessary and determined by technical staff. (b) Discretionary costs. Discretionary costs are not technically necessary and are determined by management. The management accountant explores the reduction of these costs. The scope for reduction of engineered costs are explored by engineers.

The critical areas for cost reduction of these costs are (a) design, and (b) factory organisation and production methods. The critical areas for cost reduction of discretionary costs are employee remuneration and training, marketing and distribution and finance.

COST REDUCTION SCHEMES IMPLEMENTATION

Any scheme of cost reduction is unlikely to be successful unless there is managerial commitment. The emphasis should be on profit maximization rather than cost reduction. The scheme should determine the critical areas to be researched, secure co-operation of sectional manager, to choose the techniques for cost reduction.

The techniques for the identification of cost reduction opportunities are:

(a) Organisation and work studies.

(b) Method study and work measurement.

(c) Zero base budgeting (see Chapter 10).

(d) Value analysis.

(a) *Work study*: Work study also called time and motion study in the U.S.A., is defined in the British Standard Glossary of Terms as follows: "A generic term for those techniques, particularly method study and work measurement, which are used in the examination of human work in all its context, and which lead systematically in the investigation of all the factors which affect efficiency and economy of the situation being reviewed in order to affect improvement." This definition says that work study is a systematic investigation of human work in order to find more efficient methods of carrying it out. Work study can be used to examine the existing or proposed work. The objectives of work study are:

(i) To develop optimum work methods which provide the optimum use of factors of production, particularly the use of human input into the work.

(ii) To set up standards for measuring performance.

(iii) To set up work methods and work measurement systems.

The above objectives can be achieved if the problem areas like poor morale, incentive schemes, rejected work are investigated even though the work is carried out in a routine manner. Two major techniques of work study are method study and work measurement.

(b) *Method study*: This is the breakdown of production operations or procedures into their component elements to enable the systematic analysis of these with the ultimate objective of securing a more effective use of man, machine, and material i.e. what, where, when, by whom, how and why the job is done. Following are the steps in this study:

(i) *Select an area of study*: This is done by the management of the organisation or any committee or experts.

(ii) *Collect the facts*: The facts should be collected by observation rather than by interview of people.

(iii) *Consider alternative methods*: This means to consider alternative approaches. Consideration must be given to changes in the location of work, type of people carrying it out and other factors which affect cost and efficiency.

(iv) *Develop and install the method*: The costs, safety and possibility of acceptance are some considerations to be considered before development and installing the method. There should not be interruptions of production flows.

(v) *Re-appraisal*: There must be a follow up to ensure that the new method is operating and the benefits expected are accruing from it.

(c) *Work measurement*: This means that the time that a job or operation takes should be noted. This depends on the work study because it is no use to note the time and fix the standard for doing it unless the method of doing the job is optimal one. The standard time for doing the job should be fixed on the basis of time taken by an average qualified worker. The time should be adjusted for rests and lunch break etc., work measurement is carried out by time study or motion study. The former takes into account the time taken by a worker on the job, and the latter takes into account the efficiency of placement of tools and equipment and movement of operatives. These studies should not be made secretly, otherwise the working force will oppose it. The cost of these studies can be statistically tested, e.g. the use of activity sampling. Thus, work studies help to reduce the costs or to achieve greater production from the same costs.

(d) *Value analysis*: Value analysis considers reducing the cost of performing the function. This is one of the special management technique which is used in programmes to examine cost reduction. The idea of this technique was made by L.D. Miles in early 1950s. It has been defined as:

> The analysis of the utilitarian or marketing functions of a product or producer in an organized way with the aim of identifying any alternative ways of achieving the required ends, and in choosing the least cost method of doing this form the alternatives found.

The value analysis gained force in U.K. in 1964 when Dunlop Rubber Company introduced it. Prof. Gage mentions twelve steps in value analysis. They can be grouped as under:

(a) Collect all relevant information.

(b) Think of new ideas. Consider the function of each part and the whole product. Find out other ways in which these functions could be carried out. Arrange these functions in first order and second order. First order function means which make a product and second order function means which helps the product work and sell. The cost of the first order functions cannot be avoided.

(c) Evaluate new ideas.

(d) Plan the change.

(e) Put the change into actual application.

(f) Final assessment.

The value analysis will reveal the reasons for excessive costs. These reasons may be:

(i) Designers may make last minute change under pressure.

(ii) Usage may have changed since the product was made.

(iii) New types of materials might have become available.

The other factors that effect cost reduction may be (a) Design, (b) Factory organisation, and (c) Marketing.

(a) *Design*: It is called value engineering. Product design may offer opportunities for cost reduction. Three things must be considered in this connection. The product must have acceptable aesthetic qualities, meet the functional requirements of reliability and maintenance and the production costs of the design.

Some form of simplification and standardisation should be considered to reduce the number of components or end products. Set up costs must be considered. Better design will reduce the wastage of materials, production time and overheads.

(b) *Factory organisation*: This concerns the materials, labour and work services. Cost reduction can be achieved in the use of materials in the production process e.g. at purchasing or storing or handling or manufacturing stage. In case of labour costs also, the opportunities of cost reduction are many e.g. increasing productivity by incentive schemes or training or by good working environment. The cost of work services like power and fuel supply may also be sometimes reduced e.g. trading off cost of preventive maintenance or inspection costs or minimizing clerical costs.

(c) *Marketing*: Some costs here are unavoidable and others are discretionary. The areas of cost reduction are packaging, transportation, advertisement, etc. Financial management also may be directed to reduce costs e.g. in case of working capital management.

THE NATURE OF THE COST ALLOCATION PROBLEM[1]

If all inputs could be directly associated with particular cost centres, whether they were product units, operating departments or any other cost objective (see below for definitions) there would be very few problems in measuring values and profitability and, in fact, the whole process of cost accounting would be considerably simplified. However, this is obviously

1. Adapted from A.T.C. (England).

not the case and every business faces the problem of trying to associate different kinds of indirect costs with particular cost objectives. In the final analysis there is unlikely to be a "correct" treatment of indirect costs which would suit all the various information needs of management, but the purpose of this chapter is to examine some of the problems caused by the need for cost allocation and absorption and to emphasize the arbitrary nature of most of the accounting procedures used for treating indirect costs.

The Cost Accounting Standards Board in the U.S.A. has defined the terms used in this connection. They are:

(a) *Allocate*: To assign an item of cost, or a group of items of cost, to one or more cost objectives. This term includes both direct assignment of cost and the reassignment of a share from an indirect cost pool.

(b) *Cost objective*: A function, organisation sub-division, contract or other work unit for which cost data are desired and for which provision is made to accumulate and measure the cost of processes, products, jobs, capital-projects, etc.

(c) *Direct cost*: Any cost which is identified specifically with a final cost objective. Direct cost are not limited to items which are incorporated in the end product as material or labour costs identified specifically with a contract are direct costs of that contract. All costs identified specifically with other final cost objectives of the contractor are direct costs of those cost objectives.

(d) *Indirect cost*: Any cost not directly identified with a single final cost objective, but identified with two or more final cost objectives or with at least one intermediate cost objective.

(e) *Production unit*: A grouping of activities which either uses homogeneous inputs of direct matter and direct labour or yields homogeneous outputs such that costs or statistics related to those homogeneous inputs or outputs are appropriate as bases for allocating variances.

(f) *Indirect cost pool*: A grouping of incurred costs identified with two or more cost objectives but not identified specifically with any final cost objective.

(g) *Final cost objective*: A cost objective which has allocated to it both direct and indirect costs and in the contractor's accumulation systems, is one of the final accumulation points.

(h) *Allocation vs. absorption*: It is also important to distinguish between allocation and absorption. Absorption can be used to refer to a specific case of allocation i.e., the tracing of costs to individual product units. In the main, allocation will be used to describe the general process of cost association with cost objectives.

Generally, allocation depends on:

(i) Identifying the cost objective

(ii) Defining the cost pool

(iii) Selecting a method for relating (a) and (b). The link between the two is the "cost allocation base". The base is normally units of production, direct labour hours or machine hours.

Cost Pools

Pools are simply groupings of costs and the determinants of the classification could be:

(a) on the basis of cost behaviour—i.e., all costs are divided into fixed or variable categories.

(b) On the basis of function—for example, all selling costs are accumulated irrespective of whether they are fixed or variable.

(c) On the basis of department—for example, where costs are accumulated for a maintenance department.

Ultimately, pools may themselves be aggregated depending upon the information requirements of management and certainly for external reporting purposes.

Cost Objectives

Cost objectives can be either "intermediate" or "final" and the costing for the final objective will normally involve the aggregation of cost pools established for intermediate objectives. The situation shown in Exhibit 16.1.

COST POOLS

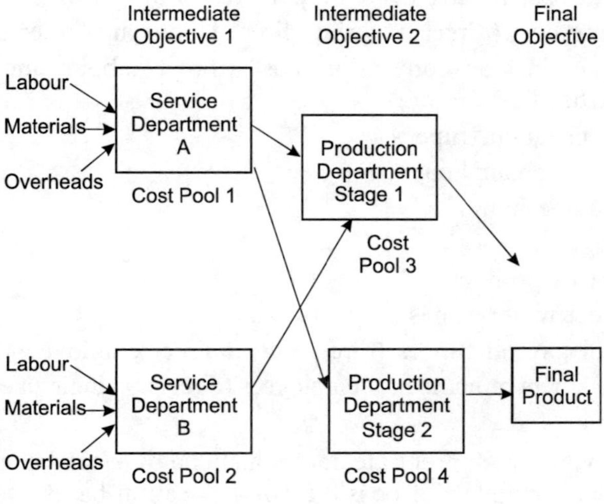

Exhibit 16.1

Exhibit 16.1 shows the individual cost pools for the service departments which would be established in order to identify the costs of running those departments. The next objective would be to establish the costs of operating the two production departments, each of which uses facilities from both service departments. New cost pools would be created, including the allocated costs of both service departments. Finally, the cost of the end product would need to be identified on a unit basis, requiring the absorption of both Cost Pools 3 and 4.

The "Key" Problem

The essence of the problem is establishing the appropriate cost-allocation base and it may only be partially possible to trace economic linkages between the cost pool and the objectives. For this reason the base selected will in many cases be completely arbitrary. Nevertheless, certain bases have tended to become acceptable through usage and the following is a list of allocation bases [extracted from the CASB disclosure statement]. These bases are the suggested recovery activities for cost pool under the following broad headings:

(a) Manufacturing, engineering and comparable indirect costs.
(b) General and administrative expenses.
(c) Service centre costs.

The bases are:

(a) Sales
(b) Cost of sales
(c) Cost input (direct material, direct labour, other direct costs and applicable overhead)
(d) Total cost incurred (cost input plus G and A expenses)
(e) Prime cost (direct material, direct labour and other direct costs)
(f) Processing or conversion cost (direct labour and applicable overhead)
(g) Direct labour rupees
(h) Direct labour hours
(i) Machine hours
(j) Usage
(k) Unit of product
(l) Direct material cost
(m) Total payroll rupees (direct and indirect employees)
(n) Headcount or number of employees (direct and indirect employment)
(o) Square feet.

Obviously, where appropriate, more than one base can be used. Having identified a large number of possible cost-allocation bases, the statement then goes on to require firms to tendering for government contracts to indicate how different types of cost pools would be recovered and an appropriate allocation method would need to be attached to each of the following pools:

	Type of pool	Allocation base
(a)	Single plant-wide pool	( )
(b)	Manufacturing	( )
(c)	Engineering	( )
(d)	Manufacturing and engineering	( )
(e)	Tooling	( )
(f)	Off-side or out-plant (geographical pool)	( )
(g)	Field service	( )
(h)	Material handling	( )
(i)	Departmental/shop	( )
(j)	Sub-contract administration	( )
(k)	Use and occupancy	( )
(l)	Quality control	( )
(m)	Fringe benefits	( )
(n)	Other pools	( )

Cost Allocation of Head Office Expenses

The statement on "Allocation of head office expenses to segments" provides some illustrations of appropriate cost allocation bases.

Home office expense or fraction	Illustration allocation base
(a) Personnel administration	(a) Number of personnel, labour hours, payroll
(b) Data processing services	(b) Machine time, number of reports
(c) Centralised purchasing and sub-contracting	(c) Number of purchase orders, value of purchases number of items
(d) Central telephone service	(d) Usage costs, number of instruments
(e) Centralised warehousing	(e) Square footage, value of material, volume

The Problem Reiterated

The above examples are sufficient indication that cost allocation is not a precise, clear-cut process but a vague attempt to take account of broad relationships and attach average costs to the objectives. Management will need to demonstrate an awareness of the allocation problem by asking questions such as:

(a) are the cost objectives generally receiving benefits from the pool in line with the proportion of costs allocated?

(b) are the allocations appropriate for stock valuation purposes?
(c) are the allocations appropriate for pricing purposes?
(d) are the allocations providing reasonable measures of product and segment profitability?
(e) are the cost allocations classified so as to not produce misleading information for planning and control purposes?
(f) are the allocations achieving goal-congruence between the various cost objectives using a common cost pool?

EVALUATION OF COST ALLOCATION SYSTEMS

The questions asked at the end of the preceding section give a firm indication as to the many purposes which cost allocation schemes have to serve, and in most cases it will not be possible for all objectives to be achieved. Ideally, the cost allocation base defines a cause and effect relationship, but this is a rise situation normally confined to direct costs. A criteria for assessing cost allocation would therefore normally be a combination of:

(a) Causal relationship
(b) Fairness
(c) Convenience—i.e., what may be ideal in terms of the other two criteria is just not cost-effective.

Irrespective of the purpose, being able to justify cost allocation on the basis of cause and effect is the ideal situation. From management's point of view, to be able to directly relate the incidence of a cost to a specific activity level means that not only is the question of fairness automatically covered by the facts of the situation, but the cost becomes controllable in relation to the activity base.

Unfortunately, few opportunities will arise where the relationship is so readily identifiable, although general connections can be found which, although not representing perfect dependency, do coincide with verifiable physical and technological relationships. For example, in a labour-intensive manufacturing process there ought to be a plausible economic connection between labour hours and indirect labour costs. Similarly, certain servicing and maintenance costs will depend to some extent on the number of machine hours worked.

The cause and effect criterion can therefore be a useful "general test", but will not assist the evaluation if the cost elements are fixed at all activity levels, such as factory rent, or are totally remote from all the normal allocation bases, such as development costs.

"Ability to Bear" Criterion

Where tests based on economic relationship breakdown, the cost allocation problem cannot be avoided, because stocks have still got to be valued (in accordance with SSAP 9) and products will still have to be priced. The only option is to construct some kind of arbitrary base and one common method is to allocate to cost objectives on the basis of "ability to bear". Effectively, this is tantamount to using the sales or market value of the cost objective as a weighting for cost allocation purposes, and this method therefore enables management to fabricate "profitability" as required.

The approach is almost opposite to the "cause and effect" rationale and its justification depends crucially on the assumption that cost inputs have a consistent relationship with the values of the end products. Importantly, this method makes no attempt to actually measure the cost input to the objective and leads to a situation where allocation depends on market prices, over which the firm may have no control.

Another problem on the motivational side is that "unsuccessful" products in terms of sales will automatically be relieved of costs irrespective of demands made on the cost pool. Similarly, if managers of cost objectives know that indirect costs will be allocated on the basis of sales value, they may feel inclined to be very conservative in their budgeting in mind that the cost budgets would be drawn up at the start of the operating period.

The Fairness Criterion

Obviously, the cause and effect characteristics would be the prime test of "fairness" but where this is not available the concept becomes far more vague. A common interpretation of fairness is that it should reflect on the benefits received by cost objectives. However, this almost inevitably leads back to the "ability to bear" approach and is, therefore, very much a second best approach.

Evaluation of Specific Cost Allocation Bases

Four common bases for allocation are:

(a) direct labour hours
(b) direct labour cost
(c) material cost
(d) machine hours.

In practice, (a) and (b) are in most common use, but each one has its merits.

(a) *Direct labour hour*—The chief rationable is that many overhead costs are time-related, and should therefore, be recovered on a time-related basis.

(b) *Direct labour cost*—This will yield a similar result to as long as rates are uniform. If rates differ, this method becomes defensible only on the assumption that higher paid workers consume more indirect costs.

(c) *Material cost*—This is unlikely to be an accurate allocation base unless a considerable proportion of the overhead is related to material processing or handling.

(d) *Machine hours*—This basis would seem to be particularly applicable where overheads were being incurred in a machine-intensive production environment. However, measurement of machine time may be more problematical than for labour costs and for this reason the latter may often be preferred.

Partial vs. Full Allocation

The arguments regarding allocation might be to some extent resolvable if the policy were only to allocate to cost objectives those elements from the cost pool which could be specifically related to the objective and which were likely to be controllable within the cost objective. The remaining costs would then be treated as "period" costs and may not be allocated at all. From a motivational point of view, to restrict cost allocation to those costs for which at least some cause-and-effect relationship could be identified would be a considerable enhancement to the purposes of the responsibility centre structure. It would also ensure that performance reports were more useful in terms of assessing cost control. Also, the formal delegation of responsibility for controllable costs could result in actual cost reduction, particularly if performance was linked to remuneration.

The opposing view is based on the idea that full cost allocation acts as a permanent reminder to managers that all the costs have to be covered. It is also argued that if the full charge is made, managers will feel more inclined to use the services, although the main concern ought to be the efficiency with which the services are used.

The Argument for No Allocation

In the final analysis, the view could be taken that if the allocation is to be carried out on a totally arbitrary basis then it is better not to allocate at all. This problem is particularly relevant to the treatment of general and administrative overheads where the relationship between the cost pool and cost objectives is necessarily arbitrary. It is almost impossible to identify a beneficial or a causal relationship. The only realistic attitude is to ensure that allocations are made only where there is no option, and in the main this should only apply to pricing decisions where in the long run these general overheads will need to be recovered. It is the current opinion of the CASB that where this kind of cost has to be allocated it should be on the basis of the total cost input of the business unit, on the ground that the costs in the general and administrative overheads pool are the expenses of the management of the business as a whole and should, therefore, be recovered on a base which measures the total activity of a business unit during a cost accounting period.

Cost Allocation and Purpose: A Summary Example

INDIA TODAY is a national publishing company mainly involved in the production and distribution of weekly and monthly magazines. National advertising costs are allocated to sales regions on the basis of circulation, weighted by an index that measures relative buying power in the territories. Indicate whether this method of allocation provides cost and profit information appropriate to the following decisions:

(a) Whether or not to close down on unprofitable territory.

Answer:

Not appropriate: Closing the territory will not change the amount of national advertising expenses. For deciding what action to take with respect to the territory, the segment margin (sales less variable expenses, less direct territorial fixed expenses) should be compared with the amount of cost which can be saved by closing that territory. This will show whether or not the territory is making a contribution to costs which will continue regardless of the decision.

(b) Whether or not a regional manager has achieved a sufficiently high sales volume.

Answer:

Possibly appropriate: It would depend on the extent to which advantages of the national advertising could be traced to the individual regions. If they could not, the allocation figure would be irrelevant. Local market research might indicate beneficiary effects and if so, sales could be matched against target responses to advertising expenditure.

(c) Whether or not the territory manager has operated his territory efficiently.

Answer:

Not appropriate: It would appear that local managers have no control over advertising expenditure, and therefore, the allocation should be excluded for performance appraisal performances. This analysis may require modification if a beneficial relationship can be identified, but basically managerial performance should be judged on the basis of controllable.

(d) Whether or not advertising costs are being satisfactorily controlled.

Answer:

Not appropriate: Control can be exercised only over the total expenditure for national advertising and at the source; control is not aided by allocating this total to territories.

ACTIVITY-BASED COSTING (ABC)

ABC is a recent development in management accounting. Under it, the overheads are absorbed on the basis of advanced manufacturing technology. It is the basis of benefits received from indirect activities, e.g. ordering, setting up, assuring quality instead of machine/labour hours, etc. It is based on the belief that activities cause, cost and the cost of activities be assigned to products based on individual products demand for each activity. This approach was developed by Kaplan and Cooper.

Many managers believe that the direct labour hour or cost or machine hours do not meet the desired goal in cost allocation. If many costs are caused by non-volume-based cost drivers, activity-based costing should be considered. ABC is a system under which first costs of each activity of an organisation are accumulated. It then applies the cost of activities to products, services or other cost objects using appropriate cost drivers. The force behind overhead costs are named cost drivers. ABC controls the costs by controlling cost drivers. Costs are grouped into pools according to activities which drive them. If say we consider financial accounting as main activity, then the cost drivers will be (a) number of accounting transactions, (b) number of times accounts produced, (c) volume of activity, (d) coordinated shipping process. There are three key areas of ABC: (1) Product cost differentiation, (2) Activities and their cost drivers, and (3) Identification of non-value added cost. Cost centre is established for each cost drive.

ABC is also called **"Transaction Based Costing"**. Most cost drivers are measures of the number of transactions involved in a particular activity. Examples of transactions that serve as cost drivers are production orders, material requisitions, machine setups, product inspections, material shipments received and orders shipped. Low volume products usually cause more transactions per unit of output than do high volume products.

ABC helps to measure the profitability of products and customers more accurately. Control of cost is also measured by ABC. Four steps are taken in ABC.

(1) Determine the cost objective, key activity centres, resources and related cost drivers. For example, in Bill department the cost drivers are as follows:

	Activity centres	Cost drivers
(a)	Account billing	Number of lines
(b)	Bill verification	Number of accounts
(c)	Account inquiry	Number of labour hours
(d)	Correspondence	Number of letters

(2) Develop a process-based route map representing the flow of activities resources and their inter-relationships.

(3) Collect relevant data concerning costs and physical flow of the cost driver units among resources and activities.

(4) Calculate and interpret new activity-based information.

ABC systems are more complex and costly than traditional systems.

Example 1

A company is manufacturing four products A, B, C, and D. The following information is available for a period:

Product	A	B	C	D
Output (units)	120	100	80	120
Cost per unit:	₹	₹	₹	₹
Direct material	40	50	30	60
Direct labour	28	21	14	21
Machine hours (per unit)	4	3	2	3

The four products are similar and are usually produced in production runs of 20 units and sold in batches of 10 units. A machine hour rate is now used to absorb overheads. The total of the production overhead for the period has been analysed as follows:

	₹
Machine department costs	10,430
Set up costs	5,250
Stores receiving	3,600
Inspection/quality control	2,100
Material handling and despatch	4,620
	26,000

The following cost drivers can be used:

Cost	**Cost Diver**
Set-up costs	Number of production runs
Stores receiving	Requisitions raised
Inspected/Quality control	Number of production runs
Material handling and despatch	Orders executed

The number of requisitions raised on stores was 20 for each product and number of orders executed was 42, each order being for a batch of 10 of a product.

Required:

(a) to calculate the total cost for each product under ABC system.

Solution

Machine Hour Basis

(In ₹)

Products	A	B	C	D
Direct material	40	50	30	60
Direct labour	28	21	14	21
Overheads (Rate × hours)	80 (20 × 4)	60 (20 × 3)	40 (20 × 2)	60 (20 × 3)
Cost of Production per unit	148	131	84	141
Output in units	120	100	80	120
Total Cost	17,760	13,100	6,720	16,920

e^1Rate per machine hour ₹ 26,000 ÷ 1300 e^2 hours = ₹ 20

e^2 hours = (4 × 120) + (3 × 100) + (2 × 80) + (3 × 120) = 1,300

Cost under A, B, C

Cost	₹	Drivers	No.	Cost/unit of driver ₹
Set-ups	5,250	Prod. runs	21*	250
Stores receiving	3,600	Requisition	80@	45
Inspection/Quality	2,100	Prod. runs	21	100
Handling/dispatch	4,620	Orders	42	110

$$* \text{ Production runs } = \left(\frac{120}{20}\right)+\left(\frac{100}{20}\right)+\left(\frac{80}{20}\right)+\left(\frac{120}{20}\right)$$

@ Requisitions = 20 for each product or 80 in total.

The machine department cost of ₹ 10,430 will continue to be absorbed on a rate of 10,430 ÷ 1,300 = ₹ 8.023 per machine hour.

Total Cost

	A	B	C	D
D/M	4,800	5,000	2,400	7,200
D/L	3,360	2,100	1,120	2,520
Set-ups	1,500	1,250	1,000	1,500
Stores/receiving	900	900	900	900
Inspection/Quality	600	500	400	600
Handling/Despatch	1,320	1,100	880	1,320
Machine Depreciation costs @ ₹ 8.023 per hour	3,851 (480 hrs)	2,407 (300 hrs)	1,284 (160 hrs)	2,888 (360 hrs)
Total	16,331	13,257	7,984	16,928
Cost per unit	136.09	132.09	99.80	141.07

Comparison

	A	B	C	D
				₹
(1) Cost of Production under traditional method	148	131	84	141
(2) Cost under ABC	136.09	132.57	99.80	141.07
Difference	11.91	1.57	15.80	0.07

From the above example, the student should note the following steps under A, B, C system:

Steps: 1. Identify activities.

2. Find cost of each such activities.

3. Determine the cost drivers (if not given) i.e., basis of cost assignment.

4. Collect activity data and calculate ABC rates.

5. Product cost calculation as per ABC.

Two Views

There are two views of ABC:

(1) Cost assignment view

(2) Process view

According to cost assignment view, cost object creates a need for activities to be performed and activities create need for resources. The cost flows from resources to activities to cost object, whereas demand flows from cost object to activities to resources. The total cost, called activity cost pool, originates from resources, then assigned to activity by a resource driver e.g. if a supervisor spends 60% of his time on machines, his 60% salary (resource) will be assigned to machines and then total machines cost will be traced to the products manufactured. Following chart shows it.

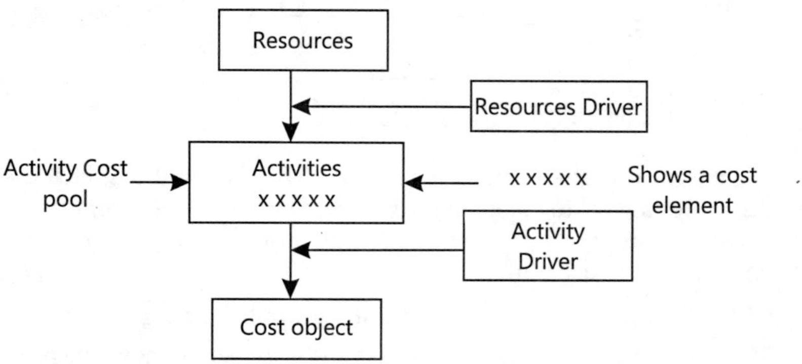

The above example has been explained by this view.

According to process view, the assignment of cost through cost drivers are assigned to performance measures like the number of defective units, unit cost of a manufacturing operation, and number of customers specifications. A performance measure indicates how well the work has been done in terms of quality, time and quantity. Performance measure for one activity becomes cost driver for next activity because first activity effects the next activity.

Activity A	Activity B	Activity C
(cost driver)	(cost driver and performance measure of A)	(cost driver and performance measure of B)

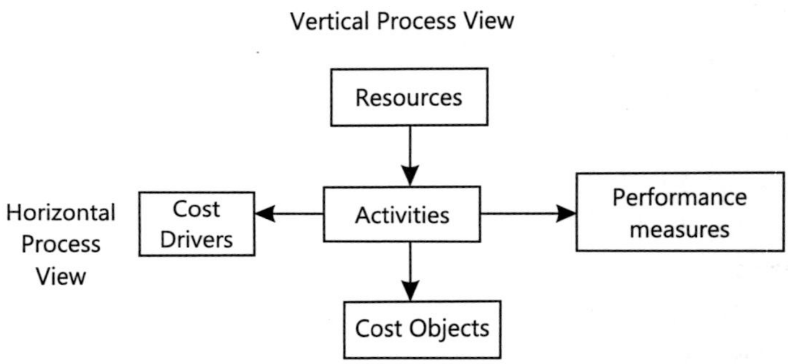

Activity Based Costing Model

Both these views can be integrated shown below, starting from inventory control department.

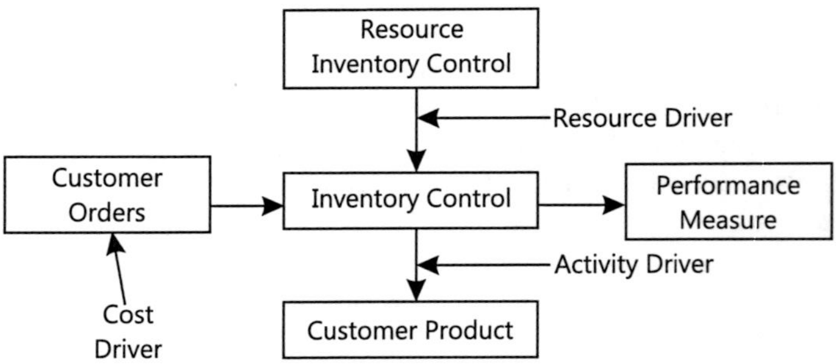

It is essential that appropriate cost driver must be selected. ABC should be reviewed to make improvements. In case of marketing costs, ABC can be used by tracing marketing costs according to products, customers, area and country.

Cost Management Systems and Value Added Costing

The purpose of cost management systems is to identify how management's decisions affect costs. This is done by first measuring the resources used in performing the organisation's activities and then assessing the effect on cost of changes in those activities. The main aim of cost management is to identify value added costs and non-value added costs. The value added costs are those necessary costs of an activity that cannot be eliminated without affecting a product's value to the customer. Costs that can be eliminated without affecting a product's value are non-value added costs, e.g. accounting costs.

Value added: It is the wealth created by reporting entity by its own and its employees' efforts and comprises salaries and wages, fringe benefits, interest, dividend, tax, depreciation and retained net profits. The value added is shared by employees, government, lenders and shareholders.

Accounting approach is to add net sales, income from services minus cost of bought in materials and services and cost of services. In preparing value added statement, there are problems as how to treat investment income, work-in-progress and stocks, pay roll costs and depreciation. There is a difference of opinion as to include or exclude depreciation.

Value added helps in comparison of performance, productivity measurement (per rupee capital employed/sales/labour cost/or per employee/ per labour/machine hour) and resource allocation.

A number of ratios are used for value added. They are:

(a) Gross Margin $= \dfrac{\text{Value added}}{\text{Sales}}$ or $\dfrac{\text{Operating profit}}{\text{Value added}}$

(b) Stock turnover $= \dfrac{\text{Gross output}}{\text{Stocks}}$

(c) Fixed assets turnover $= \dfrac{\text{Value added}}{\text{Operating assets}}$

(d) Labour productivity $= \dfrac{\text{Value added}}{\text{No. of employees or Direct hours worked or employment costs}}$

(e) Capital productivity $= \dfrac{\text{Value added}}{\text{Capital employed}}$

(f) Rate of investment $= \dfrac{\text{Capital expenditure}}{\text{No. of employees}}$

Example 2

Manju Co. Ltd. presents following information for the year 2015 of accounts statements of value. You are required to prepare for the company and value-added statement for the year. The number of employees are 95.

	₹		₹
Turnover	23,00,000	Raw materials purchased	6,25,000
Plant and Machine (net)	10,80,00	Cash at Bank	98,000
Loss on sale of Machine	75,000	Printing and stationery	22,000
Depreciation on Plant and Machine	2,00,000	Audit fee	28,000
Dividend equity shareholders	1,46,000	Retained profits (Op. Bal.)	9,94,000
Debtors	1,95,000	Retained profits for the year	2,88,000
Creditors	1,27,000	Rent, Rates and Tax	1,65,000
Total stock of all materials:		Other expenses	85,000
W-I-P and finished goods:		Share Capital Equity	15,00,000
Opening stock	1,60,000		
Closing stock	2,00,000	Interest on borrowings	40,000
Wages and salaries	3,27,000	Income tax for the year	2,76,000
E.S. Insurance	35,000		
P.F. Contribution	28,000		

Solution

Statement of value added

	₹	₹
Turnover		23,00,00
Increase in Stock of raw materials		
W-I-P and finished goods		40,000
Total		23,40,000
Less: Cost of goods and services purchased:		
Raw material purchased	6,25,000	
Printing and stationery	22,000	
Audit fee	28,000	
Rent rates and Taxes	165,000	
Other expenses	85,000	
Added value		9,25,000
		14,15,000

Statement of disposal of value added

		₹	₹
(a)	To employees:		
	Wages and salaries	3,27,000	
	E.S. insurance	35,000	
	P.F. contribution	28,000	3,90,000
(b)	To Government:		
	Income tax for the year		2,76,000
(c)	To Providers of Capital:		
	Interest on borrowings	40,000	
	Dividends	1,46,000	1,86,000
(d)	Reinvested in business:		
	Depreciation on Plant and Machine	2,00,000	
	Retained profit for the year	2,88,000	4,88,000
	Loss on sale of machine		75,000
	Total disposal of value added		14,15,000

Ratios:

1. Value added per employee $= \frac{14,15,000}{95} =$ ₹ 14,895

2. Earnings per employee $= \frac{3,90,000}{95} =$ ₹ 4,105

3. Turnover per employee $= \frac{23,00,000}{95} =$ ₹ 24,210

JUST-IN-TIME

Attempt to minimize non-value added costs have given rise to the use of "JIT" systems i.e. JUST-IN-TIME production system i.e. zero ending inventory. Produce as and when needed. The purpose is to have ZERO system. To make JIT successful, four steps are necessary:

(a) Focus on quality: This calls for TQC (total quality control)
(b) Short production life cycle time: It is the time from starting production to delivery of goods to the customer.
(c) Smooth flow of production.
(d) Flexibility in facilities and employees: Facilities should be able to produce a variety of components or products. Employees should be able to do a variety of jobs.

Some companies use TARGET costing i.e. develop costs on the basis of prices. Companies first determine the price of a product at which they can sell the product, then the try to produce less than that price to earn profit.

It is not just a technique or collection of techniques. It is a very broad philosophy, that empasizes simplification and continuously reducing waste in all areas of business activity. It depends on the communication concept of teamwork and continuous improvement. In fact, many of the assumptions, attitudes and concept of communication and capitalism are included in it. In a back flush cost system, manufacturing costs are accumulated in a few inventory accounts system using job order or process costing methods. Most of the accounting records are eliminated. The production facilities are also arranged in self-contained manufacturing cells that are dedicated to the production of a single or similar products. In this way more of manufacturing costs become direct product costs and flow cost allocations are necessary. Thus more accurate costing is obtained inspire of the fact the cost accumulation method is simplified.

This concept was first developed in Japan. It is an approach under which materials or parts are ordered in the exact quantity required and just at the time they are needed to avoid work, to control inventory. It is a purchasing method. Waste is minimised in waiting time, transport, processing, quality and inventory of materials. It adopts a total quality management approach. The main techniques uses in its implementation are: (a) Inventory management, (b) smaller batches of production, (c) production layout, (d) separation of value added functions, (e) care for uncertainties, (f) reduction of set up time. It uses a card or visible record called in Japanese "KANBAN". It is a pull system in inventory. To enforce Kanban, following rules are observed:

(1) People from downstream process only obtain parts from the upstream process via a Kanban card signal.
(2) People from upstream produce according to the information on the Kanban card.
(3) No Kanban—no production or issue of materials.
(4) Reduce the number of Kanban card, and used only when parts are needed.

JIT can be successful only if supplier cooperate, accounting is appropriate and cordial labour relations. It differs from 'Material' requirement or resource planning as they are computerised production scheduling systems. In India it is a failure, subbers put excuses live labour trouble, power shortage, transport sickness/Challans etc.

Life Cycle Costing

Some products degenerate over a period of time. The innovation of a new product and its degeneration into a common product is called 'life cycle' of a product. This cycle consists of market research, design and specification, tooling manufacturing, selling and distribution. Life cycle costing is a technique which values account of total cost of owning a physical asset or making a product during its economic life. In case of an asset, the costs associated with its acquiring, using caring for and disposing is considered. Besides the feasibility study, research, design and development, production and maintenance, replacement and disposal is also included. It is usually in a project. All these costs are evaluated together. In a project life cycle costs of capital asset can be grouped into three broad categories, (a) Initial costs, (b) operating costs, and (c) disposal costs. The project life cycle costing system developed should generate relevant financial information relating to acquiring of resources, appropriate case costs, efficient use of resources and replacement decision of an asset. The term 'Terotechnology' is used for a combination of management, financial, engineering and other practices applied to physical assets in pursuit of life cycle costs.

Example 3

A company wants to replace its machine. The types of machines are being considered, A, B and C.

The other costs are as under:

Machine	A	B	C
	₹	₹	₹
1. Cost of Machine (including installation charges etc.)	55,000	74,000	67,000
2. Misc. material	8,000	Nil	Nil
3. Labour costs (P.A.)	27,000	23,000	25,000
4. Maintenance costs (P.A.)	4,000	3,000	3,000
5. Electricity charges (P.A.)	1,000	1,000	1,000
Total operating costs	40,000	27,000	29,000

The new machines are expected to last for 10 years. The cost of capital is 15%. Which machine should be used?

Solution

Machine	A	B	C
	₹	₹	₹
Cost	55,000	74,000	67,000
Operating costs:			
A (40 × 10 × 5.019)	2,01,000	–	–
B (27 × 10 × 5.019)	–	1,36,000	
C (29 × 10 × 5.019)	–	–	1,46,000
P.V. of costs	2,56,000	2,10,000	2,13,000

Machine B is most economical as per financial considerations only. Much also depends on expectancy of life of C machine.

ALLOCATION OF SERVICE DEPARTMENT COSTS

Four basic methods are available for the allocation of service department costs:

(a) direct allocation
(b) step allocation
(c) repeated distribution method
(d) reciprocal services allocation

These can now be considered in turn.

Direct Allocation Method

Under this method, service department costs are simply allocated directly to operating departments, irrespective of whether one service department services another service department. This tends to be the most commonly used method. This and the other methods can be considered and compared in relation to Exhibit 16.2.

DIRECT ALLOCATION METHOD

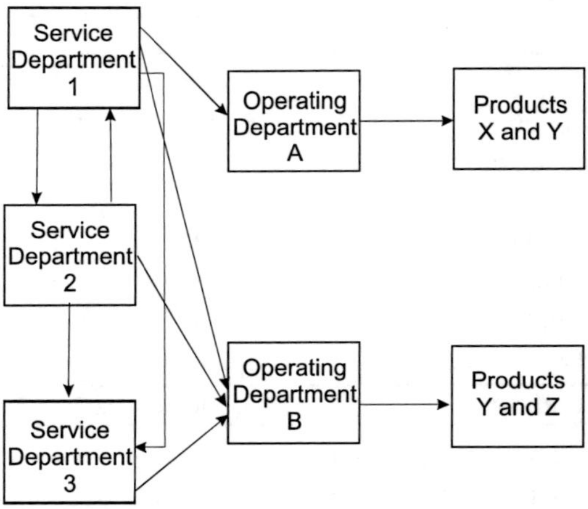

Exhibit 16.2

Example 4

Exhibit 16.2 supported by the following data regarding the utilization of output from the service departments.

Service Dept.	Service Department			Operating Department		Total units
	1	2	3	A	B	
1		200	200	1,200	400	2,000
2	40		80	60	60	240
3				150	50	200

Budgeted cost data for the service departments and operating departments is as follows:

Service Department	Cost ₹
1	1,600
2	1,200
3	1,800
Operating Departments	**Cost ₹**
A	2,000
B	2,400

Direct method computations:

Service Department	Operating Departments A		Operating Departments B	
	Ratio	Cost ₹	Ratio	Cost ₹
1	$3/4\left(\frac{1,200}{1,600}\right)$	1,200	$1/4\left(\frac{400}{1,600}\right)$	400
2	$1/2\left(\frac{60}{120}\right)$	600	$1/2\left(\frac{60}{120}\right)$	600
3	$3/4\left(\frac{75}{100}\right)$	1,350	$1/4\left(\frac{25}{100}\right)$	450
Direct costs		2,000		2,400
Total costs		5,150		3,850

Sometimes allocation may be on some basis. Consider this example.

A company has three production departments A, B & C and the expenses as per distribution summary are ₹ 30,000, ₹ 26,000, and ₹ 24,000 respectively. There are four service departments and their expenses are stores ₹ 4,000; Time keeping ₹ 300; Power ₹ 1,600, and Canteen ₹ 1,000. Other Information is as under:

	Deptt. A	Deptt. B	Deptt. C
(1) Horse power of machines	600	600	400
(2) No. of workers	40	30	30
(3) Value of stores	₹ 5,000	₹ 3,000	₹ 2,000

The costs will be distributed on following basis:

		A ₹	B ₹	C ₹
(1) Stores	(5:3:2) Value	2,000	1,200	800
(2) Timekeeping	(4:3:3) No.	1,200	900	900
(3) Power	(3:3:2) H.P.	600	600	400
(4) Canteen	(4:3:3) No.	400	300	300

Step Method

This method takes account of the services given to one service department by another and, as a result, is far more complicated than the direct method. The order in which the service department costs should be allocated must first be established. The most common solution is to allocate the costs first of that service department which services the greatest number of other service departments. An alternative approach is to select the service department first which has the largest cost to be allocated.

Example 5

Service Dept.	Service Departments				Operating Departments			
	2		3		A		A	
	Ratio	Cost ₹	Ratio	Cost ₹	Ratio	Cost ₹	Ratio	Cost ₹
1	1/10	160	1/10	160	3/5	960	1/5	320
2			4/10	544	3/10	408	3/10	408
3					3/4	1,878	¼	626
Direct costs		1,200		1,800		2,000		2,400
Total costs		1,360		2,504		5,246		3,754

Explanation of calculations:

(a) Service Department 1 is allocated first as it has the highest total service units.

(b) The ratios for Service Department 1 are:

$$\left(\frac{200}{2,000}\right), \left(\frac{200}{2,000}\right), \left(\frac{1,200}{2,000}\right) \text{and} \left(\frac{400}{2,000}\right).$$

(c) Secondly, Service Department 2 costs are allocated. Including the allocation from Service Department 1, these amount to ₹ 1,200 + ₹ 160 = ₹ 1,360. The ratios are:

$$\left(\frac{80}{200}\right), \left(\frac{60}{200}\right) \text{and} \left(\frac{60}{200}\right).$$

(d) The ratios for Service Department 3 are:

$$\left(\frac{75}{100}\right) \text{and} \left(\frac{25}{100}\right).$$

The total costs to be allocated from Department 3 are ₹ 1,800 + ₹ 160 + ₹ 544 = ₹ 2,504.

Repeated Distribution Method

Under this method, the expenses are redistributed to both the production departments and the service departments on an agreed percentage basis.

Example 6

The total expenses as per primary distribution summary of two service departments and three production departments are as follows. Redistribute the expenses on repeated distribution method basis of service departments to production departments.

Production Departments			Service Departments	
X	*Y*	*Z*	*A*	*B*
₹ 7,810	₹ 12,543	₹ 4,547	₹ 4,000	₹ 2,600

The apportionments to be made as under:

	X	*Y*	*Z*	*A*	*B*
A	30%	40%	20%	—	10%
B	10%	20%	50%	20%	—

Solution

	Departments				
	X ₹	*Y* ₹	*Z* ₹	*A* ₹	*B* ₹
	7,810	12,543	4,547	4,000	2,600
Expenses of *A*	1,200	1,600	800	(–4,000)	400
	9,010	14,143	5,347	—	3,000
Expenses of *B*	300	600	1,500	600	(–3,000)
	9,310	14,743	6,847	600	—
Expenses of *A*	180	240	120	(–600)	60
	9,490	14,983	6,997	—	60
Expenses of *B*	6	12	30	12	(–60)
	9,496	14,995	6,997	12	—
Expenses of *A*	4	5	3	(–12)	—
Total after Apportionment	9,500	15,000	7,000	—	—

Reciprocal Allocation Method

The step method provides an insight into the complexities which arise in allocation problems when service departments service each other. An exact solution to this kind of problem can be obtained using algebraic method, called 'Simultaneous Equation Method'*, although the solution

* The use of Matrix algebra can also be made. Students may see any book on Cost Accounting.

is relatively simple unless a large number of departments is included. In practice, the approximation provided by the step method is quite adequate. Under this method two following equations are solved:

x = Expenditure of "x" department + % of y department

y = Expenditure of "y" department + % of x department

In order to demonstrate the method, let us now assume that there are only two service departments and two operating departments. The data is as follows:

Example 7

Service Dept.	Service Department		Operating Department		Total units
	1	2	A	B	
1		200	700	100	1,000
2	1,600		400		2,000

The relevant costs are as follows:

	₹
Service Department 1	11,920
Service Department 2	4,000

Let x = total direct costs for Service Department 1 plus the percentage allocation of units from Department 2—(80%).

Let y = total direct costs for Service Department 2 plus the percentage allocation of units from Department 1—(20%).

Then:
$$x = ₹\ 11{,}920 + 0.8y$$
$$y = ₹\ 4{,}000 + 0.2x$$

Solving for x and y:

$$\begin{aligned}
x &= ₹\ 11{,}920 + 0.8y \\
&= ₹\ 11{,}920 + 0.8\ (₹\ 4{,}000 + 0.2x) \\
&= ₹\ 11{,}920 + ₹\ 3{,}200 + 0.16x \\
0.84x &= ₹\ 15{,}120 \\
x &= ₹\ 18{,}000 \\
\text{and } y &= ₹\ 4{,}000 + 0.2x \\
&= ₹\ 4{,}000 + 0.2\ (₹\ 18{,}000) \\
&= ₹\ 4{,}000 + ₹\ 3{,}600 \\
&= ₹\ 7{,}600
\end{aligned}$$

The allocation would then be as follows:

Allocations

Service Dept.	Total cost ₹	Operating Dept. A ₹	Operating Dept. B ₹	Service Dept. 1 ₹	Service Dept. 2 ₹
1	18,000	12,600	1,800		3,600
2	7,600	1,520		6,080	
	25,600	14,120	1,800	6,080	3,600

Note: That the total of the Service Department 1 costs and Service Department 2 costs are greater than the total costs incurred in the two departments. This is because of the reallocation of costs to the two service centres.

The total cost allocated to the operating departments is ₹ 15,920, which is the total of the costs incurred in the two service departments. The reciprocal method is only really justified as an occasional test for the step method so as to ensure that the calculations from the latter are not too remote from the correct figures. This is likely to be justifiable in the case of crucial pricing decisions using cost-plus methods.

COST ALLOCATION AND THE CONTRIBUTION APPROACH

It was emphasized earlier that the cost allocation problem was the result of the need to meet several management information purposes, but it is the nature of the exercise that ultimately the apportionment of the indirect costs will disguise the contribution being made by individual cost objectives such as products and departments. This creates special problems for the evaluation of performance and decision-making in the short run.

If financial information to be useful for measuring performance and providing relevant data for the decisions, the classification into fixed and variable categories is crucial. This should then facilitate identification of costs which are likely to be controllable and costs which would change with variations in output and sales levels. Also, it will ensure that contribution figures are obtained for the key performance areas.

The Contribution Approach

The treatment of cost allocation in terms of the format of performance statements can be demonstrated by the following general model:

The model assumes that the company is divided into two divisions and the product breakdown for one division only is shown. The allocation problem is treated in a way which ensures that the most relevant information is produced for decision-making and management appraisal purposes. Indirect costs are divided into the following categories:

(a) *Unallocated costs*: These are the general overheads of the business which cannot be controlled at any cost objective level other than the company as a whole and which would be almost impossible to allocate on the basis of causal or beneficial relationships.

(b) *Uncontrollable fixed costs*: These are indirect costs which can be associated with a particular cost objective but are not controllable at the level of the cost objective. These costs are therefore relevant in assessing the economic viability of the segment of product but not in assessing managerial performance.

(c) *Controllable fixed costs*: These costs are controllable within the cost objective's discretion but would not of course be controllable from a time span point of view, i.e. these costs could not be avoided in the short run.

	Company As a whole ₹	Branch A ₹	Branch B ₹	Branch B Product 1	Branch B Product 2	Not allocated
Sales	1,500	500	1,000	500	500	
Cost of sales	780	200	580	275	305	
Gross contribution	—	—	—	—	—	
Margin	720	300	420	225	195	
Less: Variable selling and administration cost	220	100	120	75	45	
Contribution margin	500	200	300	150	150	
Less: Controllable fixed costs	190	110	80	16	19	45[1]
Controllable contribution	310	90	220	134	131	(45)
Less: Uncontrollable fixed costs	70	20	50	18	12	20
Net contribution	240	70	170	116	119	(65)
Less: Unallocated costs	135	—	—	—	—	—
Net income	105	—	—	—	—	—

All other costs could be directly associated with either the individual segments or products.

The resultant key measures are:

(a) *Contribution margin*: This is the key figure for evaluation of marginal decisions up to the short-term capacity of the business units.

(b) *Controllable contribution*: This is the key figure for evaluation of segment and product managers.

(c) *Net contribution*: This is the key figure for the evaluation of the economic performance of segment and product cost objectives.

1. Only those costs clearly identified to product line should be allocated.

The Basis of Joint Cost Allocation

The established valuation basis for stocks is the lower of cost or net realizable value. Since separable costs present no allocation problems, the allocation of joint costs is the central problem. The methods of allocating joint cost split conveniently into two categories:

(a) *Allocation by relative physical characteristics*: Methods using relative physical characteristics involve the computation of an average and differ primarily as to whether a simple average or weighted average is used. Costs are incurred in the expectation on generating a surplus over cost and arguably higher acquisition costs would be acceptable for gold than for silver. The use of the simple average method ignores differential realizable values, yielding identical joint costs per unit for all joint products. Some attempts have been made to accommodate this criticism by attaching weight factors reflecting sales values difficulties of production, etc., to quantities produced. The choice of weight factor is of course subjective and the resulting unit costs can be no less subjective.

(b) *Allocation by relative sales value:* The simplest situation occurs when all of the joint products are sold at the split-off point without further separable costs. The method is essentially the equivalent of the weighted average costs method using the selling price as weights. The resulting unit costs and stock valuations are determined by market values, rather than subjective considerations such as difficulty of processing etc. An important consequence of adopting this method is that profit margins are the same for each joint product. Consequently, alteration of sales mix will have no effect on margins, an important consequence for management reports, since management must seek to maximize sales revenue by selling as much of the joint product (which must inescapably be produced).

Where joint products require processing beyond split-off point the addition of separable costs to joint costs allocated as above will result in total unit costs which again do not reflect differential realizable value. This problem can be overcome to some extent by allocating joint costs by net realizable value. Net realizable value for this purpose is estimated selling price less separable costs to completion.

Some mining and canning companies value joint products at realizable value. While in low margin industry such as canning, this anticipation of profit may be acceptable, it is hard to justify such a practice in the mining industry where a fall in metal prices can reduce are to worthless rock.

Criteria for Choice of Appropriate Method

Where rapid fluctuations are in market prices, it will be then concern of the accountant to avoid the danger of overvaluing joint product stocks.

The test of "lower than cost or net realizable value" could be to write-down of some stocks of joint product and undervaluation of others where the average cost method is used. Broadly, the realizable value method of allocating joint costs is to be preferred as it establishes cost allocations which are clearly market price related.

The Allocation Methods

The main methods are:

(i) Simple average cost
(ii) Weighted average cost
(iii) Relative sales value
(iv) Net realizable value

They can now be demonstrated with examples.

Simple Average Cost Method

Example 8

A mine produces 10,000 units of gold and 20,000 units of silver at a joint cost of ₹ 15,00,000.

You are to calculate the allocation of joint costs to production using the simple average method and a computation of unit costs for gold and silver.

Solution

	Units produced	Joint cost allocation ₹	Joint cost per unit ₹
Gold	10,000	5,00,000	50
Silver	20,000	10,00,000	50
	30,000	15,00,000	

Note: That unit costs are identical; stocks of gold would be valued at the same unit cost as silver, regardless of their differential realizable value.

Weighted Average Cost Method

Example 9

A mine produces 10,000 units of gold and 20,000 units of silver at a joint cost of ₹ 15,00,000. Weight factors of 10 and 8 are accorded to gold and silver respectively based on the higher realizable value of gold. Find:

The allocation of joint costs to production using the weighted average cost method and a computation of unit costs for gold and silver.

Solution

	Units	Factors	Equivalent Units	Joint cost allocation ₹	Joint cost per unit ₹
Gold	10,000	10	1,00,000	5,76,923	57.60
Silver	20,000	8	1,60,000	9,23,077	46.15
	30,000		2,60,000	15,00,000	

Note: (i) Weight factors arbitrarily defined.
(ii) Cost allocated by equivalent units.

The stocks of gold would now be accorded a higher value than that of silver.

Relative Sales Value Method

Example 10

A mine produces 10,000 units of gold and 20,000 units of silver at a joint cost of ₹ 15,00,000. Gold and silver prices have established at ₹ 120 per unit and ₹ 90 per unit respectively.

Required:

The allocation of joint costs to production using the relative sales value method and a computation of unit costs for gold and silver respectively.

Solution

	Units	Sales Price ₹	Sales Value ₹	Joint cost allocation ₹	Joint cost per unit ₹
Gold	10,000	120	12,00,000	6,00,000	60.00
Silver	20,000	90	18,00,000	9,00,000	45.00
	30,000		30,00,000	15,00,000	

This method reflects the lower realizable value of silver and is determined by the market, rather than by subjective consideration such as difficulty to processing etc. Note that the profit margin is 100% on cost for both gold and silver. This has significance for managerial decisions as it is the maximization of sales of all joint products which will optimise profits as a whole. Any method which yields differential profit margins may cause managers to push sales of "higher margin" products, rather than maximize sales of joint products in total.

Net Realisable Value Method

Example 11

Data as in above example, but assume silver requires additional separable costs to completion of ₹ 15 per unit, and gold requires no separable costs to completion.

Required:

A computation of total unit costs for gold and silver using the relative sales value method and, by way of contrast, the net realisable value method.

Solution

Allocation of joint costs by NRV method

	Unit	NRV/Unit ₹	NRV ₹	Joint cost allocation ₹	Joint cost per unit ₹
Gold	10,000	120	12,00,000	6,66,667	66.67
Silver	20,000	75	15,00,000	8,33,333	41.67
	30,000		27,00,000	15,00,000	

The two products could yield per unit as under:

	Relative Sales Value Method			Net Realisable Value Method		
	Joint costs ₹	Separable costs ₹	Total ₹	Joint costs ₹	Separable costs ₹	Total ₹
Gold	60.00	–	60.00	66.67	–	66.67
Silver	45.00	15.00	60.00	41.67	15.00	56.67

The differential sales value of silver is recognized by the net realizable value method.

Costing By-Products for Stock Valuation and Income Measurement

There are two basic approaches to this problem:

(a) recognizing income from sales as a separate item in the profit and loss or as a reduction in the cost of the major products; and

(b) costing by-products at split-off point and subsequently adding separable costs to completion if necessary.

Effectively (a) does not cost by-products at all and hence control over by-products must be weakened if this method is used e.g., no attempt is made to reflect the existence of by-products in accounting statements until they are sold. One of the many variants of costing by-products address this problem by reporting the net realizable value of by-product production as a deduction from the cost of the major product produced.

It should be remembered that if the amounts involved are unlikely to have a material effect on reported income, then sophisticated methods of accounting for by-products are unjustified on cost grounds alone.

As waste is not costed, the cost of production bears the cost of waste production. If costs are incurred in disposing of waste, then that cost is added to the cost of production in line with the matching concept. If a market can be found for waste, the proceeds, however, small, reduce the cost of production again in line with the matching concept. When waste sales proceeds become sufficiently large to justify treating waste as a by-product, no change in thinking is required—such revenue must reduce the cost of major product, either by costing the by-product separately or by bringing in revenue from sale or expected sale.

Example 12

90 units of main product and 10 units of by-product are produced at a joint cost of ₹ 90. All the main product is sold at ₹ 4 each, but only half of the by-product at ₹ one each.

Calculate the profit earned assuming (a) the realizable value of all the by-products as other income, (b) treating only the realized value of by-product sales as other income, (c) allocating joint costs to both the main product and the by-product by the physical quantity method, (d) treating all the realizable value of the by-product as a reduction in the cost of main product sold, (e) treating only the realized value of by-product as a reduction in the cost of the main product sold.

Solution

	a		b		c		d		e	
Products	Main ₹	By pro. ₹	Main ₹	By pro. ₹	Main ₹	By pro. ₹	Main ₹	By pro. ₹	Main ₹	By pro. ₹
Sales	360	10	360	5	360	5	360	—	360	—
Cost	90	—	90	—	81	4.5	80	—	85	—
Profit	270	10	270	5	279	0.5	280	—	275	—
Total Profit	280		275		279.5		280		275	

QUESTIONS

1. Outline the way in which the techniques of product design and value analysis can be utilized as part of cost reduction programme by the management accountant.
2. What is work study and what are the major objectives of a work study programme? Outline two major techniques which are commonly incorporated into a work study evaluation?
3. What is the distinction between cost control and cost reduction? Illustrate the objectives and techniques of both methods for improving resource utilization efficiency.
4. List five different accounting treatments of by-products. What is split-off point?
5. The Diversity company processes certain raw materials into three products *A, B* and *C*. During the period the company produced the following outputs:

    A — 10,000 units weight 2 pounds each.
    B — 15,000 units weight 2 pounds each.
    C — 7,500 units weight 3 pounds each.

Additional processing costs for *A* and *B* are ₹ 1 and ₹ 0.75 per unit respectively and selling price of *A* is ₹ 2.25 and of *B* ₹ 1.50. *A* unit of *C* may be sold immediately for ₹ 2 minus selling costs of ₹ 0.30 per unit or processed further to yield net revenues of ₹ 2.25 per unit (i.e., revenues minus additional processing costs). Total processing costs incurred in the period were ₹ 10,000.

You are to find how to allocate the costs to products *A*, *B* and *C* on the basis of total units of output, total weight of output and relative sales values using (a) net realizable values based on final selling prices and (b) net realizable values based on market prices of products at split off (if available)?

Suppose that 2,000 units of *A*, 1,000 units of *B* and 500 units of *C* remained unsold at the end of the accounting period. What average costs per unit should be assigned to inventories of *A*, *B* and *C* under all the above methods (except b)? Assume *A* and *B* have been processed into their finished form.

6. Dias Ltd. Manufacture two main products *X* and *Y*. Each is produced in a separate department. These operating departments are supported by two service departments, one providing power and the other material-handling.

Since the energy crisis management have carefully examined the activities of the service departments and both are now regarded as suppliers of controlled 'work-units'. The typical distribution of the 'unit' available in the service departments for an accounting period are:

Units Consumer	Service Department	
	Power	Materials-handling
Power Department	Nil	80
Material Handling Dept.	60	—
Production Dept: *X*	80	40
Production Dept: *Y*	60	80
Total 'work-units'	200	200

The costs of the service departments for a typical accounting period are:

	Power ₹	Materials-handling ₹
Variable labour and material	14,000	2,000
Supervision	2,000	2,000
Depreciation and other fixed costs	4,000	4,000

These costs include services received from each other.

Required:

(a) Compute the cost allocations to the two operating departments using the direct method.

(b) Compute the cost allocations to the two operating departments using the step method.

(c) Compute the cost allocation to the two operating departments using the reciprocal method.

7. The following information relating to the month of June is extracted from the cost records of the Aldrid Manufacturing Co. Ltd., which makes mechanical toys, the parts of which are made in Dept. *A* and assembled in Dept. *B*:

	Total ₹	Dept. A ₹	Dept. B ₹
Direct materials consumed	6,500	5,000	1,500
Direct labour	9,000	4,000	5,000
Factory rent, heat, light	1,500		
Supervision wages	600	250	350
Depreciation of machinery	500		
Power	400		
Repairs to machinery	200	160	40
Indirect labour	400	200	20
	19,100	9,610	7,090
Machine hours worked	30,000	25,000	5,000
Direct labour hours worked	80,000	30,000	50,000
Machine hours power	400 h.p.	300 h.p.	100 h.p.
Book-value of plant	5,000	4,000	1,000
Floor space	20,000 sq.ft.	10,00 sq.ft.	10,000 sq.ft.
Number of machines-ratio between departments		2	1

The costs of batch *x* 252 have been booked as follows:

	Total ₹	Dept. A ₹	Dept. B ₹
Materials	320	270	50
Labour	750	300	450
	1,070		

Direct labour hours worked on batch *x* 252 were 2,500 in Dept. *A*, 5,000 in Dept. *B*. Machine hours worked on this batch were 1,250 in Dept. *A* and 600 in Dept. *B*.

(a) Advise how overhead expenses might be allocated to batch x 252.
(b) Consider objections which might be raised against the bases and methods of allocation used.
(c) Calculate the cost of each unit in batch x 252, assuming there are 1,000 units in the batch.
(d) Say what the effect of decisions in (a) and (c) could have on the company's future revenue and on the profit for the current period.

8. Papaver (Ruritania) Inc. operates a mill in which it processes the roots, the basis of a stap dish. The roots are delivered in standard loads of 1,000 pounds by the Root Marketing Board then washed, crushed, and cooked in three sequential processes.

The washing process washes out 50 pounds of valueless waste from each delivery giving a star 950 pounds of washed roots. These are then put into the crushing process; this produces a still of 400 pints of a nutritious juice (which is sold under a long-term contract to the Ruritania Health Care Service) and 400 pounds of pulp. The process of cooking the pulp produces 40 mash, which is sold back to the Root Marketing Board in bulk containers.

The cooking is done in a detached cookhouse, near to the washing and crushing plant. No kept of roots, pulp, juice or root mash.

Each standard load of unwashed roots costs ₹ 600.

The fixed costs per week, and the variable cost per load, of the processes are as follows:

Process	₹	Variable cost of processing	Weekly fixed cost ₹
Washing	1	per standard load	1,250
Crushing	10	per load of washed roots	5,000
Cooking	20	per load of pulp	3,750
Administration	Nil		10,000

The juice is sold for ₹ 1.50 per pint, and the cooked root mash for ₹ 1.00 per pound.

The corporation tax in Ruritania, but Papaver's gross sales revenues are subject to a 10% sales deducted at source by the Root Marketing Board and the State Health Care Service. Draft an income statement for Papaver for June 19/08, a four-week accounting period 220 loads of uncleaned roots were processed, to show the total profit or loss and the attributable to the production and sale of juice and root mash respectively.

9. Consolidated Rocklode Ltd. operates a plant which processes Ferronium ore, which is delivered in standard loads of five tons. The ore is passed through three sequential processes—washing, crushing and sieving, pulverising.

The washing process washes out 2,000 lbs of valueless waste from each load. The washed ore is then crushed and sieved, a process which produces standard yield of 4,032 lbs of aggregate, which is sold under contract to Agslab Ltd. for ₹ 250 per ton. The remaining fine ore is pulverised and sold to Gnome Products Ltd. under contract for ₹ 500 per ton. The standard yield per load from the pulverising process is 5,040 lbs. There are other small losses of ore dust during the processing.

The washing, crushing and sieving and pulverising operations are linked by conveyor systems and no stocks are held of ore at any stage of the processing nor of aggregated or powdered ore.

Each standard load of raw ore costs ₹ 1,000.

The fixed costs per week and the variable cost per load, of the processes are as follows:

Process	Variable cost of processing ₹	Weekly fixed costs ₹
Washing	20 per standard load	1,500
Crushing and sieving	150 per load of washed ore	7,900
Pulverising	200 per load of fine ore	5,800
Administration and selling	Nil	2,650

Prepare an income statement for Consolidated Rocklode Ltd. for October 19/09, a five-week accounting period during which 400 loads of raw ore were processed, to show the total profit or loss and the amounts attributable to the production and sale of aggregate and powdered ore respectively.

10. *Mechanics of service department cost allocation*: Zowie Books sells paperback books of two types. Culture Books (hereafter called C Books) are intended for the college bookstores and better department store book departments. Enjoyable Books (E Books) are devoted to current fiction. Many of the functions and costs of the two lines and separate because of their totally different markets. However, some of the firm's costs are related to servicing both lines of books (i.e., they are common costs to both C and E Books). The jointly used departments are advertising design, sales and office staff. During the past period these departments incurred the following costs:

	₹
Advertising design	4,300
Sales	6,800
Office staff	3,000
	14,100

These costs must be allocated to C Books and E Books for purposes of ascertaining the two managing editor's bonuses, which are related to profits.

Operating data for the past period are as follows:

	C Books	E Books	Advertising design	Sales	Office staff
Size of departmental staff	2	8	5	10	5
Layouts requested	10	30	0	4	6
Hours spent on this function by sales force	60	90	10	20	10

(a) Allocate the departmental costs to C Books and E Books ignoring any reciprocal relationships. The allocation is made according to rupee volume of sales. C Books sales were ₹ 12,000. E Books sales were ₹ 36,000.

(b) Allocate these costs in steps ignoring any reciprocal relationships. Allocate advertising first, then sales, and finally office staff.

(c) Restate the problem in equation form, recognizing the various reciprocal relationships. However, do not try to solve the problem.

(d) Discuss the possible advantages of using the matrix approach to solve such problems. The bases for allocation for (b), (c), and (d) are:

Advertising design — number of requests for layouts

Sales — salesman's reports of how time was spent

Office staff — number of members on departmental staff.

11. *Allocation of service department costs*: *H* and *B* are producing Little League bats under their highly successful *H* and *B* label. The techniques are highly automated and consist of two steps, shaping and finishing, which are carried out in separate departments. *H* and *B* have three other departments. One is their own power plant, which supplies power to all parts of the firm both for running machinery and for heat, light, and air conditioning. The second is the accounting department. The third service department consists of the firm's repair crew, who are skilled at servicing everything from air conditioners and typewriters to heavy equipment.

The accounting department has calculated the total costs for each department shown below. The various service department heads have estimated as best they can be services rendered by their departments to the other four units.

From	To Shaping ₹	 Finishing ₹	 Power ₹	 Accounting ₹	 Repair ₹	 Total ₹
Shaping department	100%	—	—	—	—	100%
Finishing department	—	100%	—	—	—	100%
Power station	30%	30%	—	10%	30%	100%
Accounting department	20%	40%	20%	—	20%	100%
Repair and service crew	50%	20%	20%	10%	—	100%
Cost	40,000	35,000	10,000	4,500	95,000	

(a) Allocate the service department costs sequentially, and determine the total cost for the shaping and finishing departments. Allocate the power station first, then the accounting department and finally the repair crew.

(b) Solve this problem algebraically for the service departments.

17

Human Resource Accounting

Prof. Sidney Davidson defines human resource accounting as a "term used to describe a variety of proposals that seek to report and emphasize the importance of human resources—knowledgeable, trained and loyal employees—in a company's earning process and total assets".[1] American Accounting Association defines it "as a process of identifying and measuring data about human resource and communicating this information to interested parties". E. Flamholtz says: "it is the measurement of the cost and value of people for the organisation". The subject is still in its childhood. Human resource accounting is a logical and significant extension of the scope of enterprise accounting. It is the process of measuring and reporting the human dynamics of an organisation. It is the assessment of the condition of human resources within an organisation and the measurement of the change in this condition through time. It is the process of providing information about individuals and groups of individuals within an organisation to decision-makers both inside and outside the organisation.

The concept of human capital the basic to human resource accounting at the enterprise level, is not of recent origin. The significance of human resources in organisations or at the enterprise level has been recognized in the literature of organisation theory by many writers. It was in late sixties that the subject received due attention in U.S.A. There have been two approaches to this new area of accounting.

1. Historical cost-based approaches.
2. Replacement or value-based approaches.

Historical cost-based approaches remain dominant in practical accounting. Cost-based human resource accounting (or human resource cost accounting) fits into conventional accounting practices.

Techniques for Cost-based Human Resource Accounting

The techniques for cost-based HRA is similar to plant or other physical resources. They involve:

(a) recording of investments in human resources through capitalization process (i.e., as in an asset). This capitalization may involve

1. *Accounting: The Language of Business*, IInd Ed., p. 25.

salaries paid to its employees or cost of "acquiring an employee" (acquisition cost) or "start-up costs";

(b) recording of routine expirations of such capitalized items using an established amortization procedure;

(c) recording to losses to recognize special expirations due to obsolescence of investments in certain skills or knowledge capabilities or the turnover of personnel;

(d) reporting to interested parties on the condition of human resources in terms of investment therein. Prof. R. Lee Brummet has given following generalized model of cost-based HRA system that shows the fundamental aspects and some of the classification possibilities.

COST-BASED HRA SYSTEM

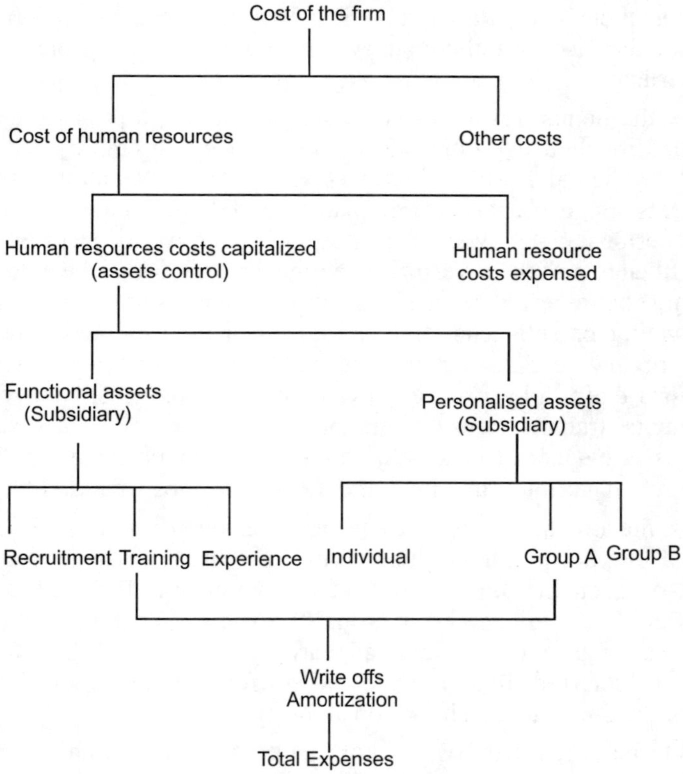

Exhibit 17.1

Another method has been proposed by a model[1] in the height of attendance at work and performance on the job.

1. Philip H. Mirvis and Barry M. Macy, *Academy of Mgt. Review* (April 1976), p. 76.

The two most well-known firms adopting cost-based HRA in practice are R.G. Berry Corporation of U.S.A. and Touche Ross & Co. of Canada.

Functional groupings of invested costs may to be made like recruitment, training and experience building. For each functional group detailed contents must be given. For example, recruitments costs may include search fees, advertising, travel expenses of candidates or interviewer, internal screening expenses, interview expenses, testing and evaluation expenses. Another grouping of investments should be made by individuals or supervisory or managerial personnel and for groups of individuals involved in relatively routine and similar job assignments. This is necessary to find the cost effectiveness. Invested costs can be found from invoices or expense vouchers or may be in the form of wages of salary paid to individuals in whom investments are made. The use of cost standards is possible if the human resource investments are classified by nature of input and identifying them with individuals. Standard costs can be established for foremen, supervisor, middle managers separately for recruitment, training and experience.

After the human resources costs are capitalized, a procedure must be established for their expiration. Because of uncertain employment tenure, physical or mental health of employees or death the human resources investments are of highly varied nature and large range of lengths of benefits periods. Each type of cost is to be amortized according to the period of benefits of the investments enjoyed by the firm. The amortization policy must be reviewed regularly because human resources are potentially self-activating or self-generating unlike physical resources. Similarly, a periodic review of human resources must be made because of changes in positions due to physical health changes of employees, changes in job requirements, transfers and resignations, etc. The cost-based system will provide asset balances (book value figures) for unamortized inputs to HR in the form of various functions and various groups of individuals.

Thus, the amount of "net increase in HR investment" can be debited in profit and loss account as an item of expense in the financial statements. In balance sheet, the amount of "net investment in HR" will be shown as an asset. The retained earnings may be shown separately as financial retained earnings and HR retained earnings in the liability side. Any amount of "deferred income tax based on full tax deduction for human resources cost" are to be shown on liability side.

It is to be noted that HRA is not recognized for external reporting as a part of generally accepted accounting principles. Nor are they recognized for income tax purposes. Some organisations are more highly human resource intensive than others. Some make larger investments in people than do others. Historically, cost-based HRA has serious limitations.

VALUE-BASED HRA MODELS

Human values are adjusted to price level changes. Standard cost of recruitment, hiring, training and development of various types of persons can be developed.

Many authors have developed models for estimating the value of human resources. Following are some of them:[1]

1. Hermanson's unpurchased goodwill model and adjusted discounted future wages model.
2. Hekimian and Jones competitive bidding model.
3. Lev and Schwartz's present value of future earnings model.
4. Brummet, Flamholtz and Pyle's economic value model.
5. Flamholtz's Stochastic rewards valuation model.
6. The Likert causal, intervening and end result model.
7. Myers and Flowers' five dimensions model.
8. Ogan's discounted certainty equivalent net benefits model.
9. Brummet and Taylor's human resource value index model.
10. Flamholtz's determinants of an individual's value to a formal organisation model.

Hermanson Unpurchased Goodwill Model

This model is based on capitalising earnings in excess of normal earnings for a group of companies of which the firm is a part. He also suggests the discounting of future compensation with an adjustment using an "efficiency ratio" to determine the value of an individual. He uses a five years period and applies an adjustment which is a calculated ratio of the average earnings rate on owned assets of the employing firm to the average rate on owned assets of all firms in the economy. This method is based on present value method.

Steps

To arrive at the value of the human assets:

(1) Estimate annual wages and salaries payment for five years into the future.

(2) Calculate the present value of the estimated wage and salary payments by applying a discount factor equal to normal rate of return in the economy.

(3) Calculate an average efficiency ratio based on the previous five years performance. This ratio is found by dividing the actual earnings of the firm by normal earnings for each year on an average in the results. In making the calculation, the later years receive more weightage than the earlier years.

---

1. For details refer to *Handbook of Modern Accounting*, Sidney Davidson & Roman L. Weil, Chapter 37.

(4) Multiply the present value of the future wage salary payments by the average efficiency ratio. The resulting figure represents the estimated present value of the human resources.

LEV AND SCHWARTZ ADJUSTED PRESENT VALUE PERIOD MODEL

(a) Calculation of the Present Value of Future Wages and Salary Payments:

Year	Estimated Wages and Salary Payments ₹ (000)	Discount Factor at 6%	Present Value of Future Payments Discounted at 6% ₹ (000)
1	10	0.94	9
2	12	0.89	11
3	13	0.84	11
4	14	0.79	11
5	15	0.74	11
Total	64		53

(b) Calculation of the "Average Efficiency Ratio" based on Previous five Years Performance:

$$\text{Efficiency Ratio} = 5\frac{RF_0}{RE_0} + 4\frac{RF_1}{RE_1} + 3\frac{RF_2}{RE_2} + 2\frac{RF_3}{RE_3} + 1\frac{RF_4}{RE_4}$$

$$= 5\frac{20}{16} + 4\frac{15}{10} + 3\frac{10}{10} + 2\frac{18}{9} + \frac{12}{10}$$

$$= \frac{6.25 + 6.0 + 3 + 4 + 1.2}{15}$$

$$= \frac{20.45}{15} = 1.36$$

RF_0 = The rate of accounting income on owned assets for the firm for the current year.

RE_0 = The average rate of accounting income on owned assets for the firm in the economy for the current year.

RF_4 = The rate of accounting income on owned assets for the firm for the previous four years.

RE_4 = The average rate of accounting income on owned assets for the firm for all firms in the economy for the previous four years.

(c) Present value of human resources:

= Efficiency ratio × Total P.V. of future payments

= 1.36 × 53 = ₹ 7,208 (000).

Hekimian and Jones Competitive Bidding Model

This model suggests a procedure by which profit centre managers bid for the services of valuable employees of their various sections. This is based on opportunity cost. The maximum bid price would be used as the "value" of the individual. The value of an employee depends upon his alternative use in the various divisions of an enterprise. Human asset is scarce if it can be alternatively used in various divisions. It would mean that if an employee has several alternative uses for deployment in various divisions, he will be termed as scarce and will have high value. The opportunity cost value of human resources is established by competent bidding within an organisation. Hekimian and Jones proposed this competitive bidding process. The division/department having the highest bid for a particular type of human resource would include its prices in the investment base. This process of evaluating human resources provides a base for optimal allocation of personnel within an organisation and a quantitative base for planning/developing the human assets of the firm. However, it does not include the opportunity cost of the employee outside the organisation. Lev and Schwartz's present value model uses the following formula to calculate estimated human capital value of a person y years old.

$$\Sigma(vy^*) = \sum_{t=y}^{T} Py\ (t+1) \sum_{i=y}^{t} \frac{Ii^*}{(I+v)^{t-y}}$$

E (vy*)	= expected value of human capital value of a person y years old
T	= person's retirement age
$Py = (t)$	= Probability of person dying or resignation or retirement
Ii^*	= expected earnings of the person in the period
r	= discount rate specific to the person.

This method is based on the value of the firm's employee force by aggregating and averaging the earning profiles of homogeneous groups of employees. The age factor is important as it affects the increase and decrease and the productivity of human earnings.

The method adopts a cost-based approach to the valuation of human capital.

The firm's human capital value obtained by the application of the aforesaid equation in this manner allows the development of a net set of ratios like the ratio of human to non-human capital value, showing the degree of labour intensiveness in an organisation. But the non-human assets values are not based upon the earning profile of the assets while the human assets values are based on the earning profile of employees, so both cannot be matched together as they have no common base.

We can also know the changes in the structure of labour forces through this approach. The method also reports 'general' and 'specific value' of human capital reflecting firm recruitment and wage policy.

Brummet, Flamholtz and Pyle's Economic value model is based on "economic value concept" involving forecasting of future earnings, the discounting of these forecasted future earnings and pro rata association of this amount to all assets including human resources. This model is similar more or less to the Hermanson model.

The economic value of an individual to an organisation is the present worth of future services he is expected to provide during his productive life, i.e. till retirement. In considering the state of future services, the different roles likely to be assigned during the service period (productive life) and the total values of different roles are to be considered. The theory takes into consideration only individual economic value and not the added value/profit by team building, and group formation as such does not reflect the value of human resource based on interpersonal relationship.

Flamholtz's Stochastic Return on Effort Employed Model

It measures the return on the quantity and quality of total effort expanded and the contribution made by individuals in the various functions of an organisation varying from purchase and manufacturing to selling. It takes into account the factors which distinguish quantity and quality of effort expanded. These factors may be as below:

(i) Level or grade of work done.
(ii) Effectiveness of individual on his job position.
(iii) Experience profile.
(iv) Measurement of total effort employed in various functions of the organisation on the basis of rating factors.

Illustration

(1) *Level on Grade of Work Done*

Different grades to jobs are distinguished for developing wage structures:

Job Grade	Factor
10 (director)	10
7 (sales manager)	7
4 (salesman)	4
1 (typist)	1

(2) *Effectiveness of Individual Job Performance*

Personal Assessment	Factor
Very good	1.5
Satisfactory	1.0

(3) *Experience which Increases, up to a Point, the Efficiency of Job Performance*

Years of Experience	Factor
0-1	1.0
1-2	1.1
2-3	1.2
3-4	1.3
4-5	1.4
Over 5	1.5

The above factors are multiplied together in measuring the effort employed by each individual. Say, a good sales manager with five years experience would be: 7 (job grade) × 1.5 (personal assessment) × 1.5 (job experience) = 15.75 for effort employed by a good sales manager.

When all the calculations for every other individual are aggregated, we obtain a figure which represents the total effort employed. We may now find out the return on total effort expanded on any functional area of business:

Measurement of Effort Employed

Business	Buying	Manufacturing	Selling	Total Effort	Total Profit	Total Profit/Total Effort
1	150	900	350	1400	1,40,000	₹ 100 per unit of effort
2	80	1000	120	1200	24,000	₹ 20 per unit of effort
3	100	2000	400	2500	5,00,000	₹ 200 per unit of effort

This method helps to identify areas where effective allocation of human resources is done.

Flamholtz's Stochastic reward value model is based on probability. It assumes the movement of individuals through different roles or positions in the organisations as a probability depending on their prior or service held by any person in the organisation. A person's expected realizable value E (*RV*) is calculated by the following formula:

$$E\ (RV) = \sum_{t=1}^{n}\left[\sum_{i=1}^{m}\left[\frac{Ri - P\ (Ri)}{(1+r)^{t}}\right]\right]$$

where Ri = value R is to be found out by the organisation in each possible position or post of a person

$P\ (Ri)$ = Probability that a person will occupy position or post i

t = time

m = Position of exit

r = Appropriate discount rate.

The organisation has to first define mutually exclusive set of "positions or posts" an individual may occupy in the organisation. Secondly, the value of each position to the organisation is to be determined. Thirdly, estimate is made of a person's expected tenure in the organisation and lastly the probability of a person occupying each position or post at a specified future time is to be found out. Flamholtz also developed a theoretical model to identify the key variables (like productivity, skills personality) that determine an individual's value to an organisation and the inter-relationships of such variables. Some of these determinants may be expressed in monetary terms and some may not be so expressed. This model is first step towards the development of a theory, claims Flamholtz.

STOCHASTIC REWARDS VALUATION MODEL BY BRUMMET, FLAMHOLTZ AND PYLE

Steps

(i) Define the mutually exclusive set of 'states' an individual may occupy in the organisation,

(ii) Determine the value of each state to the organisation,

(iii) Estimate a person's expected tenure in an organisation, and

(iv) Find the probability that a person will occupy at each possible state at specified future times.

Defining Service States and Assignment of Economic Values of Service States

Service State	Billing Rate ₹	Chargeable value	Gross Economic value ₹	Compensation ₹	Net Economic value ₹
Staff Accountant	20	2,000	40,000	20,000	20,000
Manager	40	2,000	80,000	40,000	40,000
Partner	60	2,000	1,20,000	60,000	60,000
Exit	–	–	–	–	–

Service State Probabilities for X Employee

Service State	Time Period				
	T1	T2	T3	T4	T5
Staff Accountant	0.90	0.40	0.20	–	–
Manager	–	0.50	0.70	0.50	0.20
Partner	–	–	–	0.40	0.60
Exit	0.10	0.10	0.10	0.10	0.20

Expected Condition Value of X Employee

Service State	Time Period T1	T2	T3	T4	T5	Total E.C.V.
Staff Accountant	(20,000) 1/1= 20,000	(20,000) 4/9= 8,889	(20,000) 2/9= 4,444	– –	– –	– 33,333
Manager	–	(40,000) 5/9 = 22,222	(40,000) 7/9 = 31,111	(40,000) 5/9 = 22,222	(40,000) 2/8 = 10,000	85,555
Partner	–	–	–	(60,000) 4/9 = 26,667	(60,000) 6/8 = 45,000	71,667
Total	20,000	31,111	35,555	48,889	55,000	1,90,555

Expected Realizable Value of X Employee and Present Value of Expected Future Services

Time Period	Expected Conditional Value ₹	Probability of Remaining	Expected Realizable Value ₹	Discount Factor at 63	Present Value of Expected Services ₹
T1	20,000	.90	18,000	.9434	16,981
T2	31,111	.90	28,000	.8900	24,920
T3	35,555	.90	32,000	.8396	26,867
T4	48,889	.90	44,000	.7921	34,852
T5	55,000	.80	44,000	.7473	32,881
Total	1,90,555		1,66,000		1,36,501

MODEL FOR A DISCRETE INCOME STREAM

$$V = \sum_{t=r}^{r} \frac{I(t)}{(1+r)\, t-r}$$

Where

V = the human capital value of a person r years old.
I = the person's annual earnings upto retirement.
r = a discount rate specific to the person.
t = retirement age.

Incorporation of the Possibility of Death Occurring Prior to Retirement Age in Model

$$E(V_r^*) = \sum_{t=r}^{t} P_r\ (t+1) \sum_{i+r}^{t} \frac{It}{(1+r)} \pm r$$

where $E(V_r^*)$ is the expected value of a person's human capital and $P_r\ (t)$ is the probability of a person dying at age t.

Rensis Likert's Model

This model, unlike other models, deals with group or interactive process among people. His model is based on measured relationships among three types of variables called as casual, intervening and end results. It is limited to assessment of change and does not assess existing value. He assumes the managerial leadership as casual, organisational climate as intervening and total productive efficiency as the end result. The measure of loyalty, motivation, trust and commitment helps to determine the changes in the quality of human resources. Human resources cost more if pressure is put on employees to increase production. The statistical analysis of this model is a practical problem.

Myers and Flowers Model

This model is based on the five dimensions of knowledge, skills, health, availability and attitudes. The first four are assessed by using checklist and the fifth one is assessed through perception survey. These can be expressed in terms of money. Following example will explain it.

Example

Name	Annual Salary ₹	Job grade	Period	Attitude weight	Attitude score	Weighted attitude score
1. Mohd. Ahmed	14,000	28	5	5	1.05	5.25
2. John Willy	7,000	57	11	5	1.12	5.60
3. Ram Chand	9,000	12	22	7	1.21	8.47
4. Venkat	6,500	72	3	3	1.26	3.78
5. Joseph	18,500	30	4	6	1.15	6.90
	55,000			26		30.00

$$\text{Attitude Index} = \frac{30}{26} = 1.15$$

Money measurement of attitudes = 1.15 × 55,000 = ₹ 63,250
Gain = ₹ 8,250, Gain per person = 8,250 ÷ 5 = ₹ 1,650

Under this model, weights are assigned for attitudes and score of attitude is found for each person. The total weighted attitude score is divided by attitude weight by net attitude index. The attitude index is multiplied by the total salary of all persons. This gives us to find the gain or loss per person.

Ogan's Model

This model takes into account the cost to the firm of retaining human resources.

The models considered above have ignored this factor. Ogan considers both costs and benefit aspects of human resources. It is expressed as follows:

$$K_{kj} = \sum_{j=1}^{n} \sum_{k=t}^{L-t} \frac{1}{\sqrt{(I+r)^k}} \bar{V}_{qj}$$

L = end of estimated useful life of the employee
j = jth individual j = 1, 2 …………, n
r = a discount rate external to the organisation (risk free)

$\bar{V}_{qj}$ = certainty-equivalent net benefits generated by human resources

t = sometime period from I to L which is a point in the useful life of employee to which the certainty-equivalent net benefits that occur after t are discounted

K_{kj} = adjusted total net present values of human resources in a professional organisation

$q = k + t$

This model is used to sum the discounted "certainty equivalent net benefits".

Brummet and Taylor Model

This model proposes the development of a Human Resource Value Index (HRVI). The initial value of an organisation's human resources may be estimated and then "tracked" with successive calculations of this HRVI.

The HRVI is determined by applying an interactive multiplier (IM) to the summation of the products of individual performance ratios (IPRs) and corresponding measures of position contribution potential (PCPs), i.e.

$$\text{HRVI} = \text{IM} \quad [\Sigma \text{ (IPR} \times \text{PCP)}]$$

The individual performance ratio is calculated on the basis of performance for each person to standard performance. These ratios are then weighted by the firm according to importance of each position e.g. on the basis of salary or length of service. These two factors for each individual are multiplied and then totalled. The total then is multiplied by IM i.e. measure of interactive condition. IM may be measured by scaling the results to show 1.0 as neutral condition, less than 1.0 as detractive and more than 1.0 contributive.

The value-based models quoted above do not facilitate the recording of second order variables such as attitude changes that are by nature non-transactional. Both value-based and cost-based data are analogous. But still conceptual relationship of these two approaches has set up a stage for further development.

Uses and Problems

The following are the uses of human resource accounting:

1. *Correct profit disclosure:* If the human resource investment is not shown, the profit may be under or overstated. This causes misleading disclosure to the owners and public. If human resources are not accounted for a high profit may not mean that oganisation's performance is satisfactory because employee's attitude may not be good.

2. *Return on assets:* To measure the return on assets the changes in human resource assets must also be included in profit contribution. For transfer pricing also, the transfer price of people must be taken into account when transferred from one section to another.

3. *Employee turnover:* HRA can help to identify unrecovered investments in present workers and by providing continuously updated cost information

for those activities that are occasioned by personnel turnover. It can help to determine wage policy of the firm.

4. *Efficiency of personnel functions:* HRA helps to bring under close check the costs and benefits of personnel departments.

5. *Impact on management behaviour:* HRA encourages the managers to take a longer run view of their decisions. When managers are evaluated, it will affect their decisions and behaviour.

6. HRA will have an impact upon *corporate financial* reporting. This information will show the management's attention to building human assets. However, there appears to be little chances for inclusion of HRA as an integral part of generally accepted accounting principles.

There are problems in implementation of HRA, both technical and conceptual.

American Accounting Association has pointed out the following problems:

(a) HRA has to some managers seemed hastily constructed discipline made of "recycled parts" from other disciplines. The parts have not functioned satisfactorily in their original habitat.

(b) HRA unfortunately has no exploitative connotation to some people.

The technical problem of HRA is of value-based approach. The conceptual hurdles are that HRA may cause discrimination. Accountants capitalize any asset only if an organisation legally owns it. It is not the case with people. The necessity of inter-disciplinary involvement is a serious hurdle to HRA.

Example

Following is an example that demonstrates the possibilities of integration of HRA within the conventional accounting.

Income statement for quarter ended March 2020

	₹	₹
Sales		20,00,000
Expenses:		
Depreciation on plant	82,000	
HR expenditure	7,15,000	
Other expenses	9,13,000	17,10,000
		2,90,000
Income tax 48%		1,39,200
Income before recognizing charge in estimated value of HR		1,50,800
Additions to HR	95,000	
Less Amortization and write off	60,000	
Net increase in investments of HR		35,000
Net increase in excess of estimated value of HR at over cost		61,000
Income including charge in estimated value of HR		2,46,800

Balance Sheet

	As on 1-1-2020 ₹	As on 31-3-2020 ₹
Assets:		
Current assets	7,00,000	8,32,000
Plant	13,00,000	13,18,000
(a) Investment in HR	5,00,000	5,35,000
(b) Excess of estimated value over cost of HR	3,00,000	3,61,000
Estimated value of Human organisation	8,00,000	8,96,000
Total assets	28,00,000	30,46,800
Capital & Liabilities:		
Capital	10,00,000	10,00,000
Current Liabilities	3,00,000	3,00,000
Retained earnings:		
Financial, product and plant resources	7,00,000	8,50,000
Human resources—cost	5,00,000	5,35,000
Human resources—additional value	3,00,000	3,61,000
Total liabilities	28,00,000	30,46,000

It is interesting to note that in first three months of 2020, a new investment of ₹ 95,000 was made while the estimated value of HR increased ₹ 96,000 and book value write off amounted to ₹ 60,000 accounting for ₹ 61,000 increase of the excess of estimated value of human resources over their book values.

Indian Example

Now in India also many companies are showing HRA as a part of their financial statements. Here is the example of NTPC.

A company is known by men it keeps. NTPC can boast of having best techno-managerial brains in power sector. NTPC management always endeavours to bring out best of them by keeping them motivated. Well-planned HR strategies focus its attention on overall development of the employees to face a challenging power scenario, emerged after opening up of power sector in liberalized economy. NTPC thrives on quality manpower rather than on quantitative one. There has not been significant increase in manpower during the last five years despite capacity addition. Year-wise manpower strength is as under:

Year	Executives	Supervisors	Workmen	Total
2010-11	6499	3040	12258	21797
2011-12	6604	3005	12318	21927
2012-13	6841	3010	12445	22296
2013-14	6914	2951	14414	24279
2014-15	7014	2951	14429	24394

NTPC treats its human resource as an asset like other assets. The value of its human resources has been worked out using Lev & Schwartz economic model and applying company's policies. The present worth of future earnings has been worked out by considering a discount factor of 12% per year. Category-wise break-up of the same is depicted in the table below:

Category	No. of Employees	Per Capita ₹ lakhs	Total ₹ crores
Executives	7014	24.36	1708.61
Supervisors	2951	22.18	654.53
Workmen	14429	20.09	2898.79
Total	24394	21.57	5261.93

The comparison of human resource value with that of other assets over the last five years is depicted in the following table:

S. No.	Details	2014-15	2013-14	2012-13	2011-12	2010-11
1.	Gross fixed assets	22727	19722	15377	13349	12047
2.	Capital work-in-progress	1928	4117	7372	7081	5718
3.	Net current assets	6107	5009	4550	4726	4948
4.	Total human resources	5262	4649	3375	3065	2764
	Total Resources	36024	33497	30674	28221	25477

Performance Indicators

Based on above data, various ratios are presented to assess the trend in performance parameters as under:

S. No.	Details	2014-15	2013-14	2012-13	2011-12	2010-11
1.	Value added (₹ crores)	5486	4500	3288	2993	2297
2.	Turnover* (₹ crores)	9840	8344	6360	5918	4485
3.	Generation (MU)	97609	89838	76470	76474	66092
4.	Manpower	24394	24279	22296	21927	21797
	a. Value added/Emp. (₹ lakhs)	22.49	18.53	14.75	13.65	10.54
	b. Turnover/Emp. (₹/lakh)	40.34	34.37	28.53	26.99	20.57
	c. Generation/Emp. (HU)	4.00	3.70	3.43	3.49	3.03

* Excluding income from consultancy and other incomes and provisions written back.

QUESTIONS

1. In recent years, the concept of human resource accounting has been theorized in management and accounting literature.
   (a) How could this theory be defined?
   (b) What are the objectives of the concept?

(c) State the theoretical proposals that have been made in favour of human resource accounting.

(d) What are the more serious drawbacks of this new accounting concept?

2. Following is a statement of changes on human resources value given by Pekin Ogan.

Human resources were increased by:		$
New employees		3,00,500
Increase in the values of current employees		8,000
Employees transferred in		1,75,000
Total increase		4,83,500
Human resources values were decreased by:		
Termination	23,000	
Retirement	75,000	
Decrease in the value of current employees	45,000	
Death	38,000	
Decrease in the value of current employees	52,500	
Total decreases		2,33,500
Net increase		2,50,000
Add: Previous HRV balance		5,00,000
Current human resource value		7,50,000

Considering Ogan's model, offer your comments as compared to other models.

[*Hint:* This model considers both cost and benefits to the firm, though it is difficult to determine and quantify them. The model fails to recognize the importance of interaction among individuals to group or organisational performance.]

3. The following is an excerpt from the Elvin and Ronen Corporation annual report for 2020. The company is a manufacturer of shoes. The data are supplementary to the usual audited human resource accounting are possible, such as using some approximation of current values, but corporation has confined to its historical records.

Balance Sheet	2020 Conventional & HRA $	2020 Conventional only $
Assets:		
Total current assets	1,83,11,713	1,83,11,713
Net property, plant & equipment	35,00,227	35,00,227
Excess of purchase Price over net assets acquired	12,85,829	12,85,829
Deferred financing costs	1,73,278	1,73,278
Net investments in human resource	19,64,243	—
Prepaid income tax & other assets	2,13,500	2,13,500
	2,54,48,790	2,34,84,547

Balance Sheet	2020 Conventional & HRA $	2020 Conventional only $
Liabilities & Stockholders' equity		
Total current liabilities	39,09,083	39,09,083
Long-term debt excluding current instalments	69,70,000	69,70,000
Deferred income tax based upon full Tax deduction for HR costs	9,82,122	—
Stockholder's equity:		
Capital stock	19,02,347	19,02,347
Additional capital in excess of par value	56,76,549	56,76,549
Retained earnings:		
Financial	48,83,418	48,83,418
Human resources	9,82,121	—
	2,54,48,790	2,34,84,547
Statement of Income:		
Net sales	4,31,61,564	4,31,61,564
Cost of sales	2,86,21,050	2,86,21,050
Gross profit	1,45,40,514	1,45,40,514
Selling, general & admin. expenses	1,07,83,922	1,07,83,922
Operating income	37,56,592	37,56,592
Interest expenses	5,98,846	5,98,846
Income before income tax	31,57,746	31,57,746
Net increase in HR investment	1,84,293	—
Adjusted income B.I.T.	33,42,039	31,57,746
Income Tax	16,15,147	15,23,000
Net Income	$17,26,892	$16,34,746

The annual report explains "Human resource accounting is an attempt to identify, quantify and report investments made in recruiting, acquiring, training, familiarising and developing people. Outlay costs connected with these activities are accumulated and capitalised where they are expected to have beyond current accounting period. The basic outlays in connection with acquiring and integrating new people are amortized over their expected tenure with the company. Investments made for training or development are amortized over a much shorter period of time. Total write-off an individual's account occurs upon his departure from the company."

Required:

(a) Were there more write-off of human assets during 2020 than new investments? Explain, using numbers given in statements.

(b) Why do you think that advocates of HRA prefer such a normal approach instead of less informal measures like employee attitude surveys, absenteeism and employee turnover measures and the like.

(c) Do you support the use of HRA? Give reasons.

[*Hint*: The impetus of HRA is due to perceived need for the information internally compare total investment in management and non-management resources and total amortization and write-off. The investment shows more people are participating in developing activities, increased reliance on growth and development of internal human resources and systematic planning and evaluating formal and informal development activities.]

18

Management Accounting in Non-Profit Organisations

INTRODUCTION

"Non-profit organisations" (better to use not-for-profit) are the organisations whose goal is something other than earning a profit for its owners. Usually, their goal is to provide service. They include government units, universities, colleges, schools, clubs and charitable institutions. The role of management accounting in these organisations is affected by certain characteristics of such organisations.[1]

1. The absence of profit measure.
2. Their tendency to be service organisation.
3. Constraints on goal and strategies.
4. Less dependence on clients for financial support.
5. The dominance of professionals.
6. Differences in governance.
7. Difference in top management.
8. Importance of political influences.
9. A tradition of inadequate management controls.

Because of these characteristics, it is difficult to relate costs and benefits to measure performance and to compare different organisational units. Moreover, the principal concepts and techniques used by business are not followed in these organisations. These are accrual concept, cost accounting, standard costs, variance analysis and responsibility accounting.

Despite the difficulties associated with measuring the results of the activities of non-profit entities, some evaluation of results can be made by applying some management accounting techniques. It will depend on the accounting concept that the NPO is following.

---

1. *Management Control in Non-profit Organisation*, Anthony, R.N. and Herzlinger, R.E. (IRWIN 1990).

There are three concepts in use for measurement of income and recognition of expenses in NPO. They are earning concept, stewardship concept, and compromise revenue concept.

The three principles in accounting are called (a) cash receipt and expenditures, (b) accrued revenue and expenditures, and (c) accrued revenue and expenses principles. The NPO are advised to follow the last principle. Under first approach all receipts, except unrestricted contributions, must be "earned" in order to be retained like in a commercial organisation. The restricted contributions are not shown in statements until spent. Under second concept followed in health and welfare, focus is on stewardship responsibility of the entity. Operating statements show the changes in assets made available to the organisation to conduct its programme, certain revenues are matched with related costs e.g. special programme. The third concept requires reporting property and endowment gifts in the determination of net changes in stewardship for the year with appropriate segregation and disclosure of the 'capital' nature of these gifts. But gifts restricted for operating purposes are shown as 'deferred liabilities' until spent. Traditionally, NPOs have followed what is called "Fund Accounting" concept.

The operating statement of NPOs shows, what Anthony suggests, operating capital maintenance (not the government organisation), i.e. the extent to which NPO equity was increased or decreased as a result of operations in a given accounting period. Transactions are revenues if they increase their equity and also result from operating activities during the period e.g. sale of goods and services. Membership dues, pledges, contribution or grant or appropriation are not earned revenue until funds have been spent for that purpose. Most NPOs show spending in terms of expenditure rather than in terms of expenses. The expenditure basis of reporting relate to inventories, fixed assets, and fringe benefits.

However, some expenses in NPO are to be measured. They relate to the measurement of expenses for programmes and for responsibility centres. The full cost of a responsibility centre or a programme is the sum of direct cost plus equitable share of its indirect cost. However, there are difference in the way the line between direct and indirect costs is drawn in various NPOs. Similarly, the distinction is made between variable and fixed, opportunity costs and inputed costs, capital costs and operating costs.

BENEFIT-COST ANALYSIS

The counterpart of volume-cost-profit analysis for NPOs is sometimes called benefit cost or cost utility analysis or cost effectives. This analysis can be shown in two kinds of situations:

(a) those that generate revenues by themselves.

(b) those in which there are both revenues and costs.

(a) *Costs*: One of the most important but difficult steps in this analysis is determining the cost of each programme and to assess the cost of continuing that programme. It is necessary to separate fixed and variable component of the cost, the discretionary from the committed, so that one can determine how much more it would cost to continue the programme. Sometimes, enough information may not be given but we can make reasonable assumptions. The cost of programme is difficult to predict. Two elements of uncertainty must be distinguished in estimating costs of future programmes.

(i) Cost estimating uncertainty and (ii) programme uncertainty i.e. lack of information about what will be required by a given programme.

Suppose there is a job-training centre which can handle 200 trainees. To house and train 100 men, following expenditures are incurred for six months training period.

	₹
Food	22,000
Rent	6,000
Salaries of staff	68,000
Administration	30,000
	1,26,000

The average cost per man is ₹ 1,260. If 200 men are trained, the total cost for six months training period is as follows:

	₹
Food	44,000
Rent	6,000
Salaries	96,000
Administration	38,000
	1,84,000

The average cost comes to ₹ 920.

Now question is whether to expand it or maintain it at existing levels. Using high and low method the fixed and variable cost of this centre are:

₹ 1,84,000 – 1,26,000 = ₹ 58,000

This ₹ 58,000 is variable cost that will increase if instead of 100 men we train 200 men i.e. ₹ 580 per men.

The fixed costs are ₹ 1,84,000 – (580 × 200) = ₹ 68,000

Or ₹ 1,26,000 – (580 × 100) = ₹ 68,000

So, the answer to question whether to train 200 men instead of 100 men depends upon the variable cost of ₹ 580 and not the average cost of ₹ 1,260.

(b) *Revenues and costs*: The measurement of cost of any programme lies in the inter-relationship among various programme components. There are some NPOs that earn some revenue. For example, the training will enable to earn more. In that case one has to compare the cost of training and the revenues earned from that training. The intangible benefits are to be measured. Some governmental activities generate little or no revenue except in a very indirect sense. These include national defence, police protection and legislatures. In some of these activities, it is difficult to define the output, let alone assign it a money value to compare with input. Benefits of programme are difficult to quantify. The danger to quantify is that wrong objectives may be considered and ancillary benefits may be ignored. For such cases, effort will have to be made to select some unit of output instead of money in terms of rupee. The choice of the unit should be made with care.

Zero base budgeting, function classification of expenses and other budgeting tools necessitate detailed information on the costs and benefits of alternative programmes. Following points are worth noting for cost benefit analysis[1] in a non-profit organisation.

1. *Value*: Some attention must be given to weighing the value of particular programmes in other than monetary terms. In the long run this analysis will not be a totally accurate process.

2. *Opportunity costs*: They are the foregone revenues or advantages that the organisation sacrifices by putting your resources into a particular programme rather than applying these same resources to their best use.

3. *In-kind resources*: Determine if any of the alternative programme you are examining allow for significant amounts of in-kind resources. "Free" resources are valuable and hard to find. Consider their worth as equal to their cash value. Be careful not to let the free resources alter your purpose. Examine any restrictions associated with their use. Only if there in-kind contributions allow you to further your purpose should be seek to take advantage of them.

4. *Analyse your resources*: Determine the extent of both private and public support for the organisation. Do not be over optimistic. Also do not under estimate your revenues. The ways to develop resources other than cash are to be considered. The possibilities of receiving endowments, grants, membership fees, interest on savings and investments etc. are to be explored. The duration and time of resources, along with their source and size, are also to be analysed. To sum up, following steps are necessary in this analysis: (1) Systematic consideration of alternative means of accomplishing a stated objective, (2) Estimation of the economic costs and benefits to be derived from each of the alternative, (3) Consideration of time phasing of costs and benefits, (4) Assessment of the effects of

1. Tracy, *Handbook of Non-Profit Organisations*, McGraw Hill.

uncertainty, and (5) Consideration of ancillary costs and benefits of each alternative from the point of view of the whole organisation.

BUDGET AND VARIANCE

Two basic classifications of budgets for non-profit organisations are same as those for commercial organisations—operating budgets and capital budgets. These organisations may employ any one type of the operating budgets viz. traditional budget or programme budget or performance budget or planning, programming, budgeting system, or zero-base budgeting (see details in Chapter 10). In developing the budget, revenues are classified by source and expenditures are classified by function with further sub-classification related to activity, character and object. For example, the activities of an educational institution may be classified as (a) instructional and (b) administrative and auxiliary instructional activities include both resident and extension instruction, public service, research and operation of libraries—administrative activities include staffing and promotion, registration and enrolment, operation of educational plant. Auxiliary activities include the hostels, college unions, book stores, health centres and sports and cultural programmes. Revenues in support of these different activities are provided by such varied sources as governmental grant and appropriations, contributions, student fees, endowment, incomes and revenues from sales of goods and services.

In case of hospitals, major activities centre about inpatients, outpatients and emergency services. They may carry on special activities such as teaching, research and nurse training. The auxiliary activities include services like chemist and pharmacy shop and cafeterias for staff and visitors. The administrative activities cover the hospital staffing, registration of patients, operation of physical plant, food and laundry, housekeeping and accounting. The major source include government grant, charges from patients for various services like room rent, fees or medical tests, gifts and donations, endowment funds.

Example 1

Rajdhani College has asked your assistance in developing its operating budget for the coming academic year ending June 30, 2020. You are supplied with the following data for the current year:

		Graduate ₹	Post-graduate ₹
(1)	Average number of students per class	25	20
	Average salary of faculty members	10,000	10,000
	Average number of hours carried each year per student	33	30
	Enrolment	2,500	1,700
	Average teaching load in hours per year (10 classes of 3 hours)	30	30

For the year ending June 30, 2020 the graduate enrolment is expected to increase by 10%, while the post-graduate enrolment is expected to remain the same. Salaries of lecturers will be increased by a standard 5% and individual selection grade to teachers shall be awarded ₹ 90,750 for graduate and ₹ 85,000 for post-graduate teachers.

(2) The current budget is ₹ 2,10,000 for operation and maintenance of plant and equipment. This includes ₹ 90,000 for salaries and wages. It is expected that 5% increase in salaries and wages and ₹ 9,000 in other expenditures for operation of plant and equipment.

(3) The budget for the remaining expenditures for the year ending June 30, 2020 is as follows:

	₹
Administrative and general	2,40,000
Library	1,60,000
Health and recreation	75,000
Athletics	1,20,000
Insurance and retirement	2,65,000
Interest	48,000
Capital outlay	3,00,000

(4) The college expects to award 25 tuition free scholarship to graduates and 15 to post-graduates.

(5) Budgeted revenue for the year 30-6-2020 is as follows:

	₹
Endowments	1,14,000
Net income from auxiliary	2,35,000
Services	1,80,000

You are to prepare a statement showing expected enrolment, total hours to be carried and the number of faculty members needed.

Prepare also the budget for salaries and tuition revenue.

Solution

Statement of Details

	Enrolment	Teaching Hours		Per faculty member	Total faculty
		Average	Total		
Graduates	2,750[1]	33	90,750	750[2]	121
Post-graduates	1,700	30	51,000	600[3]	85

1. 110% × 2,500 = 2,750.
2. 25 × 30 = 750.
3. 20 × 30 = 600.

Faculty Salaries Budget

	Average salary ₹	Total Faculty ₹	Total Basic ₹	Increments ₹	Total Salaries ₹
Graduates	10,500	121	12,70,500	90,750	13,61,250
Post-graduates	10,500	85	8,92,500	85,000	9,77,500
			21,63,000	1,75,750	23,38,750

Revenue Budget

	Fees paying Students ₹	Average hours ₹	Total hours ₹	Fees per hour ₹	Total fees ₹
Graduates	2,725	33	89,925	22	19,78,350
Post-graduate	1,685	30	50,550	22	11,12,100
			1,40,475		30,90,450

Example 2

Jaslok Hospital gives you following information:

Type of patient	Total Patients	Average number of days in the hospital		Percentage of regular patients		
		Regular	Medicare	Private	Semi-Private	Ward
Medical	2,100	7	17	10%	60%	30%
Surgical	2,400	10	15	15%	75%	10%

Out of the patients served, 10% are expected to be medicare patients, all of whom are expected of select semi-private rooms. The number and proportion of medicare patients have increased over the past few years. Daily charges for rent per patient are ₹ 40 for private room, ₹ 35 for semi-private and ₹ 25 for a ward.

Operating charges are based on man-minutes (number of minutes the operating room is in use multiplied by number of persons assisting in the operation). The per man/minute charges are 13 Paisa for inpatients and 22 Paisa for outpatients. Operations are as follows:

Operation	No.	Average number of minutes per operation	Average number of persons
A	800	30	4
B	700	45	5
C	300	90	6
D	200	120	8
	2,000		

The same proportion of inpatients operations are expected for next year and 180 outpatients are expected for operation. The outpatient operations require 20 average minutes and three assistants. The department costs budget for the year ending June 30 is given below:

	₹
General services:	
Maintenance of plant	50,000
Operation of plant	27,500
Administration	97,500
All other	1,92,000
Revenue-producing services:	
Operating room	68,440
All other	7,00,000
Total budgeted costs	11,35,440

The following informations provided for cost allocation purposes:

	Square feet	Salaries ₹
General services:		
Maintenance of plant	12,000	40,000
Operation of plant	28,000	25,000
Administration	10,000	55,000
All other	36,250	1,02,500
Revenue-producing service:		
Operating room	17,500	15,000
All other	86,250	3,02,500
Total	1,90,000	5,40,000

Basis of allocations:

Maintenance of plant—salaries

Operation of plant—square feet

Administration—salaries

All other—8% to operating room

Instructions: Prepare working papers showing the computation of:

(a) The number of patient days (number of patient multiplied by average stay in hospital) expected by type of patients and service.

(b) The total number of man-minutes expected for operating room service for inpatients and outpatients. For inpatients show the breakdown to total operating room man-minutes by types of operation.

(c) Expected gross revenue from routine services.

(d) Expected gross revenue from operating room services.

(e) Cost per man-minute for operating room services assuming that the total man-minutes computed in part B is 8,00,000 and that the step-down method of cost allocation is used (that is costs of the general services departments are allocated in sequence first to the general services department that they serve and then finally to the revenue-producing departments).

Solution

(a) Computation of expected number of patient days for year ending June 30.

Type of Patient	Total Patients		Type of Service			
				Semi-private		
	Regular	Medicare	Private	Regular	Medicare	Ward
Medical:						
Patients	1890 (1)	210 (2)	189 (3)	1134 (3)	210	567 (3)
Average stay (days)			×7	×7	×7	×7
Patient days			1323	7938	3570	3969
Surgical:						
Patients	2160 (4)	240 (5)	324 (3)	1620 (3)	240	216 (3)
Average stay (days)			×10	×10	×15	×10
Patient days			3240	16200	3600	2160
Total patient days			4563	24138	7170	6129

(1) .90 × 2,100
(2) .10 × 2,100
(3) Expected number of patients × applicable percentage
(4) .90 × 2,400
(5) .10 × 2,400

(b) Computation of total number of man-minutes expected for operating room services for year ending June 30.

	Number of Operations[1]	Time in Minutes		Personnel	Man-
		Average	Total	Required	Minutes
Inpatient:					
Type A	960	30	28800	4	115200
B	840	45	37800	5	189000
C	360	90	32400	6	194400
D	240	120	28800	8	230400
Total inpatient	2400				729000
Outpatient:					
Operating room man-minutes	180	20	3600	3	10800
					739800

1. 2,400 patients × last year's proportion for this type of operation.

(c) Computation of expected gross revenue from routine services for year ending June 30.

	Private	Semi-private	Ward	Total Charges
Number of patient days	4563	31308	6129	
Charge per day	×40	×35	×25	
Revenue	₹ 1,82,520	₹ 10,95,780	₹ 1,53,225	₹ 14,31,525

(d) Computation of expected gross from operating room services for ending June 30.

Type of Patient	Charge per minute	Man-minutes	Revenue
Inpatient	₹ 0.13	7,29,000	₹ 94,770
Outpatient	₹ 0.22	10,800	2,376
Total revenue			₹ 97,146

(e) Computation of cost per man-minute for operating room services for year ending June 30.

	Total Direct Expenses ₹	Maintenance of Plant ₹	Operation of Plant ₹	Administration ₹	All Other ₹	Total after Distribution ₹
General Services:						
Maintenance of plant	50,000	(50,000)				
Operation of plant	27,500	2,500	(30,000)			
Administration	97,500	5,500	2,000	(1,05,000)		
All other	1,92,000	10,250	7,250	25,625	(2,35,125)	
Revenue-producing services:						
Operating room	68,440	1,500	3,500	3,750	18,810	96,000
All other	7,00,000	30,250	17,250	75,625	2,16,315	10,39,440
Total	11,35,440	0	0	0	0	11,35,440

From above examples, we find that in NPOs the approach to budgeting should be to estimate the available resources and secondly to plan spending to match the available resources, neither more nor less. However, the policy that budgeted revenue sets the limit on expenses is not available sometimes.

The two general format for spending portion of the budget are:

(a) Line item budget, which focuses on objects of spending.

(b) Planning, programme budget system, which focuses on programmes.

Examples adapted from *Modern Advanced Accounting*, Meigs, Mosich & Larsen.

There are many variations of PPBS and such systems generally have following four basic elements:

(1) A programme budgeting structure oriented toward end objectives. The budget merely specify *lump sum* amount of appropriations for each aging. It may be either on the basis of objects of expenditure i.e. specific categories of inputs or may be on the basis of programmes i.e. focus is on end items—the ultimate output of service of the organisation. (2) A multi-year programme and financial plan i.e. extending planning and budgeting cycle from a single year to several years in future. (3) Programme evaluation. (4) Analytical studies e.g. capital budget inventory management or cost effectiveness analysis.

Like in a commercial organisation "variance" analysis should be made in NPOs. The common variances used are (a) volume variance. It may be of revenue or of expense, (b) price variance, (c) efficiency variance, and (d) effectiveness variance. By variance analysis one can find that the NPO is exactly on target with some items and is off by some amount on some items. For such items adjusting action is needed.

Volume variance:

(a) Revenue volume variance =

(Actual quantity of service rendered – quantity budgeted or planned volume) × unit revenue

(b) Expense volume variance = (Actual expenses – Budgeted expenses) variable expense per unit i.e.

Variable expenses per unit plus variable portion of semi-variable expenses.

Example 3

In Ram Manohar Lohia Hospital following information was available:

Budgeted quantity of service (volume) = 10,000 patient days

Actual quantity of service = 11,000 patient days

Unit revenue = ₹ 200 per day

Variable expense per unit = ₹ 4

(A) (a) Revenue volume variance = Budgeted revenue – Actual revenue = (10,000 days × ₹ 200) – (11,000 × ₹ 200) = ₹ 2,00,000 (F).

(b) Expense volume variance = (Actual – Budgeted) × V.C. per unit (11,000 patient days – 10,000) × ₹ 4 = ₹ 4,000 (U).

(B) Price variance = (Budgeted price per unit – Actual price per unit) × No. of units.

(C) Efficiency variance = Actual expense – Budgeted variance.

(D) Effectiveness variance cannot be measured.

OUTPUT MEASUREMENT

Though efficiency and effectiveness cannot be measured, yet to find them is a necessity. Many different measures are used to classify output measures e.g. result measures, process measures and social indicators. A result measure is a measure of output expressed in that are related to the organisation's objectives. It the output measure cannot be measured in quantitative terms, then it is called surrogate or proxy i.e. it represents the closest feasible way of measuring the accomplishment of an objective. Process measure, also called production measure, is a means-oriented measure rather than end-oriented measure. Like result measure, it relates to an activity carried on by an organisation e.g. the number of hours lines typed in one hour or number of purchase orders written in one month. Output per man-hour called productivity measure. Social indicators refer to the result of the work of an organisation like police, court. Output measures may be objective, subjective, quantitative and non-quantitative or satisfactory and unsatisfactory. However, the type of output measures are appropriate for use in a given NPO depends upon the purpose for which it is used e.g. in a hospital the total cost of the hospital or over all cost per patient per day or cost per unit of service be measured. However, output measures must be related to individual programme element. Sometimes even inputs are a better measure of output measures.

CONTROL OF OPERATIONS

A budget is the most important control device in NPO. Then there is specific restrictions by guarantors on the purposes for which fund may be spent. In addition to the financial controls, NPOs are guided by rules and procedures for specific matters. Internal audit is another control, though it is not so perfect device. The accounting system affords also as a tool of control.

Nowadays in NPOs there is a shift from what is called "line item control" to "Programme control". In line item control the amount is fixed for each item e.g. so much for salaries, travel, repairs, etc. A programme is a planned course of action that is intended to help the organisation to achieve its goal. To analyse any proposed new programme benefit/cost or systems analysis is used. But there is no point in making a benefit/cost analysis unless there is some measure of agreement on what the goals are. A programme should not be adopted unless its benefit exceeds costs and among two competing proposals, the one with more benefits or the one with lower costs. However, in NPOs there are problems that arise in making the use of benefit/cost analysis. The problems are: How to quantify the value of a human being, the use of discount rates, risk and inflation and taxes. Moreover, it is difficult to determine the cost of each programme zero-based budgeting, PPBS, functional classification of expenses and other budgeting tools necessitate detailed information on benefit/cost of alternative programme. In the long run this analysis will not be totally accurate process. While this analysis is made "Opportunity costs must be taken into account".

PRICING

Prices charged for services rendered are important for management control in NPOs. As a general rule in NPOs the principles of pricing (including transfer pricing) are that service should be sold rather than given away, prices should affect consumer actions, it should ordinarily be equal to full cost, unit or service that is priced should be narrowly defined and prospective pricing is preferable to cost reimbursement. There are, however, exceptions and disagreement, about these rules. The basis for pricing in NPOs may be any of the following:

(a) *Full cost pricing*: Some specific services may be fixed above or below full cost.

(b) *Market-based prices*: It is for certain services e.g. research and development services.

(c) *Subsidy and penalty prices*: It is the price of that service whose price should set to encourage or discourage the use of that service e.g. outpatient charges, postal service for villages. The smaller is the specific unit of service that is priced, the better is the basis of decision about allocation of resources.

(d) *Distributional prices*: These prices are used for those services whose use should not be governed by ability to pay e.g. bus fare for blind. Such price is set before the performance of the service.

Whether or not depreciation should be provided should depend (not on that existing capital assets that was a gift) on financing of the next asset. If existing asset was provided by gift, and there is no intention of replacing it, there is no need to charge depreciation on it. Depreciation should be funded, i.e. an amount equal to depreciation charge should be invested in a separate fund and be kept completely shielded from current operations.

The interest paid on borrowed money to finance an asset is a cost. Should the amount of revenue from contributions and endowment income be deducted from costs before calculating price. The answer depends on "what is the intention of donors" i.e. if it is used to help finance general operation, then it may be deducted from the cost of these operations. Imputed costs sometimes are included in calculating prices, though sound practice is not to include them.

CASH FLOW ANALYSIS

In NPOs, it is very important to see how the receipts will come to the organisation. The best way to do this is to follow cash as it comes into, through, and out of the organisation with a cash flow analysis chart like the following:

Example 4

Cash Flow Analysis Chart

	January		February		March	
	Expected ₹	Actual ₹	Expected ₹	Actual ₹	Expected ₹	Actual ₹
Beginning balance	10,000	10,000	8,000	7,500	11,000	12,000
Increase	5,000	4,000	10,000	12,000	12,000	9,000
Total Cash in hand	15,000	14,000	18,000	19,500	23,000	21,000
Monthly Expenses	7,000	6,500	7,000	7,500	8,000	9,000
Ending balance	8,000	7,500	11,000	12,000	15,000	12,000

It is good if income figures are divided into several different sources such as grants, membership fees, service fees and so on.

The schedule can be prepared for the whole year. To determine the "expected" figure, the historical data available, contracts and other documents that call for payment to the organisation are helpful.

For those organisations that have many sources of income, many of whom are variable in payment, the use of expected value can be made to determine the "expected" figure. Following is an example:

Expected Value Table

Donors	Donation ₹	Expected value ₹
A	10,000 (0.8)	8,000
B	10,000 (0.8)	8,000
C	5,000 (0.8)	4,000
D	5,000 (0.8)	4,000
E	8,000 (0.7)	5,600
F	10,000 (0.7)	7,000
G	10,000 (0.3)	3,000
H	20,000 (0.1)	2,000
		41,600

The list of potential donors is made, then the amount of the probable contribution and the best guess of the probability of that contribution are shown. In final column the expected value of contributions is found by multiplying the probable donation by the probability of donation. These figures can be applied to cash flow analysis chart showing the timing of the probable grant. This helps to recognize the probability of expected funds and to plant for their use. This chart works to the extent of the accuracy of the estimates. For those donations that are extremely large, they should not be included in analysis except at extremely conservative estimates. To expected value table estimates of grants with alternative estimates of probability can be added e.g. 0.5 probability for ₹ 10,000 or 0.9 probability for ₹ 2,000 depending upon circumstances.

QUESTIONS

1. How does non-profit organisations differ from commercial and government organisations?
2. What is benefit-cost or cost utility analysis? What are its limitations? Explain the term "proxy or surrogate".
3. Describe how you might measure the benefits associated with a community swimming pool, a community hall, an enlarged police force and a public library.
4. (a) A university wants to change its budget structure from "line items" orientation to a programme orientation. What programme categories might be used to operate such a budget? Will the last year's budget be of any relevance?

   (b) Describe the three primary basis of revenue and costs recognition that are used by non-profit organisation.
5. (a) A common practice of NPOs is to cut back all budget requests by a set percentage, ignoring the merits of the specific requests. What are advantages or disadvantages of such an approach?

   (b) Critics of costs benefit analysis object to placing or monetary values on human lives. Yet this valuation is implicit in many decisions that must be made by NPOs. Give some examples of decision that might imply a value for life? Could these decision be made in a more rational manner if cost benefit that analysis is not used?

6.[1] A large hospital has been given ₹ 20,00,000 for the treatment of two major diseases. A special study commissioned by the Board of Management has estimated the number of lives that could be saved annually in the community by various levels of expenditure follows:

Amount spent ₹	Lives Saved	
	Disease A	Disease B
5,00,000	50	25
10,00,000	90	40
15,00,000	120	50
20,00,000	140	55

(a) Assuming that the Board wish to maximize the number of lives saved, how much of ₹ 20,00,000 should be spent on each programme?

1. Adapted from *Managerial Accounting*, Drebin, A.R. and Jr. Bierman, H. (Holt-Saunders).

(b) Because of resources limitations, it is not possible to save all lives based on the above figures, determine an implicit value of a life in the hospital population.

7. The government is considering possible ways of reducing unemployment. Two alternative programmes have been suggested. One is a training programme for unskilled workers. The other is a relocation programme in which unemployed workers are moved to areas in which jobs are available. In a particular area there are 10,000 unemployed workers, all unskilled. Jobs could be found in the area for as many as 4,000 of these workers if they possessed the proper skills and up to 5,000 workers could be placed in unskilled jobs in other communities. The training programme would last from 5 to 10 weeks. It is estimated that 50% of these enrolled could be given the necessary skills in a five week programme, 75% could be given these skills in ten week programme. Programme between these two lengths would produce proportional results, it is assumed that 25% of these enrolled cannot be properly trained regardless of the length of the programme. Cost of training programme are estimated to be ₹ 1,00,000 for administration, plus ₹ 100 per student per week of the course. All the unemployment persons have expressed their willingness to take part in either programme. The cost of relocation programme is expected to ₹ 50,000 for administration, plus ₹ 1,500 per worker relocated. Total funds available for the programme are ₹ 50,00,000.

   Assume that the benefit of these programmes are to be measured by the number of unemployed workers placed in jobs. Determine how available funds should be used i.e. how many persons should enrolled in the training programme, how many weeks should the training programme last and how many persons should be offered relocation assistance. At this level of effort, what are the costs and benefits of each programme.

19
Management Reports

Introduction

A report is a statement of facts relating to a particular subject, prepared after an independent inquiry or investigation and presented to the responsible persons with or without opinions and suggestions.*

One of the major responsibilities of a management accountant is to prepare a report to the management. It may be about any activity of the firm e.g. responsibility performance report, cost of production report, man-power performance report and so one. Reports may be short run, interim or periodic report (e.g. weekly or monthly). The purpose of all reports is to be an aid to the management, to communicate information, to perform managerial functions, to measure executive performance and to establish contacts with outsiders. The management, on the basis of the report, takes the corrective action to bring performance in line with standards. Any report prepared for higher management may be divided into two categories: (a) The written report, and (b) Graphs and charts.

Kinds of reports: They can be divided on two bases: (a) functional and (b) formality. A functional report is further divided into three types: (i) Informational, (ii) Analytical, and (iii) Research/Examination. On the basis of formality report may be (a) Statutory and (b) Non-statutory (General or Voluntary). Non-statutory reports may either be (i) periodic (routine) or (ii) special.

The written report must be prepared by the management accountant prior to the meeting. In preparing any written report, following guiding principles must be taken into consideration.

Essentials of a Good Written Report

1. The number of reports should be kept at minimum. Every report should save a definite purpose.
2. The reporting system should be kept under constant review.
3. Reports should be kept as simple as possible, containing only the essential information. The exceptions should be highlighted. It should be clear and unambiguous.

---

* "Report Writing for Business" Lesikar, Raymond V. (Richard D. Irwing.)

4. Reports should be tailored to the person who will use them and not to a function or a job.
5. Report should be accurate, but only to the degree required for their purpose. Accuracy is relative.
6. Reports must be timely to be of value.
7. Reports should not only communicate, but should motivate the persons.
8. It should state by whom it is submitted, be dated and duly signed. Sections should be headed and paragraphs numbered for easy reference. The contents should follow a logical sequence i.e. present position, courses of action which might be taken and recommendation.
9. Professional opinions should not be expressed assertively, since they are opinion and not facts.
10. Report should be impartial. The report should not become a decorative piece of the shelf.

Report Preparation

While preparing a report following seven steps are necessary:

(1) Know the preliminaries. It means to know who is to receive it, what is its purpose and time factor within which report is to be submitted.

(2) Collect the facts and figures.

(3) Analyse, interpret and draw conclusions.

(4) Arrange the subject matter. In arrangement a report should have:

   (a) Heading or title.
   (b) Table of contents.
   (c) Introduction and background—main body of report.
   (d) Recommendations (Summary and Conclusions).
   (e) Arguments—further general conditions of report.
   (f) Appendix.

This arrangement is suggestive. Sometimes "Executive Summary and Conclusions" may follow before introduction and background.

(5) Draft the report suitably.

(6) Edit the report.

(7) Present the report.

In report preparation, following seven principles of report preparation must be kept in mind.

(i) Principle of sound purpose.

(ii) Principle of proper planning.

(iii) Principle of clarity.

(iv) Principle of brevity and accuracy.

(v) Principle of scheduling and timeliness.

(vi) Principle of cost.

(vii) Principle of relevance.

The reports by a management accountant are internal reports and not external reports. They are not meant for shareholders or the outsiders. The most common examples of a written reports are the report by internal audit or "Management Audit" report.

MANAGEMENT AUDIT

Internal audit is a "review of operations and records, sometimes continuous, undertaken within a business by specially assigned staff". Actually, management audit is even broader form of auditing. It is a systematic approach to the appraisal of overall performance of management. It not only verifies all multifarious accounting statements produced for management, but also investigates the administrative system up on which they are based besides examining the accounting methods and principles of the firm.

The task of management accountant becomes difficult sometimes because of individual personalities. Few people may take kindly to their work being investigated by someone they know has immediate excess to high authority. He has to proceed with great patience and tact.

The increasing size of businesses today creates an ever-widening gap between management and actual field of operations, and it is here that the management accountant can provide the essential connecting link throughout the whole organisation. For as the chain of responsibility lengthens, so does the possibility grow of delays, misinterpretations and misjudgements which hinder the running of what would otherwise be an efficient and prosperous business.

One of the better known methods of appraising managerial performance is the management audit developed by Jackson Martindell[1] of the AIM (American Institute of Management). The AIM audit evaluates the performance of a company in relation to the performance of other companies in the same industry and in relation to the performance of outstanding companies in other industries. Some of the information needed for the management audit is a matter of public record, but much of it comes from the answers to a 300 item question. Point values for the answers given to each question are assigned, with the maximum number of points being 10,000. Managerial performance in each of the following 10 categories is evaluated.

1. *Economic function*: It determines the public value of company. It is related to the product or service chosen by the company and is evaluated in moral or ethical sense. It is a measure of stature in the eyes of the public.

---

1. *The Scientific Appraisal of Management*, Jackson Martindell (Harper & Row), 1962.

2. *Corporate structure*: The organisation of the company is evaluated in respect to its appropriateness for that particular company. How far the organisation structure permits effective control of the enterprise?

3. *Health of earnings*: It is not only measured in terms of money by R.O.C.E., but also in terms of potential that might be realised with full utilization of the company resources.

4. *Service to the shareholders*: The questions to be answered here are: Has the investment of shareholders in the company been subjected to an undue degree of risk?, to what extent has their equity in the company appreciated in value?, and has there been a fair return on investment in the form of dividends? The nature and openness of communications between the company and its shareholders through annual reports and meetings is also an important factor.

5. *Research and development*: It helps to measure the future growth potential. It is more than product research like the development of new markets, improving methods of distribution and selecting the most efficient advertising media.

6. *Directorate analysis*: The members of the board of directors is analyzed to determine whether or not there are conflicts of interests rising as the result of other business activities on the part of directors. The board's method and degree of influence on management is assessed.

7. *Fiscal policies*: Poor fiscal policies cause most corporate financial debacles. The fiscal policies are rated in respect to the organisation structure available for the establishment of such policies, the soundness of capital structure of the company and effectiveness of such policies.

8. *Production efficiency*: The concept is not only applicable to manufacturing organisation, but also to organisations providing services. It can be expressed as a ratio between sales and number of production employees, between sales volume and payroll cost and between value of production and invested capital.

9. *Sales vigour*: Comparative rating of the sales policies and practices of many companies is difficult because of differences in sales methods of companies. The method of distribution is appraisal, the media and amount spent for advertising, and the capability and size of sales force is considered. The method of pricing and development of new markets are also weighed.

10. *Executive evaluation*: This is the most important of all other factor. The factors have to be considered are ability, industry and integrity of the executives of the firm. Moreover, executive turnover, compensation, method of selection of executives, training and the extent of participation by key executives in public affairs are also considered.

The criticisms against AIM audit have been that it is oriented too much towards investment concept of business management. The total points of 10,000 have been allowed as follows:

(a) Corporate structure	500 points
(b) Executive evaluation	2,200 points
(c) Directorate analysis	800 points
(d) Production efficiency and sales vigour	2,000 points
(e) For remaining	4,500 points

Secondly, the audit rates past performance too heavily and does not evaluate future performance. Some companies evaluated on this basis were found "excellently managed" during two or three years and later year they followed several financial difficulties.

However, the concept can be used as part of an overall control programme. The management audit focuses attention upon many aspects of managerial performance rather than upon one or two easily measured performance areas. It emphasizes the measurement of the result of managerial performance, which other types of audits generally fail to do. It encourages a systematic reconsideration of where the organisation should be headed in the next five or ten years.

There are differing views about the extent to which management audit should be future oriented as opposed to present and past oriented. John C. Burton has suggested that the audit should avoid making forecasts and should concentrate instead on the organisation's past and present performance (like AIM audit). The public will be able to make its own prediction about the future success/failure of the organisation. Robert B. Buchele, however, suggests that management audit need to be more future oriented. Past performance is no longer a reliable indicator of future viability because the external environment of organisations is undergoing increasingly rapid changes. Buchele's auditing approach focuses on aspects of the organisation that he feels are the most relevant to predicting future success or failure. He includes the following:

1. Rate of expansion or contraction of markets.
2. Determination of success potential for products the firm will be able to produce in the future.
3. Cost-benefit analysis of the R&D programme.
4. Degree of co-ordination between R&D and long-range planning.
5. Flexibility and appropriateness to the future of the organisation's manufacturing processes and skills.
6. Adequacy of the styles and characteristics of top management for meeting probable future challenges.

Buchele does not, of course, suggest that the present and past record should be ignored. Management's past approaches to its future needs, for example, will help auditors estimate how prepared for the future the organisation is today.

GRAPHS AND CHARTS

Sometimes the help of graphs and charts is taken to depict factual information. This justifies the use of graphs in reports to management.

A graph is a pictorial presentation of the relationship between variables. Many types of graphs can be used in reports, depending upon the nature of the data involved and the purpose for which the graph is intended. The disadvantages of graphs is that they are not precise in their definition or if they are, that they cannot be read to the degree of exactness to which they are drawn. Since management does not have much time to go into lengthy reports, graphs save much time and effort.

A graph is used to show the relationship between two variables by means of either a curve or line. One of the variables should be taken as independent variable and this variable is plotted along the x-axis. Where graphs show absolute changes, the zero line should normally be shown. Too many lines should be avoided on one graph. The scale should be on left hand lines wordings should not be shown vertically. Where number of curves are necessary, colouring or dotted or pecked lines should be used:

1. Line graph.
2. Bar graph, bar chart or bar diagram.
3. Percentage component part graph and semi-logarithmic scale graphs.
4. Pie graph, circular graph or area diagrams.
5. Z charts.
6. Flow charts.
7. Gantt charts.

1. *Line graph*: Points are located by co-ordinates from the table. Successive points are connected by a straight line. For this reason it is called line graph. Note that zero is indicated on a vertical-axis (Exhibit 19.1).

Example 1

A company produced sugar and sweets during the year 2010 to 2020.

Year	Sugar (Tons)	Sweets (Tons)
2010	200	75
2011	185	90
2012	225	100
2013	250	85
2014	240	80
2015	195	100
2016	210	110
2017	225	105
2018	250	95
2019	230	110
2020	235	100

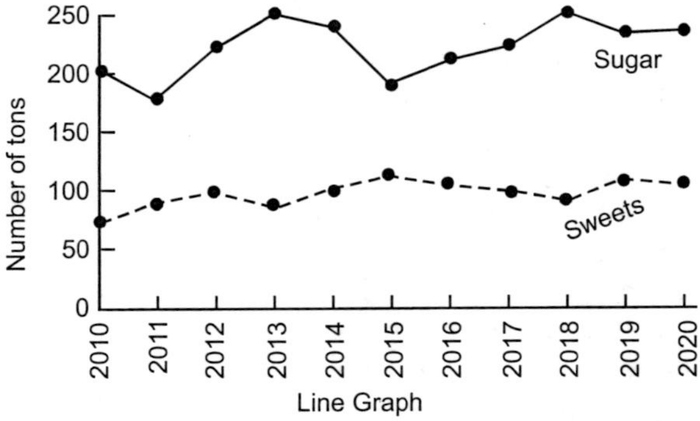

Exhibit 19.1

Where the attention to omission of zero is drawn, line graph will be shown either by removing the lower line graph or by use of zig-zag line. The disadvantage of this method is that the reader may not notice omission of zero.

2. *Bar charts or graphs*: This type of chart facilitates quick visual comparison. It must always begin at zero, otherwise the comparison will be distorted. The simple bar chart reveals increases or decreases in magnitude of any particular item. The width of bars, which are all equal, have no significance in this case and can be taken any convenient size so long as such charts show relative rate of change. Instead of comparing the production with total production, the production of two periods may be compared e.g. the production of sugar in 2010 and 2012 compared, the increase wads [(225/200) × 100] = 112.5% and of sweets in the same period is 133.33% [(100/75) × 100]. In such a case, percentage will be shown on left side. But line graph will be drawn, preferably using logarithmic ruled graph paper.

3. *Pie graph or area diagrams*: These charts are used to show the relationship of parts to the whole. They are formed on the basis of a circle divided into sectors, after the method of slices from a cake or pie, hence the name. The disadvantage of such a graph is that it is difficult to judge from them difference between the size of "slices". They are of little use for management control purposes. Area diagrams differ from it only in that they show relative differences by squared blocks of various sizes. Consider the following example:

Continent	Production of Sweets (million tons)
Africa	30.3
Asia	26.9
Europe	4.9
North America	24.3
Oceania	8.5
South America	17.9
U.S.S.R.	20.5

To construct the graph, we assume that the total production of 133.3 million tons of sweets is equal to 360° in a circle. So, 1 million ton is equal to 360°/133.3. The production for each continent is as follows:

Africa 82°, Asia 73°, Europe 13°, North America 60°, Oceania 23°, South America 48° and U.S.S.R. 55° of a circle. Using a protractor, the required dividing lines can be drawn as shown in Exhibit 19.2.

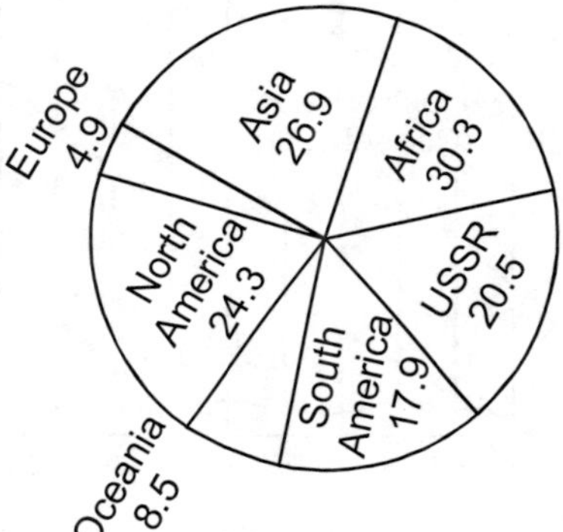

Pie Graph

Exhibit 19.2

4. *Z charts*: Comprising three curves on a single graph the *Z* chart is so-called because on completion, it is similar to the letter *Z*. These three curves are (a) the current figure for the period concerned, (b) the cumulative amount of the latest date, and (c) the moving annual total or trend.

There is one disadvantage of this chart. Because the trend curve begins at the cumulative figure for the previous period, it is separated rather widely from the current monthly or other period figure. Consider the following example that gives sales figures of a firm.

	₹		₹		₹
January	4,000	May	5,900	September	8,600
February	5,200	June	7,000	October	7,910
March	6,800	July	7,390	November	8,900
April	6,300	August	9,200	December	12,100
				January (next)	10,100

The trend figure is calculated as follows:

	₹
Total sales for the year	89,300
Add January next year	10,100
	99,400
Less January beginning	4,000
Trend for January next year	95,400

As the figures for previous year are not available, a budgeted trend curve has been shown in Exhibit 19.3 for illustrative purpose.

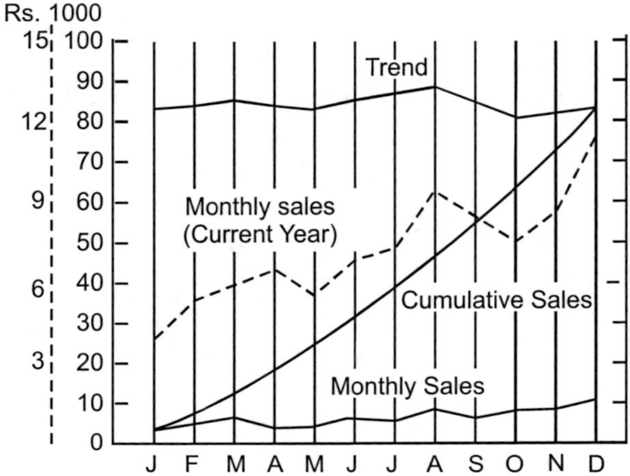

Z Chart

Exhibit 19.3

5. *Flow charts*: This type of chart is useful for management control purpose. It enables an overall picture of a system or systems to be obtained, and when adjustments are made to increase efficiency or eliminate unnecessary procedures, the prevailing flow of work and probable effects may be seen clearly.

It is useful for internal audit purposes. It can facilitate planning and lead to the organisation working more efficiently, as well as elucidating procedures of instituting or improving an internal check system. A flow chart for the raw material purchases is shown in Exhibit 19.4. Two symbols are used as key and the letters show the following activities.

(a) Prepare purchase requisition.

(b) Prepare purchase order.

(c) Count and inspect incoming shipment and prepare receiving report.

(d) Compare quantity of materials received with quantity listed on receiving report-shortage to accounts section.

(e) Compare data on purchase order, receiving report, and vendor's invoice and prepare voucher.

(f) Send voucher to payment section.

6. *Gantt charts*: The non-repetitive project or programme is becoming an increasingly frequent phenomenon in today's large organisations. As these projects also increase in scale, complexity, and cost, new methods for planning and controlling them have been and are being developed.

The best known of the older approaches in Gantt chart (after the name of Henry L. Gantt). This relatively simple chart has made a significant contribution to project management. It is also the foundation upon which the other sophisticated types of project and programme control techniques—milestone scheduling, PERT and CPM—are based.

Gantt chart is appropriate for scheduling a series of unrelated activities. It is a graphic control method for a project with a specified completion date (see Exhibit 19.5). The project is broken down into separate tasks or assignments, and estimates are made of the amount of time necessary to carryout each task. The date of completion by which task is likely to be completed is also included.

This information is translated into a pair of brackets for each task. Each bracket pair on the chart indicates the task's starting date and completion date. With each set of brackets a contrasting bar is filled in representing the degree of accomplishment of that particular task. The result is a graphic representation of the state of each phase of the project on each day of the production period. In other words, the manager can see what particular tasks are behind or ahead of schedule and how much. If you select a date when a certain decision, accomplishment or event is to take place and indicate that data on the horizontal bar of a chart, you have created a milestone.

MANAGEMENT INFORMATION SYSTEM (MIS)

The reports to management are facilitated if there is MIS. There are many definitions of MIS. Some definitions of MIS stress the role of computers and EDP. For our purpose, MIS is defined as "a formal method of making available to management the accurate and timely information necessary to facilitate the decision-making process and enable the organisation's planning control and operational functions to be carried out effectively". The system provides information on the past, present and projected future on relevant events inside and outside the organisation.

The managerial activities are of three categories, namely strategic planning, management control, and operational control. MIS must provide the different types of information that these three managerial activities require. One major company designed the manufacturing component of its MIS in this way.

(a) Supervisors: receive daily reports on direct and indirect labour, material, usage, scrap, machine down time.

(b) Superintendents and departmental heads: received weekly departmental cost summaries and product cost reports.

(c) Plant managers: received weekly and monthly financial statements and analyses, product cost reports, etc.

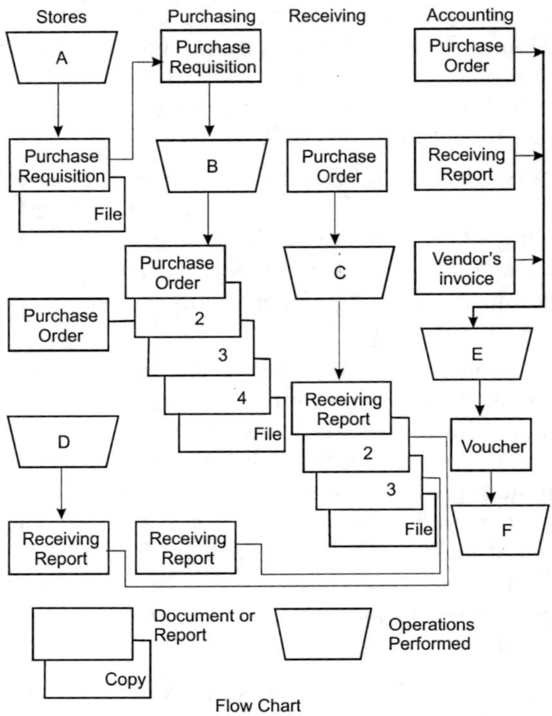

Flow Chart

Exhibit 19.4

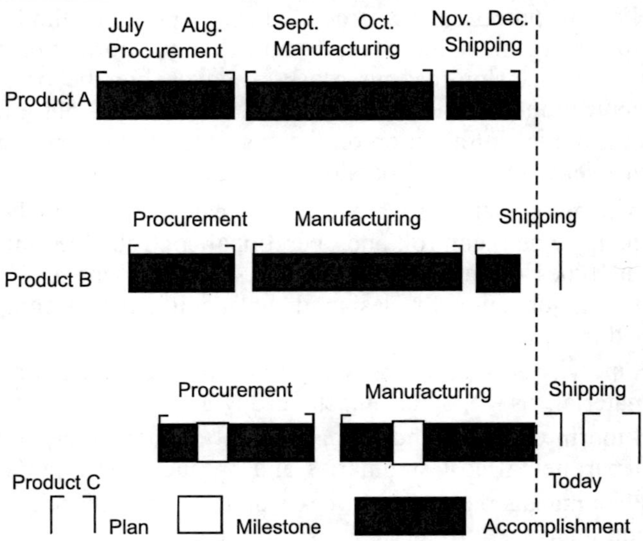

Gantt Chart for Manufacturing Deptt.

Exhibit 19.5

(d) Divisional managers: receive financial planning reports, product cost summaries, plant cost control reports.

(e) Top manager: receive overall monthly and quarterly financial reviews, financial analysis and divisional performance reports.

Many steps have been suggested by many authors to be followed in designing and implementing on MIS, and they are out of purview here. An organisation may face problems in implementing a computer-based MIS. It will disrupt the establishment departmental boundaries, and the present informal system. It will affect the organisational climate of human behaviour. Therefore, the MIS should meet the user's needs, make the users to participate in the system, make the communication easy and must be accompanied by a satisfactory reward system.

QUESTIONS

1. Describe the use of graphs and charts in presenting management accounting information and describe the kind of chart, you would suggest to illustrate actual and budgeted production and labour control (*Hint.* Gantt and Flow charts).
2. What is the purpose of management audit? What ten areas does management audit appraise?
3. What are the basic essentials for a report prepared for the management?
4. Present a *Z* chart from the following data through the year to 31-8-2015.

Sales in ₹ '000

	2013 Actual	2014 Budgeted	2015 Actual
September	60	70	80
October	70	70	60
November	900	100	60
December	100	110	110
January	120	130	120
February	120	130	110
March	120	120	130
April	150	150	140
May	100	110	
June	100	110	
July	80	90	
August	70	70	

20

OR Techniques and Management Accounting

OPERATIONAL RESEARCH

During World War II, certain mathematical techniques were developed to aid in the resolution of complex military problems and in recent years have been applied to aid managers in their decision-making. A general term used to describe these sophisticated mathematical techniques is "Operations Research". The term "operation" is used to mean any sequence of actions which is required to achieve a desired result. Operations Research (OR) is applied to problems that concern how to coordinate and conduct these activities in an organisation. It may be defined as (1) "an application of the scientific method to (2) problems arising in the operations of a system which may be represented by means of a mathematical model and (3) the solving of these problems by resolving the equations representing the system". The following major phases would probably be encountered by any researcher in any OR project, big or small.

1. Formulating the problem.
2. Constructing a mathematical model to represent the system under study.
3. Deriving a solution from the model.
4. Testing the model and solution derived from it.
5. Establishing controls over the solution.
6. Putting the solution to implementation.

OR has been applied to problems in government, military and in almost all types of business and industry. The specific areas of application include:

1. Accounting and auditing procedure designs;
2. Advertising, bidding and pricing strategies;
3. Capital investment planning and portfolio selection;
4. Controlling large-scale construction projects;
5. Developing quantity discount schedules;
6. Estimation of credit and investment risks;

7. Forecasting manpower, capital requirements, production capacity and developing plans for their acquisition;
8. Locating points of distribution and warehousing and determining the best distribution methods;
9. Locating within the plants and controlling the movements of required production materials and finished goods inventory;
10. Scheduling medical examinations;
11. Selecting the building site for a plant, scheduling and controlling its development and designing its layout;
12. Selecting R&D projects and allocating budgets, facilities and personnel to these projects; and
13. Studying personnel recruitment procedures, absenteeism, accident rates and labour turnover.

Recurring Decision Situations

In Operations Research studies certain types of decision situations arise over and over again. Each of these types makes use of specific techniques and models designed to handle the specific decision problems associated with it. Some examples of these types of situations follow:

1. *The allocation situation*: Most organisations have to operate within limitations of resources. Many important management decisions involve and allocation of scarce resources to the different activities. The objective of the allocation could be any of the following:

(a) Maximize profit, or machine utilization, or returns on investment,

(b) Minimize costs, or total time.

2. *The competitive situation*: This situation, where one individual's decisions are affected by the decision of one or more other individuals, is rather common in marketing, sales, or contract bidding.

3. *The inventory situation*: Inventories are ideal resources but they are necessary. The question is how much? The decision problem is usually concerned with controlling the quantity of inventory required per order and its frequency of acquisition.

4. *The replacement situation*: Both obsolescence and breakdown may result in such a situation. Cost minimization is sought after and in situations of obsolescence, the decision problem is that of determining the optimum point in time, or in cumulative usage, to replace the equipment as well as the selection of the equipment with which the replacement should be made. In case of permanent equipment breakdowns, the decision problem concerns the determination of item to be replaced and their frequency so that the total cost is minimized.

5. *The sequencing situations*: The sequencing problems encountered in job shop problems or general routing problems are recurring in

nature. These are repetitive activities involving decisions regarding the determination of the best way of sequencing. The objectives may include cost minimization, profit maximization or minimization of process times.

6. *Waiting-time situations*: Waiting time processes involve the arrival of units requiring service in one or more service stations. In most cases, waiting is required of either the unit requiring services, or the service units, or both. In each case of waiting costs are associated. Minimization of the total cost is the objective in such cases and has to be done by controlling arrivals or by organizing the service facilities.

7. *Combined processes*: Real life situation, which seldom involve only one process, are generally a combination of processes. They are solved in sequence by using one or more OR techniques.

The above are not exhaustive examples, but are those which have been so far faced in practice.

The following introduction to operations research techniques and applications indicates a few major applications of OR and touches briefly upon some of the underlying mathematical techniques.

It should be noted that OR does not make a final choice nor translate the decision, into action. The effectiveness of OR is limited to the analysis and comparison of relationships that may be expressed quantitatively and transformed into a mathematical model. Even so, there are times when subjective judgment of the decision-maker must override the recommendation of OR techniques are not adaptable to the prediction of customer reaction to a given style or colour, nor do they clarify alternatives in human relation problems.

The following[1] are some OR technique:

(a) Linear programming.
(b) Duality theory and sensitivity analysis.
(c) PERT/CPM network analysis.
(d) Theory of games.
(e) Queuing or waiting line models.
(f) Simulation.

LINEAR PROGRAMMING

Linear Programming (LP) is one of the recently developed Operations Research techniques that can be effectively and successfully used in solving certain types of business problems. It is one of most widely used techniques of Management Sciences. There are three main reasons which are responsible for its wide applicability. These are:

1. For detailed mathematical discussion reader should refer to any standard book on OR.

1. Linear programming is one of the oldest techniques;
2. The method is flexible enough to solve many different problems; and
3. Finally, the very nature of Linear Programming is such that it can be very easily solved by a general purpose computer.

A business executive is often confronted with the allocation of his firm's limited resources. These resources may be conveniently used to provide optimal solutions to these kinds of allocation problems. The problem of maximizing contribution margin, selection of a portfolio investment, minimization of cost and decision-making with more than one scarce resource can be solved by it. The term 'Linear' refers to the relationship between or among two or more variables—a relationship which is directly and precisely proportional. On the other hand, 'Programming' refers to the use of certain types of mathematical technique that results in the best solution to a problem involving limited resources.

Areas of Application

It has already been mentioned that Linear Programming, commonly known as LP, is generally used in solving allocation problems. Many types of allocation problems are found in business and industries. Some examples to which LP has been successfully used are:

1. *Assignment problems*: These types of problems involve matching system components on a one-to-one basis with a view to achieve maximum efficiency from the total system. Suppose, P men must be assigned to M machine so that the efficiency of d; the total work system is maximized. The application of LP can identify the best man/machine combination to satisfy the stated objective.

2. *Blending or mixing problems*: Products like paint, animal feed, petroleum products, etc. are manufactured by blending or mixing various ingredients. Several combinations meeting the minimum product requirement are possible. But costs do differ. Linear programming methods may be used to identify the least cost mix and minimize the cost of production.

3. *Determination of produce mix*: The determination of the types and quantities of products to be manufactured during the next planning period is a typical industrial problem. Different items in the product line has different profitability. Furthermore, there may be constraints of capacity, demand as well as distribution. LP can be used to find out the optimal product mix to maximize profit.

4. *Distribution problems*: In many situations, products are to be shipped from several manufacturing facilities having limited capacities to field warehouses that anticipate a given demand over a given time period. Shipping or transportation costs and/or production costs vary among the alternative methods of supplying the warehouses. The firm in question aspires to minimize the total cost buy at the same time, fulfil destination

requirements within the constraints imposed by source capacitiès. LP can be effectively used to find out the best solution in such situations.

5. *Machine loading*: Consider the case of a factory where a series of order are to be processed through a group of machines. The processing cost of each order depends in part on the particular machine to which it is assigned. Machine capacities are limited and as such precludes assignment of each order to the lowest cost one. LP can be used to identify that capacity allocation to the series of orders which should result in minimum total processing costs.

6. *Production scheduling and inventory planning*: Many products have seasonal demands. A producer may naturally be faced with the problem of adjusting his production operations to account for such demands. In such circumstances, LP can be used to determine the production schedule and the inventory levels for the next planning period that will met expected demand and also result in minimum cost.

Besides the above-mentioned situations, LP has also been used in solving problems listed below:

1. Optimum crop rotation plan;
2. Optimal bombing patterns;
3. Design of weapons systems;
4. Optimal purchasing policy;
5. Trim loss problem;
6. Water quality management; and
7. Oil drilling and production.

Basic Assumption and Major Requirements of a Linear Programming Problem

Linearity and certainty are the two basic and central assumptions of linear programming methods. By linearity we mean that all problem relationships can be expressed in the form of linear equations. In mathematical terms this relationship is expressed as:

$$Y = g\ (X)$$

meaning a change in X produces a constant change in Y. Straight line method of depreciation is a good example of linearity.

The term certainty, on the other hand, indicates that no significant variations are expected in the numerical value for a problem factor. The use of average cost in making a decision can be cited as an example of certainty.

While these two basic assumptions are crucial for formulating an allocation problem into a linear programming problem, there are certain other requirements which a problem must meet in order to be solved by linear programming methods. These requirements may be listed as follows:

1. There must be a tangible objective that the firm wants to achieve. It could either be maximization of total contributions or minimization of total costs. Usually, we do not use the term profits maximization as profit may not be related to sales volume.
2. Alternative courses of action (one of which will eventually achieve the objective) must be there.
3. Resources must be in limited supply.
4. The variables in the problem must be interrelated.
5. The decision-maker must be able to express the firm's objectives as well as its constraints, in the form of linear mathematical equations or inequalities.

Methods of Solutions

Linear programming problems can be solved by graphical, algebraic and simplex methods. The first two methods are relatively easier, but to solve for a larger number of variables, they are not suitable. Graphical solution become complex if the number of variables is more than two. Similarly, for more than three variables, algebraic methods of solution gets complicated. In real life situations, however, the number of variables are not restricted to two or three only. They can be in tens, or much more. In such cases, simplex algorithm is used. Certain special types of allocation problems are solved by less complex versions of the simple method known as Transportation Methods. Index method is another variation which involves minimal computational requirements and gives approximate solutions.

All linear programming solution methods are basically search procedures aimed at determining the optimal solutions to allocation problems. The computational rules and procedures for the search are, however, well defined and marked. As such, they are very easily adaptable to modern electronic computers. As a matter of fact, nowadays, standard programmes are available which makes the application easier.

FINANCIAL APPLICATIONS

Portfolio Selection

Selecting a portfolio is an important financial application

A problem frequently encountered by managers of banks, mutual funds, investment services, and insurance companies is the selection of specific investments from among a wide variety of alternatives. The manager's overall objective is usually to maximize expected return on investment, given a set of legal, policy, or risk restraints.

For example, the International City Trust (ICT) invests in short-term trade credit, corporate bonds, gold stocks and construction loans. The board of directors has placed limits on the amount that can be committed to any one type of investment in order to encourage a diversified portfolio. ICT has ₹ 5 lakhs available for immediate investment and wishes to do two things: (1) maximize the interest earned on the investments made over the next six months and (2) satisfy the diversification requirements as set by the board of directors.

The specifics of the investment possibilities are:

Investment	Interest Earned (%)	Maximum Investment
Trade credit	7%	₹ 10 lakh
Corporate bonds	11%	₹ 25 lakh
Gold stocks	19%	₹ 15 lakh
Construction loans	15%	₹ 18 lakh

In addition, the board specifies that at least 55 per cent of the funds invested must be in gold stocks and construction loans, and that no less than 15 per cent be invested in trade credit.

To formulate ICT's investment decision as a linear programming problem, we let:

X_1 = ₹ invested in trade credit
X_2 = ₹ invested in corporate bonds
X_3 = ₹ invested in gold stocks
X_4 = ₹ invested in construction loans

Objective: Maximize dollars of interest earned =

$$.07X_1 + .11X_2 + .19X_3 + .15X_4$$

Subject to:

$$\begin{aligned}
X_1 &\le 10{,}00{,}000\\
X_2 &\le 25{,}00{,}000\\
X_3 &\le 15{,}00{,}000\\
X_4 &\le 18{,}00{,}000\\
X_3 + X_4 &\ge .55\ (50{,}00{,}000)\\
X_1 &\ge .15\ (50{,}00{,}000)\\
X_1+X_2+X_3+X_4 &\le 50{,}00{,}000
\end{aligned}$$

ICT maximizes its interest earned by making the following investment: X_1 = ₹ 7,50,000, X_2 = ₹ 9,50,000, X_3 = ₹ 15,00,000, and X_4 = ₹ 18,00,000.

Linear Programming and the Minimization of Cost

The simplex method and as well as graphic method can also be used in problems in whose objective is to minimize variable cost.

For example, assume a pharmaceutical firm is to produce exactly 40 gallon and ₹ 15 per gallon respectively. No more than 12 gallons of *x* can be use *d* and at least 10 gallons of *y* must be used: The firm wants to minimize cost.

The cost function objective can be written as

$$C \text{ (cost)} = 8x + 15y$$

The problem illustrates three types of constraints,

=, ≤, and ≥ as follows:

$$x + y = 40$$

$$y = 12$$

$$y = 10$$

The optimum solution is obvious. Since x is cheaper, as much of it as possible should be used i.e. 12 gallons. Then enough y, or 28 gallons should be use to obtain the desired total quantity of 40 gallons.

DUALITY THEORY AND SENSITIVITY ANALYSIS

The concept of duality and its many important ramifications constitute a very important part in any discussions relating to linear programming. Every linear programming problem has associate with it another linear programming problem called its dual. The original problem from which the dual is formed, is known as the primal. The properties of the primal and the dual problems are very closely related and the optimal solution to one problem reveals complete information about the other.

A sensitivity analysis of the optimum solution to a linear programming problem reveals the sensitivity of the solution to changes in the parameters. It also provides insight into economic problems. The changes in LP problem usually studied by sensitivity analysis include:

1. Change in per unit profits (or costs),
2. Change in resource limits,
3. Change in technological coefficients,
4. Addition of new variables,
5. Addition of new constraints.

In general, these changes may result in one of the following cases:

(a) The optimal solution remains, unchanged, i.e., the solution variables and their values do not change;

(b) The solution variables remain unchanged, but their values change; and

(c) The optimal solution changes completely.

The end result of a sensitivity analysis for 1 and 2 above is a set of values (maximum or minimum) which indicates the range over which the solution remains optimum. The analysis, in the first instance, involves the *ceteris paribus* condition, change in one parameter is examined holding all others fixed.

Undertaking a sensitivity analysis for the changes in technological coefficients is a bit complicated. These changes can affect the left hand side of the corresponding dual constraints and hence the feasibility of the dual. One should keep in mind that it has been mathematically proved that while the primal problem seeks optimality, its dual automatically seeks feasibility. If the primal is non-optimal, its dual is infeasible and *vice versa.*

PERT/CPM NETWORK ANALYSIS

Gantt[1] charts are appropriate for scheduling a series of unrelated activities, such as separate production runs in a job shop operation. The milestone methods can be used to divide a major project into sub-activities so that managers can achieve greater control. Neither approach, however, can adequately deal with the interrelationships among activities or events. These interrelationships form an important aspect of more complex projects and programmes in which one activity or even will often depend on the successful completion of other activities or events. In such situations, some form of *network analysis* is necessary to ensure that the entire project ore programme is moving ahead as planned.

The two major forms of network technique are PERT, with stands for Programme Evaluation and Revive Technique, and CPM, the Critical Path Method. The systems were developed independently, although virtually at the same time, around 1957-58. PERT was first developed for the U.S. Navy in connection with the Polaris weapons system and is credited with reducing the completion time of the programme by two years. CPM was developed by Du Pont in order to facilitate its control of large complex industrial projects.

The two systems are similar in most essential respects. The main difference lies in the treatment of time estimates. PERT was created primarily to handle research and development projects in which time spans are based on probabilistic estimates. CPM, on the other hand, is usually concerned with projects that the organisation has had some previous experience with. Time estimates, therefore, can be made relatively accurately.

The use of both PERT and CPM has spread rapidly and made a significant impact on the planning and control of projects and programmes. Both systems are most appropriate for controlling special, complex, non-repetitive projects such as the development of a large weapons system highway construction shipbuilding, or the installation of a large-scale data processing system. However, PERT and CPM have also proved useful in managing relatively simple projects.

Establishing and using a PERT or CPM system involve considerable expense particularly if the system is computerized. In deciding whether or not to use a system, managers must determine to what extent the project to be controlled is time-critical. For example, projects such as reinforcing a weak dam, constructing a building at an olympic site, or completing contracts that include penalty payment clauses are highly time-critical. The expense of a complete CPM or PERT system would probably be justified

1. *Management*, J.A.F. Stoner (Prentice Hall).

for such projects, since these systems make it much more likely that the projects will be completed on time.

Developing the Network

There are a number of PERT and CPM techniques with different names and slight variations of methods. All, however, are essentially systems for planning, scheduling and controlling projects. Their purpose is to divide the project into separate operations and then chart the order in which the operations should be carried out, when they should be started and completed, and when the entire project should be completed. Since PERT and CPM are basically similar in technique, we will discuss them together, pointing out the differences between then whenever appropriate.

Translating a programme into a PERT or CPM network involves essentially four requirements:

1. The activity must be broken down into individual tasks. These tasks will then be put into the network in the form of events and activities. Events will usually be indicated in circles on the chart; they will represent those parts of the tasks to be accomplished at specific points in time. Activities will represent the time or the resources required to progress from one even to another. They will usually be indicated by arrows on the chart. For example, the official start of a design project would represent the chart's first event; the five weeks necessary to prepare preliminary blueprints would represent the chart's first activity.
2. Events and activities are placed in the chart in a highly logical, sequential and integrated way. For example, each activity is preceded and followed by the appropriate event; no activity may start until its preceding event (or events) has been completed. Similarly, no event is considered completed until all the events leading up to its have been completed.
3. The length of time required for each activity is estimated and written in on the network. In CPM, as we indicated earlier, a single time estimate is established for each activity. In PERT, however, each activity may be assigned three time estimates, plus a fourth with is based on the other three. The first three estimates are known as the optimistic most likely, and pessimistic time estimates. They are expressed in sequence above the arrow. The "optimistic" time estimate is the length of time in which the activity could be completed under ideal condition; the "most likely" estimate is the normal time such an activity should take; the "pessimistic" estimate takes into account the possibility that just about everything will go wrong. The fourth time estimate which appears beneath the arrow, indicates the length of time the activity is actually expected to take. It is based on a probability analysis of the other time estimates.

The times are shown on the network diagram as:

$$\frac{\text{optimistic, most likely, pessimistic}}{\text{expected}}$$

expressed, of course, in figures such as:

$$\frac{3, 5, 9}{5, 3}$$

4. A critical path through the network must be determined.

In PERT network events are generally drawn as circles and activities are represented as arrows joining two circles.

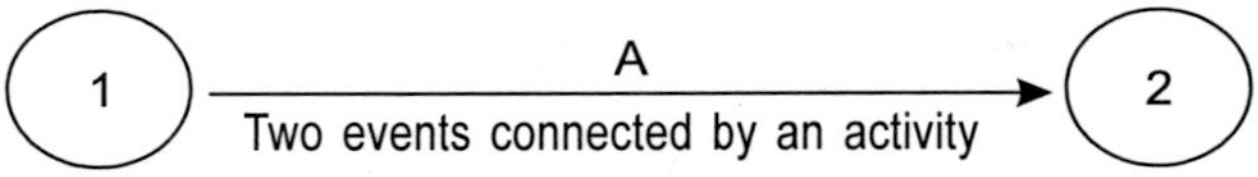

Exhibit 20.1

Events 1 and 2 are connected by activity A. Activities are denoted by alphabets line A, B, C, D, etc. but they may also be denoted by numerical such as 1-2, 3-5, 54-71, etc.

A grouping of activities and events is called a network. Events activities, as well as other pertinent information (specially estimates of time) are displayed in the PERT diagram.

Exhibit 20.2 shows a PERT network in its simplest form.

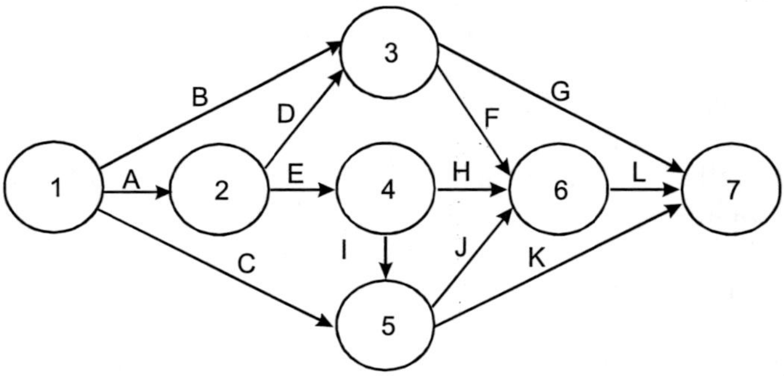

PERT Network

Exhibit 20.2

Events : 1, 2, 3, 4, 5, 6, 7.

Activities : A or (1-2), B or (1-3), C or (1-5), D or (2-3), E or (2-4), F or (3-6), G or (3-7), H or (4-6), I or (4-5), J or (5-6), K or (5-7), L or (6-7).

It must be remembered that number of activities do not have any mathematical relationship with the number of events. Only relationship which can be identified is that in an *n* event network, there are generally more than *n*-1 activities.

The origin of an activity is usually denoted as the 'tail' event or starting node (*i*) whilst the conclusion of an activity is known as the 'head event' or the ending node (*j*). The starting of activities in a network is always unidirectional. They flow from left to right.

In constructing a network, following rules must be remembered:

1. An event cannot be said to be completed until all activities leading into it are complete.
2. No activity can start until its tail event is reached.
3. Head events (*j*) must be higher than tail event (*i*).
4. The first event of the network must have a number which is (1) or greater than (1)—but never zero.
5. A network must have one starting point and one ending point.

Two Common Errors in Network Logic

In drawing networks, two errors in logic may occur. These are known as: (1) Looping and (2) Dangling.

Looping takes place when in a network activities are arranged in following ways (Exhibit 20.3). Dangling, on the other hand, occurs when a particular activity dangles, i.e., is undertaken without any result. When the terminal event of an activity does not have a head event, but it is not the terminal event of the total project, the activity is said to be dangling. Exhibit 20.4 gives an example where activity 9.11 is not dangling.

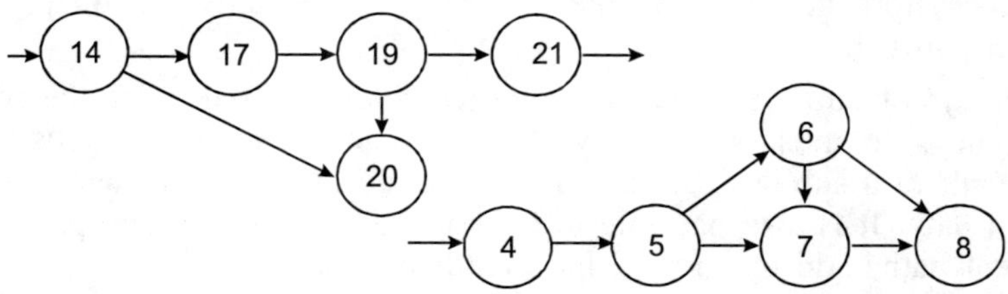

Looping Activity

Exhibit 20.3

Determining the Critical Path

The critical path is simply the longest path through the network in terms of the amount of time the entire project will take. It is determined by totalling the amount of time each sequence of tasks will take (as opposed to tasks that are performed simultaneously). The task chain with the longest time is the critical path.

The significance of the critical path lies in the fact that it will determine the total length of time, or completion date, for the entire project. If events on the critical path are delayed, then the entire project will be delayed, and the scheduled completion date will not be met.

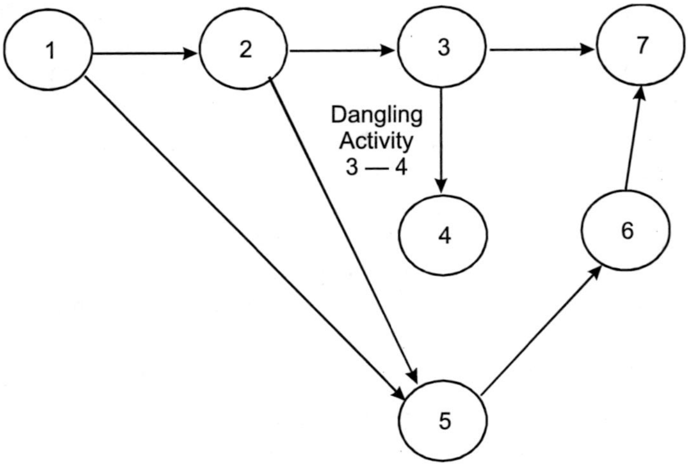

Dangling Activity

Exhibit 20.4

Paths other than the critical path are called sub-critical. These paths contain some slack since the total time for their completion is less than the critical path. One of the ways in which PERT and CPM provide for completion time to be reduced is to find ways to transfer resources from activities on the critical paths to activities on the sub-critical paths.

Delays on sub-critical paths are less serious than delays on the critical path. They, too, must be carefully controlled, however, since serious delays can result in a sub-critical path becoming the longest, and therefore, the critical path. It is also possible to have more than one critical path when different paths add up to the same number of days.

Extension of the PERT and CPM Techniques

So far we have discussed the main function of PERT and CPM, the determination and control of the time required to complete a project. The main benefit to be gained from these techniques is time saved through the initial scheduling of tasks and also time saved as the project progresses. Since time and cost are closely related saving time usually also leads to savings in cost.

In addition to these "time is money" relationships, both PERT and CPM have been adapted and applied to the explicit treatment of costs. For example, an optimum cost efficiency schedule can be developed. It will help managers to determine both the savings and the costs involved in achieving a shorter production schedule. Using extra labour to reduce the time span of an activity, for instance, may cost more in wages than would be received in a bonus for early completion.

Most of the extensions of PERT and CPM are more complex than the simple examples given here. They do, however, make significant contributions to the usefulness of PERT and CPM to managers.

Direct Costs and Times

Direct costs can be subdivided into normal costs and crash costs for each activity. Associated with these costs are a normal time and crash time. The activity costs associated with the normal time. Normal time is the time to complete the activity under normal conditions, i.e. expected time. Crash costs are associated with crash time. The shortest possible time to complete the activity is called crash time. If the indirect costs exceeds the limit, they are called penalty costs. Such division is done in case of PERT/CPM.

Advantages and Limitations of PERT and CPM

The increasing use of PERT and CPM is an indication of the fact that managers can gain significant advantages from them. These advantages include:

1. *Illustrating task relationships*: By providing a graphic representation of how the performance of each task is dependent on others, networks offer a distinct advantage over simpler graphs such as bar charts.

2. *Encouraging effective planning*: Drawing up a network requires that the project managers plan the project from start to finish in considerable detail.

3. *Pinpointing problem areas*: Bottlenecks and potential trouble spots are discovered early enough for preventive measures to be applied or for corrective action to be taken.

4. *Improving communication*: The network diagram provides a common frame of reference for all the different parties involved in project, such as designers, managers, contractors and other employees.

5. *Comparing alternative actions*: Managers are provided with an opportunity to compare different methods for reaching the project goal.

6. *Allowing concentration on key jobs*: By identifying critical tasks, CPM and PERT allow managers to apply their attention where it is most needed. At the same time, the network will indicate when other tasks are falling behind schedule. This will allow managers to take immediate action.

7. *Creating flexibility*: In a complex project, the critical path may change a number of times as time estimates prove inaccurate PERT and CPM provide managers with the ability to identify the current critical path on a continuing basis. Thus, they can keep their resources concentrated on those activities that are critical for completing the project on time.

There are also a number of limitations to PERT and CPM. The cost of setting up such systems, especially in terms of computer time, should obviously be considered before the systems are adopted. More importantly, these systems will certainly not help managers to solve all their problems. Manager-subordinate relationships, relations with suppliers, difficulties with quality control—all the day-to-day pressures that make up the manager's job—will not be relieved by PERT of CPM. Nor will these systems substitute for managerial planning and control. In fact, the reverse is true. In order for the system to be effective, they must be carefully planned and controlled. The network schedules are always tentative and not firm.

THEORY OF GAMES

The term 'Games' is probably not unknown to anybody. Basically, it is a competitive activity between two or more players who conform to specific predetermined rules, which precisely state how an eventual winner is to be decided. Thus, the generic term 'games' refers to general situations of conflict over time. Certain situations of business conflict can be easily equated with certain characteristics of simple games, where the players make use of deductive as well as inductive mathematically techniques in an attempt to determine an optimum strategy for winning.

In Operations Research, the Theory of Games applies to a very special kind of game where each of two competing players is able to choose just one of predetermined number of possible strategies. Each players makes his choice without any knowledge whatsoever of the choice that his opponent will make. Once the choices have been made, the consequent results, i.e., gain or loss to each player is immediately identifiable. As a matter of fact, theory of games is a part of decision theory under uncertainty. Here we will discuss the two person zero-sum games with the following variations:

1. Strictly determined games.
2. Not strictly determined games and finally.
3. Games against nature.

Before discussing the above situations, we should understand the standard language of games.

Standard Language of Games

Let us consider the cases of two players *X* and *Y* who are equal in their ability and intelligence. Each aware of the outcomes or payoffs for every possible combination of strategies—which are shown in following Table 1.

TABLE 1

		Player-*X*	
		Strategy A	Strategy B
Player-*Y*	Strategy P	*X* wins 4 pts	*X* wins 6 pts
	Strategy Q	*Y* wins 2 pts	*Y* wins 4 pts

It can be noted that this particular game is biased against player *Y*. This situation is roughly equivalent to a business situation where short-run loss is inevitable and this loss must be minimized by adopting a good strategy. Using certain universal languages, we can write the above-mentioned game in a much more concise format as shown below:

$$\begin{matrix} & Y \\ & \begin{pmatrix} 4 & 6 \\ -2 & -4 \end{pmatrix} \end{matrix}$$

$$X$$

The game has now been expressed as a matrix which is commonly known as a payoff or payout matrix. The four individual payoff possibilities are expressed as numbers: as positive entry indicates a payoff to the player playing row-strategies and the negative entries indicate a payoff to the player playing column strategies. For *X*, the possible strategies are row 1 and 2 (reading from top to down as in standard matrix form); and for *Y*, the possible strategies are column 1 and column 2 (reading from left to right) as in standard matrix form. Similarly, we can consider the situations presented in Table 2 which express in the universal language.

TABLE 2

		Player-*Y*		
		Strategy P	Strategy O	Strategy R
Player-*X*	Strategy M	*X* wins 5 pts	*X* wins 4 pts	*Y* wins 4 pts
	Strategy N	*X* wins 3 pts	*Y* wins 5 pts	*Y* wins 6 pts
	Strategy O	Nobody wins	*X* wins 3 pts	*Y* wins 5 pts

Expressed in universal language, the above presentation is reduced to:

$$\begin{matrix} & Y \\ X & \begin{pmatrix} 5 & 4 & -4 \\ 3 & -5 & -6 \\ 0 & -3 & -5 \end{pmatrix} \end{matrix}$$

Two Person Zero-Sum Games

Problems presented in Tables 1 and 2 illustrate two-person games and they are also two-person zero-sum games. The term zero-sum is used because the sum of the gains (or losses) of *X* exactly equals the losses (or gains) of *Y*. These types of games are a special case of decision-making in which the following conditions are applicable.

1. Only two players play the game. Each player has finite set of strategies available to him.
2. Each of the competitors knows the alternative actions available to him as well as his opponent and the outcome or payoff for any possible combination of these actions.
3. Each competitor has an order of preference for the plays—and this order is known by his opponent. That is to say each player will

play using a prescribed decision rule and all available decision rules are known by the other player. Given this known set of decision rules, each player will play assuming that his opponent will select his optimum move.

4. Each player has only one move or strategy and the rules are undertaken in concurrently or in such a way that each player does not know the particular more selected by the other player, although he is aware of the rules available to the other player.
5. Each player is assumed to try to do the best that he can give the fact that each has the capabilities to decide about the best strategy.

A situation of collective bargaining involving the trade union and management resembles a two-person zero-sum game. Both the trade union leaders and the management have certain preferences within the sets of plays available to them, but neither side is willing to commit itself completely at one time.

WAITING LINE OR QUEUING MODELS

Within a given period of time, much of managements efforts within the firm is concentrated on satisfying demands which are made upon specific activity levels. A telephone operator may be capable of handling 60 calls in 10 minutes provided the calls are received evenly. But this even distribution of calls may not be the real case. It may so happen that 15 calls are received in first five minutes whereas the rest 45 calls come in the next five minutes. If the second situation is true, then, the callers in the second five-minute span may have to endure delay. This kind of situation may arise in gasoline stations, super-market cash counters, banks or hospitals. Delays may annoy customers, and to avoid delays, number of service centres may be increased, to satisfy customers. But it will raise the cost of service. More service centres means more costs. But the queuing is 'how to ascertain the number of service centres'? From firm's viewpoint, the problem is to balance off the costs of service and the standard of service.

Queuing models may be used in aiding decision-making in the situations described above. A mathematical treatment is quite cumbersome and complex.

Example

Suppose a small hotel employs one waiter and serves breakfast 7 AM to 11.30 AM. Arrival times and service times are both exponential. The average arrival rate is 3 parties per 15 minutes and average service time (i.e. the time between the taking of a party's order and the serving order) is 3¾ minutes. With the help of queuing models different probabilities that the service time of a party can be found e.g. without waiting or time a party can expect to wait, or expected number of parties waiting for their order or a party must wait.

Manufacturers commonly face a problem of machinery breakdown. The breakdown time of a machine is non-productive time which may be due to parts failure or to scheduled stops for preventive maintenance. In establishing the cost for breakdown, the queuing models can help to consider three components costs i.e. the cost of non-productive time itself, part replacement cost and cost of labour. So the queuing models can be used in aiding decision-making. But the mathematical treatment is quite cumbersome and more complex.

SIMULATION

The quantitative techniques and models discussed so far sometimes fail to solve very complex real life problems. The models described earlier mathematically expressed the interrelationships of the elements from the real life situation. Then they were analyzed and solved to reach a solution.

However, there are situations which are so complex that these types of model building become rather impossible. In such situations, simulation models are used. A simulation model is nothing but an abstract representation of a real-life phenomenon which must adequately replicate the behaviour of the system concerned over a predetermined time span. Compared to standard quantitative decision-making techniques such as Linear Programming, Integer Programming and Markov Process Simulation requires less restrictive assumptions—but, on the contrary, it gives solutions which in most cases are less precise.

In developing a simulation model, the first step is to identify the individual elements of the system. In the second step, several trial alternatives to the problem in question are tested by combining these elements in their natural order. In the third step, the results of the alternative solutions are compared. Obviously, the best outcome is chosen as the solution to the problem. It is quite likely that the best possible solution to the problem would remain undiscovered since very often, simulation models are limited to the comparison of a relatively small number of all possible solutions. As such, the quantitative tools discussed earlier are the first choice for solving a problem. If they are not adequate, only then simulation techniques should be used.

The use of simulation method as a decision-making tool is not restricted only to management decision problems. They have been successfully and effectively used in the field of engineering as well. The general concept behind the simulation model building are similar—although their contents are different.

Types of Simulation

Typically, the simulation models fall into four major categories. These are:

1. Monte Carlo Simulation,
2. System Simulation,
3. Heuristic Simulation, and
4. Games.

In Monte Carlo Simulation models, probabilistic processes are used. These models make use of random variables to explore the relationship within a system. A System Simulation model, on other hand, is a complex reproduction of some operating system. In this case, variables are not generated randomly—they are derived from samples of actual population. Furthermore, mathematical decision rules are used to reach a solution. In situations where actual decision process cannot be easily expressed mathematically, heuristic models may be used. Heuristic Simulation models are flexible and provide a sense of order even is anlaysing a large scale problem which cannot be easily solved by common quantitative techniques or by other simulation models.

Games models are rather different from the other three types discussed earlier in the sense that these simulations usually involve human participants or players who try to simulate business condition. These are very useful tools for executive and student training.

Advantages and Limitations of OR

Advantages: Management science-OR techniques have but one purpose to help managers make better decisions. They can fulfill this purpose because they have three major advantages. First, they make it possible to break down a complex, large-scale problem into smaller parts that can be more easily diagnosed and manipulated. Second, in building and analyzing OR models researchers have to pay close attention to details and to follow logical, systematic procedures. This improves the likelihood of a good decision. Errors creep in more easily when decisions are made on the basis of subjective judgment past experience, or "rules of thumb", rather than on the basis of a systematic approach. Third, OR is helpful in assessing possible alternative for the manager. If managers are more aware of the risks and opportunities inherent in the alternatives available to them, they will be more likely to choose the right alternative.

Limitations: As might be expected, OR projects are costly. The expense of the OR specialists' time alone often makes OR too expensive for many organisations or many types of problems. For this reason, each OR study has to be subjected to its own cost-benefit analysis before the decision is made.

Another disadvantage of OR is that it cannot be effectively applied in many situations. Some problems are simply too complex to be handled by the mathematical tools that are now available. The intuitive judgment of managers will still be required. In crisis situations, there will be no time for the extended analysis of OR; managers will have to respond quickly on their own. Similarly, there are many situations where the available information is inadequate for an OR study. This is particularly true in situations involving human qualities and interpersonal relationship, which cannot yet be quantified.

Perhaps the greatest drawback or OR is that it can easily become a technique divorced from reality—either because of defects in the initial assumptions, about a problem or because certain crucial variables are ignored. As we have already mentioned, an OR analysis cannot be more sound than the information it is based upon. Accounting records, for example, are far from exact they depend heavily on estimates and crude approximations. If an OR analysis relies on such records for figures on manufacturing costs and profits, it may turn out to be faulty. The other great danger in using OR is that researchers may ignore important aspects of a problem because they are not measurable.

An OR recommendation to increase productivity by changing the work sequence may be logical but irrelevant if the entire plant goes out on strike because of poor working conditions. OR can provide guidance on a problem, but it is not a substitute for managerial judgment.

Despite the fact that OR has been successfully used to solve many problems in business, non-profit organisations, and government, OR findings are not always put into effect. For example, in a survey of corporate-level OR groups, Efraim Turban found that only about 60 per cent of OR projects were "completely" or "mostly implemented". C. Jackson Grayson, Jr., a manager with a management science background, found OR methods useless when he served as chairman of the Price Commission (which set up and monitored price controls) from 1971 to 1973, in U.S.A.

Of course, Grayson had to deal with large-scale problems that had political implications, and the nature of his assignment made fast action particularly important. Still, he was unusually familiar with OR techniques and presumably predisposed toward using them. This fact makes his failure to find OR useful more compelling than if the bad been a "stodgy" old manager resisting new technologies.

Grayson offers five reasons of OR technique which many managers do not use:

1. *Shortage of time.* Managers bypass OR because it is too time-consuming.

2. *Inaccessibility of data.* It requires too much time, effort, and expense to obtain the information an OR model requires.

3. *Resistance to change.* Everyone encounters resistance in trying to induce people to change well-established ways of doing things. The fact that OR techniques seem so sophisticated and mysterious that many managers make it even more difficult for the techniques to be accepted.

4. *Long response time*. Management scientists approach problems in a methodical fashion, rather than begin working on a solution as soon as a problem arises. Managers, however, often need to find solutions quickly. A methodical approach may not seem helpful to them.

5. *Invalidating simplifications.* Because so many of the important areas of management—people problems, organisational politics, power struggles—are hard to quantify OR simply excludes them from its mathematical equations. The model that result may lead to elegant solutions, but these may be completely useless, because the simplified assumptions they were based on were too far removed from reason.

Grayson does not call for the abandonment of OR rather, he reaffirms its potential, provided its practitioners rid OR of its defects and limitations to gain acceptance of their methods. Grayson suggests that management scientists need to become more sensitive to the messy, complicated, time limited environment of the manager. They also need to try to put all important information in their models, no matter how imprecise and unquantifiable such information may be. Their solutions may then be ruder, but they will more workable and useful to the manager.

The Effect of Management Styles

An interesting analysis of why the management scientists have problems getting their findings implemented is provided by James McKenney and Peter Keen. These authors suggest that managers differ from management scientists in their information-gathering and problem-solving styles, and that these differences can affect how fully managers will accept OR recommendations.

A person's method of information gathering can either be perceptive or receptive. Those of us who are perceptive individuals bring preconceived notions to bear on a situation. We focus on the way various items relate to each other and how they conform to or deviate from our expectations. Those of us who are receptive individuals keep our preconceptions under control. We prefer to develop conclusions about the information we have by examining it carefully and in detail.

There are also two problem-solving styles, suggest McKenney and Keen intuitive and systematic. Those of us who are intuitive tend to approach to error methods and readily switch from one problem-solving another. We quickly jump to conclusion based on our past experience. Those of us who are systematic tend to approach a problem methodically we may formally structure a problem in the hope that we will then be more likely to find a solution.

Many types of managerial jobs (such as those in marketing and production) are particularly well suited for those of us with preceptive-intuitive styles. Management scientists, on the other hand, are much more like to have systematic style of problem-solving and, while their information gathering styles may vary, they would seem to be more toward the receptive mode.

McKenney and Keen hypothesize that managers who are more amenable to systematic approaches and whose own styles are systematic are more likely to be comfortable working with management scientists and to find OR helpful. Intuitive managers who deal in their day-to-day work with more loosely structured problems are less likely to find OR helpful or to feel comfortable working with management scientists. To learn to accept OR, say McKenney and Keen, such managers should interact informally with management science specialists and experiment with using the simpler OR techniques on some of their problems.

The Keys to Implementation

It is obviously to a manager's advantage to increase OR's usefulness and to make it more likely that helpful OR suggestions will be implemented. Wagner has suggested that the most beneficial OR programmes contain the following eight elements:

1. *Sponsorship by top management*: Without the support of top management, an OR programme will be less likely to have a manager's co-operation. It is also top management's job to make sure an OR programme serves the needs of the entire organisation, rather than only one part.

2. *Managerial responsibility for the programme*: If managers have the ultimate responsibility for the success of an OR project, they are more likely to become actively involved in it. When responsibility for the programme is left to the OR staff, it is easier for managers to ignore OR's findings.

3. *Manager participation*: If managers participate in establishing programme objectives, the OR models will be much more realistically based. In turn, the solutions suggested by OR studies will be more useful.

4. *Use of managerial judgment*: A manager's advice must be obtained at carefully chosen points in the OR process. Such a procedure will prevent an OR project from going off on a wrong track. It will also make us more open to the solutions offered by OR.

5. *Technical aspects not permitted to dominate*: The mathematical and technical procedures of OR must, of course, be performed competently if the technique is to have any value. However, OR personnel must take into account the less measurable aspects of a problem. They should be particularly aware of how people affect and are affected by the solutions they suggest.

6. *Rapid data collection*: A long, extended process of information gathering will not be helpful to the manager who needs to make decisions as soon as possible. Collecting data quickly and efficiently will shorten the OR process and thus make it more useful.

7. *Preparation for initial difficulties*: When a new OR system is being tested and installed temporary difficulties are to be expected. If managers anticipate problems and prepare for them the effectiveness of the system will not be hindered. For example, to prevent resentment when an OR programme is begun, managers can work with their subordinates in developing ideas and suggestions to make the programme work.

8. *Accurate record keeping*: As an OR programme progresses, the assumptions and facts that originally went into models may become outdated. So, the original models are to be kept up to date.

QUESTIONS

1. What are the major features of a meaningful OR programme? What are the steps in OR approach to problem-solving?
2. What are the various models used in OR and on what basis would you decide to use any OR mode?
3. What are the major defects and limitations of OR and how can they be overcome?
4. How are PERT and CPM networks developed?
5. What is critical path? How is it determined?
6. What are the advantages and limitations of PERT and CPM?

21

Accounting for Changing Price Level

PRICE LEVEL AND FAIR VALUE ACCOUNTING

The price level does not always remain same. It increases or decreases. Most of the countries are facing increase in price level (called inflation). As a result, it has been suggested that financial statements would be more useful if historical costs were adjusted for the changing value of currency or if historical costs were abandoned entirely and replaced with current economic values.

Money is the common denominator used in the preparation of financial statements. The rupee or any other currency, represents a unit of value i.e. it measures the amount of purchasing power available to obtain goods and services through exchange transaction. In the use of money it is implicit, as a measuring unit, assumption that the rupee is a stable unit of value, just as a metre or acre. But unlike the metre or acre, the rupee is not a stable measuring unit. The value of rupee shrinks with change in prices.

The financial statements are prepared on historical cost basis. Many accountants are unhappy with this basis on the ground that cost figures of a year ago are not comparable to current cost levels. Historical cost reporting model does not show (a) the maintenance of capital in real terms. (b) Calculation of profits in real terms. (c) The balance sheet does not reflect current worth of an enterprise as cost-based accounting shows assets at their historical costs. So inflation brings substantial diminution in operational capital and therefore the profit is shown at exaggerated and illusory figure. (d) The cost of goods sold charged to the profit and loss account is understated. Hence, the accounting for changes prices, also called inflation accounting is adopted.

One must note that in historical accounting reduces to a minimum the extent to which accounts may be affected by personal judgment of those responsible for their preparation. Further, the transactions relating thereto are capable of being easily verified by reference to the relevant documentary and other evidence.

To meet these criticisms, following different solutions have been offered:

1. *Current purchasing power or general price level model*: Here the historical cost is restated for general price level changes. The principle is to change the measuring unit but retain the historical cost reporting model.

2. *Current value accounting*: It abandons historical cost model. It can take two forms:

(a) Current value without separate identification of the effects of general price level changes, i.e. depart from the historical cost reporting mode but retain the measuring unit. This approach of current value accounting abandons historical cost and shifts to some measure of value.

(b) Current value, with the effects of general price level being shown separately.

Under it both the unit of measurement and historical cost model should be changed.

Even if historical cost model financial statements are restated to reflect the changing value of the rupee, the resulting statements would still be presented in terms of historical costs and would not reflect current (fair) value of assets. For example, a plot of land costing ₹ 10,00,000 would be restated at ₹ 15,00,000 if the general price level has risen by 50%. However, the current value (fair value) of that land might be ₹ 50,00,000 because the price of land had risen more than the general price level. Historical cost model reflects the current fair value at the date of acquisition, but a significant change in the current value of the asset after acquisition tends to make historical cost irrelevant for decision-making purposes. Therefore, many people have urged that current fair value of asset should be used in place of historical costs as a valuation basis.

The use of current cost accounting does not mean that changes in price level would be ignored. Price level accounting and current value accounting are complimentary responses to different measurement problems. They are neither mutually exclusive or a substitute for each other. General price level changes used for restatement of financial statement do not deal with specific price changes and current value accounting does not deal with inflation as such. Both approaches can be used for a single set of financial statements.

EFFECTS OF CHANGING PRICE LEVELS

The effects of changing price level are:

(a) It is possible for the distribution of money profits earned by a business to involve a distribution of real capital, which results in the undermining of the real value of interests of contributors of business capital. (b) The measurement in terms of money of the results of the operations of a business do not reflect the results, in terms of real values, of these operations.

We can illustrate these points by examples. Suppose a company acquired land in 2011 for ₹ 1,00,000 and sold it for ₹ 2,00,000 in 2020. The general price level index, say, doubled in these ten years, thus the value of money is cut to half. It means that the company is not better off since the value of ₹ 2,00,000 is equal to ₹ 1,00,000 of 2011. But the accountant would record a gain of ₹ 1,00,000 and may conclude that company is better off. Consider the following example. A company had capital of ₹ 10,000 and invested in an asset with a five-year life depreciated on the fixed instalment basis. The asset is rented at ₹ 3,000 per year. It has no scrap value after five years and can be replaced with same type of asset for ₹ 15,000. The profits during five years were not withdrawn. On historical basis, the position in the beginning year and last year will be as follows:

At the end of 1st year

P & L Account

	₹		₹
Depreciation	2,000	Rent	3,000
Profit	1,000		
	3,000		3,000

Balance Sheet

	₹			₹
Capital	10,000	Asset	10,000	
Profit	1,000	*Less* Dep.	2,000	8,000
		Cash		3,000
	11,000			11,000

At the end of fifth year

Balance Sheet

	₹		₹
Capital	10,000	Cash	15,000
Profit	5,000		
	15,000		15,000

After replacement by new asset

Balance Sheet

	₹		₹
Capital	10,000	Asset	15,000
Profit	5,000		
	15,000		15,000

When the financial statements are not adjusted for changing price level, the carrying values of asset and depreciation and mis-stated. In fact, during five years no profit has been made. If profits were withdrawn, it would mean distribution of real capital. We can conclude that failure to consider the changing value of money in preparation of financial statements in a period of rising price level means that what is reported as income may be in part, a recovery of capital. The same is time of stock, cost of goods sold, other assets and expenses. In a period of inflation taxable income, income tax expense, and net income may be overstated. Taxable income may be overstated because charges are not large enough of offset the inflation in prices of fixed assets. This is the most strong argument in favour of price-level accounting and against historical cost model. However, failure to recognize the effect of price level changes during inflation does not necessarily result in an overstatement of net income.

Because there may be offsetting G.P.L. gains from borrowing.

In addition to above points, changing price levels may have the following effects where historical cost model is followed:

(a) Data are neither comparable through time nor additive as well. The data of different firms is not comparable.

(b) Financial statements are difficult to interpret e.g. increase in sales may be not real. Sales, volume may not increase, though in amount sales increased because of rise in prices.

(c) The items in accounts are affected differently by changing price level e.g. prices of stock and wages may not more at a similar rate.

(d) Selling price may be fixed at too low a level to maintain the real capital of the business.

GENERAL PRICE LEVEL OR CURRENT PURCHASING POWER ACCOUNTING MODEL (GPL OR CPP METHOD)

The real value of money is called "purchasing power". The aggregation of specific prices at any particular time is called General Price Level (GPL) or Current Purchasing Power (CPP). A general price level change recognizes the change in the value of money in all its uses. The use of index numbers is made of show GPL. The Reserve Bank of India, Central Statistical Organisation, Economic Times and Commerce magazine are some organisations that publish different index numbers from time to time. It is better to select that index number which reflects the average change in retail prices of a fairly broad but select "basket" of consumer goods. This is the opinion of the author. There is actually no perfect general price index. Accounting Standard Committee of U.K. recommends also retail price index. In U.S.A., Financial Accounting Standards Board (FASB) recommends the use of consumer price index for all urban consumers (CPI-U).. Without entering into arguments as to which index number or one general index or several specific indexes, the procedure for GPL accounting is as follows:

(a) Restatement or conversion in common rupees.
(b) Monetary and non-monetary classifications.
(c) Purchasing power gains or losses on net monetary items.

(a) Restatement or Conversion in Common Rupees

The procedure for restating the rupees of varying purchasing power reported in historical cost financial statements in rupees (or any currency for that matter) of current purchasing power is mathematically simple, although sometimes time-consuming process. The restatement or conversion (also called translation) is found by using conversion factor and multiplying it by the amount.

$$\text{The conversion factor} = \frac{\text{Index for current prices}}{\text{Index for price prevailed at the data related to the amount being restated}}$$

For example, the cost of an asset on 1-1-2010 is ₹ 1,000 and in 2010, the index was 87. In 2016, the index was 225. Then the cost of the asset in terms of 2016 = 225/87 × 1,000 = ₹ 25,86.20. Technically, the index at the date of acquiring the asset be used. But average index for 2010 may be used, in the absence of rampant inflation or deflation, with satisfactory results.

(b) Monetary and Non-monetary Classifications

The second step is to distinguish between (i) the amounts that by their nature already stated in current rupees and therefore, require no conversion. Such items are called monetary items, and (ii) the amounts that require conversion in order to be stated in terms of current rupees. Such items are called non-monetary items. Examples are given below:

Monetary Items

Assets	Liabilities
1. Cash in hand and at bank	1. Creditors and bills payable
2. Preference shares (non-convertible and non-participating)	2. Accrued expenses 3. Cash dividend payable
3. Debentures (other than convertible)	4. Advances from customers (not on fixed price)
4. Debtors and bills receivable	
5. Allowance for doubtful debts	5. Refundable deposits
6. Loans to employees	6. Bonds payable
7. Cash surrender value of life insurance	7. Long-term debt
8. Long-term investments (fixed interest)	8. Unamortized premium or discount on bonds or bills payable
9. Refundable deposits	
10. Deferred income tax charges	
11. Advance to suppliers (Not on fixed price contract)	

All assets and liabilities not classified as monetary items are classified as 'non-monetary'. Non-monetary assets are items whose prices in terms of monetary unit may change over time, while non-monetary liabilities are obligations to provide given amounts of goods or services.

Non-monetary Items:

Assets	Liabilities
1. Inventories	1. Advances received on sales contract
2. Investment in equity shares	2. Liabilities for rent collected in advance
3. Land, building plant & machinery	3. Deferred credits
4. Accumulated depreciation on fixed assets	
5. Patents, trademarks	
6. Goodwill	
7. Other intangible assets	
8. Deferred expenses	

Note that inventories, fixed assets and intangibles are non-monetary and most liabilities are monetary because they involve a fixed claim to pay cash (except liabilities that are liquidated through exchange of goods or services). Equity share capital, and additional paid-up capital are non-monetary in nature. Some items are computed separately, e.g. reserves and surplus are computed by adding constant rupee net income less any dividends to the beginning balance of reserve and surplus. Investments in preferences stock and convertible debentures are monetary if the market values the security as a bond or debenture and if it values as a share, it is non-monetary.

(c) Purchasing Power or General Purchasing Power Gains or Losses on Net Monetary Items

Changes in the general price level give rise to gains and losses as a result of holding monetary items. It is called purchasing power or general price level gains or losses (PP or GPL gain or loss). For example, in the case of debtors or bills receivable or any claim to a fixed amount of money, the amount of money expected to be received represents a diminishing amount of GPL simply as a result of inflation. Similarly, creditors, bills payable or any fixed amount of money payable in the future becomes less burdensome during inflation because they are payable in dollars of reduced GPP.

When the general price level index is rising, it is advantageous to be in a negative monetary position i.e. to hold an excess of liabilities over monetary assets. A positive monetary position (excess of monetary assets over liabilities) results in a loss of purchasing power when prices are rising. See the following example:

	X Co. ₹	Y Co. ₹
Cash, debtors and bills receivable	12,000	2,000
Stock, fixed assets (net)	6,000	16,000
Total Assets	18,000	18,000
Liabilities (current & long term)	4,000	13,000
Equity share capital	14,000	5,000
Total liabilities	18,000	18,000

In the general price-level index increased by 10% (from 100 to 110). The Balance Sheets will appear as follows on current purchasing power accounting basis:

	X Co. ₹	Y Co. ₹
Cash, debtors and bills receivable	12,000	2,000
Stock & net fixed assets	6,600	17,600
Total Assets	18,600	19,600
Liabilities (current & long term)	4,000	13,000
Equity share capital	15,400	5,500
Net GPL (loss) or gain	(800)	1,100
Total liabilities	18,600	19,600

Workings:

Loss from holding cash, debtors and B/P	$= 12{,}000 \times 0.10 = 1{,}200$
Gains from liabilities	$= 4{,}000 \times 0.10 = 400$
X Company has positive monetary position	800
Similarly for *Y* company	
Gains from liabilities	$= 13{,}000 \times 0.10 = 1{,}300$
Loss from holding cash, etc.	$= 2{,}000 \times 0.10 = 200$
Y Company has a negative monetary position	1,100

Example 1

P&L Account of Bell Ceramic Ltd. for the year ending 31st Dec., 2020, and opening and closing balance sheets are as follows:

P&L Account
For the year ending 31-12-2020

	₹	₹
Sales		8,00,000
Cost of goods sold:		
Opening stock 1-1-2020	2,50,000	
Purchases	5,20,000	
	7,70,000	
Closing stock 31-12-2020	3,00,000	4,70,000
Gross profit		3,30,000
Selling & administrative expenses	1,70,000	
Depreciation provision	10,000	
Income tax	75,000	2,55,000
Net profit		75,000
Reserves & surpluses 1-1-2020		Nil
Cash dividends		10,000
Reserves & surplus 31-12-2020		65,000

Balance Sheets (summarised)

	1-1-2020 ₹	31-12-2020 ₹
Cash, debtors and other monetary assets	2,00,000	3,25,000
Closing stock	2,50,000	3,00,000
Machinery (net)	1,50,000	1,40,000
Land	4,50,000	4,50,000
Total assets	10,50,000	12,15,000
Current liabilities (all monetary)	1,00,000	2,00,000
Long-term liabilities	6,50,000	6,50,000
Equity share capital	3,00,000	3,00,000
Reserves and surplus	Nil	65,000
Total liabilities and capital	10,50,000	12,15,000

Notes:

(1) The above figures are on historical basis.

(2) The index number was as follows:

1-1-2020	100
During the year	160
31-12-2020	200

(3) The machinery and land were purchased at the beginning of the year. The machinery is depreciated on straight line method, with no salvage value and is estimated 15 years life.

(4) Dividends are declared and paid on 31-12-2020.

(5) The inventory is priced on FIFO basis. The opening stock was purchased on the first day of the year and closing stock was acquired in November when index was 180.

(6) All revenues and expenses are earned or incurred evenly throughout the year except the beginning inventory.

You are required to present the above financial statement on constant rupee of GPL accounting basis.

Solution

(a) ***Adjustment of Balance Sheet Items***

(1) *Monetary items*: The amounts of these items at the end of Dec. 31, 2020 need not be converted as they are given in the end of the year rupees. The amount of the 1-1-2020 be converted in terms of purchasing power at the end of the year. They are as follows:

(*a*) Cash debtors and other monetary assets

	₹	₹
31-12-2020	3,25,000	= 3,25,000
1-1-2020	$2{,}00{,}000 \times \frac{200}{100}$	= 4,00,000

(*b*) Current liabilities and long-term liabilities

31-12-2020	8,50,000	= 8,50,000
1-1-2020	$7{,}50{,}000 \times \frac{200}{100}$	= 15,00,000

(2) *Stocks*: Stocks-in-trade involve some problems for conversion. There are many methods of valuation of stock e.g. FIFO, LIFO or average cost. Sometimes, it is not known which method has been used. It also requires the information about the dates of purchase and historical cost. If it is known, then the amount of stock is multiplied by current index and dividend by the index for the data of purchase or acquisition for conversion. In this example, the FIFO method is used and the closing stock consists of goods acquired during last two months at an average index for these months.

		₹	₹
31-12-2020	Stock — Closing	$3{,}00{,}000 \times \frac{200}{180}$	= 3,33,333
1-1-2020	Stock — Opening	$2{,}50{,}000 \times \frac{200}{100}$	= 5,00,000

If LIFO is used, then problem is that price-level changes occur since the data of last purchase of goods. Some people suggest to use replacement prices in such a case.

(3) *Machinery and Land*: They will be converted in terms of the end of year rupees.

		₹	₹
Machinery	31-12-2020	$1,40,000 \times \frac{200}{100}$	= 2,80,000
	1-1-2020	$1,50,000 \times \frac{200}{100}$	= 3,00,000
Land	31-12-2020	$4,50,000 \times \frac{200}{100}$	= 9,00,000
	1-1-2020	$4,50,000 \times \frac{200}{100}$	= 9,00,000

(4) *Equity Capital, Reserves and Surplus*: The equity share capital will be converted to end of the year rupees.

	₹	₹
31-12-2020	$3,00,000 \times \frac{200}{100}$	= 6,00,000
1-1-2020	$3,00,000 \times \frac{200}{100}$	= 6,00,000

Reserved and Surplus are calculated to balance the balance sheet.

31-12-2020	Reserves and Surplus	3,88,333
1-1-2020	Reserves and Surplus	Nil

It should be noted that the amount of reserves and surplus on 31-12-2020 should be reconcilable to the amount of restated income for the year 2020, taking into consideration dividends paid during the year.

While preparing the financial statements under purchasing power accounting, equity capital, additional paid up capital, reserves and surpluses are all treated as one residual, in separable sum. It means that equity capital after price level adjustments the difference between Total restated assets minus total restated liabilities plans preference share capital, i.e., on 31-12-2020 it will be:

	₹
₹ 18,38,333 – ₹ 8,50,000	= 9,88,333
On 1-1-2020 ₹ 21,00,000 – ₹ 15,00,000	= 6,00,000
(Total assets) – (Total liabilities)	

The balance sheet after conversion will appear as follows:

Balance Sheets (Converted)
On General Price Level Basis

	1-1-2020 ₹	31-12-2020 ₹
Cash, debtors and other monetary assets	4,00,000	3,25,000
Closing stock	5,00,000	3,33,333
Machinery (net)	3,00,000	2,80,000
Land	9,00,000	9,00,000
Total assets	21,00,000	18,38,333
Current liabilities (all monetary)	2,00,000	2,00,000
Long-term liabilities (-do-)	13,00,000	6,50,000
Total liabilities	15,00,000	8,50,000
Equity share capital	6,00,000	6,00,000
Reserves and surpluses	Nil	3,88,333
Total shareholders equity	6,00,000	9,88,333
Total liabilities and shareholders equity	21,00,000	18,38,333

(b) *Conversion of P and L A/c Items*

(1) Sales: The average index is to be used because sales are evenly spread throughout the year.

$$₹\ 8{,}00{,}000 \times \frac{200}{160} = ₹\ 10{,}00{,}000$$

(2) Cost of goods sold: It will be found as follows:

	₹		₹
Opening stock	2,50,000	$\times \frac{200}{100}$	= 5,00,000
Purchases	5,20,000	$\times \frac{200}{160}$	= 6,50,000
	7,70,000		11,50,000
Less closing stock	3,00,000	$\times \frac{200}{180}$	= 3,33,333
Cost of goods sold	4,70,000		8,16,667

(3) Selling and administrative expenses:

$$₹\ 1{,}70{,}000 \times \frac{200}{160} = ₹\ 2{,}12{,}500$$

It is assumed that these expenses were incurred evenly throughout the year.

(4) Depreciation $= ₹10,000 \times \frac{200}{100} = ₹20,000$

(5) Income tax $= ₹\ 75,000 \times \frac{200}{160} = ₹\ 93,750$

(6) Cash dividends = No adjustment is necessary because dividends were paid at the end of the year.

(c) *Purchasing Power Gain or Loss*

This can be found out by preparing a statement of sources and uses of monetary items for the year 2020. The items that were occurring continuously during the year like sales or selling expenses are converted using the average index. The statement will be as follows:

Purchasing Power Gain or Loss

	2020 Historical ₹	Index	Restated to 31-12-2020 ₹
Net monetary items 1-1-2020	(5,50,000)	$\times\frac{200}{100}$	(11,00,000)
Add (Sources)			
Sales	8,00,000	$\times\frac{200}{160}$	10,00,000
	2,50,000		(1,00,000)
Deduct (Uses)			
Purchases	5,20,000	$\times\frac{200}{160}$	= 6,50,000
Selling and Admn. Exp.	1,70,000	$\times\frac{200}{160}$	= 2,12,500
Income-tax	75,000	$\times\frac{200}{160}$	= 93,750
Cash dividends	10,000	$\times\frac{200}{200}$	= 10,000
Total uses	7,75,000		= 9,66,250

	₹
Net monetary items —Historical 31-12-2020 ₹ (5,25,000)	
Net monetary items—Converted 31-12-2020 —if there was no gain or loss	(10,66,250)
Net monetary items—Historical—31-12-2020 (as above)	(5,25,000)
Purchasing power gain on net monetary items	5,41,250

Figures 1, 2 and 3 are calculated as follows:

Net Monetary Items	1-1-2020 Historical ₹	Index	Converted to 31-12-2020 ₹	31-12-2020 Historical shown 31-12-2020 ₹
Cash, debtors and Other monetary assets	2,00,000	$\times\frac{200}{100}$	4,00,000	3,25,000
Current liabilities (monetary)	(1,00,000)	$\times\frac{200}{100}$	(2,00,000)	(2,00,000)
Long term liabilities (monetary)	(6,50,000)	$\times\frac{200}{100}$	(13,00,000)	(6,50,000)
Net monetary items	(5,50,000)	$\times\frac{200}{100}$	(11,00,000)	(5,25,000)

Now the converted P & L Account will appear as follows:

P&L A/c 31-12-2020 (Converted)

	₹	₹
Sales		10,00,000
Cost of goods sold:		
Opening stock 1-1-2020	5,00,000	
Purchases	6,50,000	
	11,50,000	
Less: Closing stock 31-12-2020	3,33,333	8,16,667
Gross profit		1,83,333
Selling and administrative expenses		2,12,500
Depreciation		20,000
Loss before Income-tax		(49,167)
Income-tax		93,750
Loss before PP gain on net monetary items		(1,42,917)
PP gain on net monetary items		5,41,250
Constant rupee (GPL) net income		3,98,333
Reserves and surpluses 1-1-2020		Nil
Cash dividends		(10,000)
Reserves and surpluses 31-12-2020		3,88,333

Example 2

The summarised Balance Sheets of Bharat Forge Ltd. as on 31-12-2019 and 2020 with the profit and loss account for the year ended on the latter date. They are prepared on conventional historic accounting method. The company was incorporated on 1-1-2016 with a capital of ₹ 60,000 in ₹ 1 Equity shares, fully paid at par on that date.

Bharat Forge Ltd.

31-12-2019 ₹	Balance Sheet as on Non-monetary assets	31-12-2020 ₹
70,000	Fixed assets at cost	79,000
17,500	*Less* accumulated depreciation	24,950
52,500		54,050
16,000	Stocks	25,400
	Net monetary assets:	
4,000	Cash & debtors less creditors	9,000
72,500		88,450
60,000	Equity shareholders capital	60,000
12,500	Retained profit	28,450
72,500		88,450

P&L Account
For the year ending 31-12-2020

	₹	₹
Sales		1,60,000
Less Opening Stock	16,000	
Purchase	1,09,400	
	1,25,400	
Closing stock	25,400	
Cost of sales		1,00,000
Gross profit		60,000
Less: Depreciation of fixed assets	7,450	
Other overhead expenses	36,600	44,050
Net profit		15,950

Additional Information

(1) Analysis of fixed assets and depreciation as at 31-12-2020, with conversion rates to be used on an index of current purchasing power:

Year ended 31st December	Capital expenditure each year written off offer 10 year ₹	Depreciation ₹	Conversion rate ₹
2016	30,000	10,500	1.154
2017	20,000	5,000	1.119
2018	10,000	1,500	1.087
2019	10,000	500	1.056

(2) Assume that the fixed assets and stocks are acquired evenly and that cash flow in even in 1920.

(3) The price level index on different dates was:

31-12-2020	150
31-12-2019	144
31-12-2018	140
31-12-2017	128

Show the balance sheets and profit and loss account according to general purchasing power (constant rupee accounting) model.

Solution

There are three steps involved to solve this problem:

First step: To convert the Balance Sheet as on 1-1-2020

Fixed Assets and Depreciation

Year ending 31st December	Conversion rate	Capital cost ₹	Expenditure Converted ₹	Depreciation On cost ₹	Depreciation Converted ₹
2011	1.154	30,000	34,620	10,500	12,117
2012	1.119	20,000	22,380	5,000	5,594
2013	1.087	10,000	10,870	1,500	1,631
2014	1.056	10,000	10,560	500	528
		70,000	78,430	17,500	19,871

Stocks: Average index for 2019 is 142 $\left(\frac{140+144}{2}\right)$

The conversion factor is $=\frac{150}{142}=1.056$

Net monetary assets: Only opening balances require to be restated i.e. on 31-12-2019 at the conversion rate

$$=\frac{150}{142}=1.042$$

Net monetary assets converted value = ₹ 4,000 × 1.042 = 4,168

Equity shareholders capital:

$$\text{Conversion rate } \frac{150}{142}=1.172$$

Converted equity share capital = 1.172 × 60,000 = ₹ 70,320.

Balance Sheet 2020
(Converted)

	₹	₹
Net monetary assets at Value		
Fixed assets at value	78,430	
Less: accumulated depreciation	19,871	
Stock		58,559
Net monetary assets		16,896
Cash and debtors less creditors		4,168
		79,623
Represented by:		
Equity shareholders capital		70,320
Retained profit		9,303
		79,623

Second step: To convert the balance sheet at the end of the year 2019

Fixed assets

Additional asset in the year: ₹ 9,000 (79,000 – 70,000)

The average index for 2020 $=147\left(\dfrac{150+144}{2}\right)$

The conversion rate is $\dfrac{150}{147}=1.020$

	₹
Additional fixed assets converted value = 9,000 × 1.020	= 9,180
Opening balance of fixed assets already converted	= 78,430
	= 87,610

Accumulated depreciation: On the additional assets during the year, the depreciation was charged for six months.

	₹	₹
$\dfrac{9,000}{10 \text{ years} \times 2}$ ·	450	
$\dfrac{₹\ 70,000}{10 \text{ years}}$	7,000	
Depreciation for the year	7,450	
Revised depreciation for the year:		
Additional assets $\dfrac{₹\ 9,800}{10 \text{ years} \times 2}$	459	₹
Assets at the beginning of the year	7,843	8,302
Add: Opening balance of accumulated depreciation		19,871
Converted accumulated depreciation balance		28,173

Stock

₹ 25,400 × 1.020 (average rate for 2020) = ₹ 25,908

Net monetary assets: Already given in current purchasing power.

Balance Sheet 31-12-2020
(Converted in Current Purchasing Power)

Net monetary assets:	₹	₹
Fixed assets at value	87,610	
Less: accumulated depreciation	28,173	
Stock		59,437
Net monetary assets		25,908
Cash debtors *less* creditors		9,000
		94,345
Equity shareholders capital		70,320
Retained profit		24,025
		94,345

Third step: Converting P&L account. The profit figure of ₹ 15,950 in historical system is to be reconciled.

		₹	
Sales		1,63,200	(1,60,000 × 1.02)
Less: Opening Stock	16,896		(as per opening converted balance sheet)
Purchase	1,11,588		(₹ 1,09,400 × 102)
	1,28,484		
Closing stock	25,908		(as per closing converted balance sheet)
Cost of sales		1,02,576	
Gross profit		60,624	
Less: Depreciation fixed assets		8,302	(see conversion calculations)
Less: Other overhead expenses		37,332	
		14,990	
Less: Loss from holding Net monetary assets		268*	
Net profit before tax and appropriations (Converted)		14,722	

*Loss for monetary assets

		₹
Loss at the beginning of the year (4,168 – 4,000) =		168
Add: loss in the year 2019		
Converted amount (₹ 9,000 – ₹ 4,000) × 1.02	= 5,100	
Current net monetary assets difference (₹ 9,000 – 4,000)	= 5,000	100
Net loss from monetary assets		268

ADVANTAGES AND DISADVANTAGES OF CONSTANT RUPEE (CPP) ACCOUNTING MODEL

Advantages

1. It provides management with an objectively determined quantification of the impact of inflation on its business operations.
2. It eliminates the effects of inflation from financial information by requiring each enterprise to follow the same objective procedure and use the same price level index, thereby preserving comparability of financial statements between firms and of a single firm as well.
3. It eliminates the necessity of price level changes without having to develop a new structure of accounting i.e. it preserves the historical based accounting system that is nowadays used.
4. It eliminates the necessity of the attraction of the "Piece meal" approaches used in combating the effects of inflation of financial statements i.e. LIFO method and accelerated method of depreciation of fixed assets.

Disadvantages

The accounting neither shows present value nor net realizable value or current cost accounting:

1. This method of accounting starts with an assumption that the effect of inflation on all firms, assets and costs falls equally and which is far from truth.
2. The additional cost of preparing the final accounts on GPL accounting basis is not offset by the benefit of receiving sufficient relevant information.
3. The purchasing power gain from monetary is misleading concept because it does not necessarily represent successful management or provide funds for payment of dividend or purchase of new asset or other purposes.
4. Restating the "value" of non-monetary items at historical cost converted of GPL changes is no more meaningful than historical cost alone, i.e., if suffers all shortcomings of historical cost method. This method causes confusion and is misunderstood by users.

CURRENT VALUE ACCOUNTING

Under this approach historical cost accounting is abandoned as a basis for financial statements and shifts to some measure of current value. But there is no single definition of value. Value actually is what assets are work to a particular person, for a particular purpose and at a particular point in time. In accounting value may mean going concern value, re-sale value, market value, liquidation value, present value, current value, fair value, book value, net realizable value and so on. To determine which basis of valuation to adopt depends upon the answer to the question. What is the objective of financial statements?

Value should not be confused with valuation. The term "current value" these days is commonly advocated for (a) present value (discounted future cash flows), (b) net realizable value (the selling price of the asset in the market less cost of disposal), and (c) current cost.

Current Cost Accounting (CCA)

Since the accounting profession has accepted CCA as a useful mechanism for better presentation of financial statements, this method is discussed in detail. Current cost is the cost of replacing the identical asset owned i.e. one of the same age and of the same operating capacity. Although replacement cost and current cost are used interchangeably, yet there exists a difference. The former is the current purchase price of assets which will replace existing asset and the latter is the current purchase price of an asset owned. Sometimes both may be same e.g. in case of stocks.

Current cost is approximated in many ways. But common method is to apply a specific price index.

Based on SSAP 16 and Hyde guidelines (U.K.) the accounts produced on a historical basis remain the same. A current cost P&L Account is to be prepared to show:

(a) Extra depreciation.

(b) A cost of sales adjustment (COSA).

(c) A gearing adjustment of take into consideration the way business if financed.

(d) Monetary working capital adjustment (MWCA). Also required is a current balance sheet. The effect on the presentation of such CCP & L account will be as follows:

	₹
Profit before taxation as in the historical cost account	—
Less: Current cost operating statement:	—
Depreciation	—
Cost of sales operating statement:	—
Monetary working capital adjustment	—
Current cost operating profit	—
Add: Gearing adjustment	—
Current cost profit before taxation	—
Less: Tax	—
Current cost profit attributable to shareholders	—
Less: Proposed dividends	—
Retained current cost profit for the year	—

Example 3

Following is the Balance Sheet and P&L Account of ABC Ltd., for the year ending 31-12-2020, based on historical cost accounting system.

A current cost P&L Account and a current cost Balance Sheet is to be prepared, based on SAAP 16 (U.K.).

P&L Account
For the year ending 31-12-2020

	₹	₹
Sales		20,00,000
Less Depreciation:		
Buildings	7,500	
Plant and Machinery	40,000	47,500
Interest payable		24,000
Net profit before tax and Extraordinary items		2,26,000
Less: Taxation		1,10,000
		1,16,000
Extraordinary items (net) (Dr.)		20,000
Net profit		96,000
Dividends for the year:		
Preference shares (paid)	10,000	
Equity shares (paid)	20,000	
Equity shares (proposed)	40,000	70,000
Profit retained		26,000

Balance Sheet
As on 31-12-2020

Share Capital	₹	₹	Fixed Assets	₹	₹	₹
Equity	4,00,000		Land		50,000	
Preference	1,00,000	5,00,000	Buildings	1,50,000		
			Less Depr.	30,000	1,20,000	
			Plant & Mach.	4,00,000		
Reserves:						
Share Premium A/c	20,000		*Less*: Depr.	70,000	3,30,000	5,00,000
P&L Account	1,00,000	1,20,000				
Debentures		2,00,000	Current Assets:			
Deferred tax		20,000				
Current year tax		90,000	Stock	3,50,000		
Current Liabilities:			Debtors	2,00,000		
Creditors	1,50,000		Cash/Bank	70,000		6,20,000
Proposed Dividend	40,000	1,90,000				
		11,20,000				11,20,000

Additional Information

1. *Stocks*
   (a) 31-12-2019, ₹ 3,00,000 (FIFO) average purchase date 30-11-2019
   (b) 31-12-2020, ₹ 3,50,000 (FIFO) average purchase date 30-11-2020

(c) Price Indices for Industry

Nov. 2019—110, Dec. 2019—112, Nov. 2020—130, Dec. 2020—134, Average 2020—123.

2. *Fixed Assets*

(a) Land, professionally valued on 31-12-2020 for ₹ 1,20,000

(b) Building purchased 1-1-2017 for ₹ 1,50,000, depreciation 5% P.A. on cost, accumulated 2018 was ₹ 2,25,000. Gross replacement cost 31-12-2020 ₹ 2,70,000.

(c) Plant and machinery purchased 1-1-2018 for ₹ 1,50,000 Depreciation, 10% P.A. on cost, accumulated 4 ₹ 30,000; purchased 1-1-2019 for ₹ 2,50,000. No depreciation at the date. Price indicates for plant

January 2018—120

January 2019—150

January 2020—170.

3. *Retail price Index*

Dec. 2019—188

Dec. 2020—204.

4. *Taxation rate 52%.*

Solution

First calculate current cost adjustments:

(a) *Depreciation adjustment*

	₹
Buildings $= ₹\ 75{,}000 \times \dfrac{2{,}70{,}000}{1{,}50{,}000} - ₹\ 7{,}500$	= 6,000
Plant purchased 1-1-2017 ₹ 1,50,000 × $0.10 \times \dfrac{170}{120}$ – 15,000	= 6,250
Plant purchased 1-1-2020 ₹ 2,50,000 × $0.10 \times \dfrac{170}{150}$ – 25,000	= 3,333
Total depreciation	= 15,583

(b) *Cost Sales adjustment*

	₹
31-12-2019 = ₹ 3,00,000 $\times \dfrac{123}{110}$ = 3,35,455 – 3,00,000	= 35,455
31-12-2020 = ₹ 3,50,000 $\times \dfrac{123}{130}$ = (3,31,154) – 3,50,000 + 3,50,000	= 18,846
	54,301

(c) *Gearing adjustment (see current cost Balance Sheet on 31-12-2020)*

Net monetary liabilities:	₹
Preference shares	1,00,000
Debentures	2,00,000
Deferred Tax	1,44,670

	₹
Taxation for current year	90,000
Cash/Bank	(70,000)
	4,64,670
Equity share Capital and Reserves:	
Equity shares	4,00,000
Share premium account	20,000
Capital maintenance (before adjustment for gearing)	1,94,288
P&L A/c (before adjustment for gearing)	31,561
Proposed dividend	40,000
	6,85,849
Total (Fixed assets 7,39,750 + Stock 3,60,769 + M.W.C. ₹ 50,000)	= 11,50,519

Gearing Adjustment: $(₹\ 15,583 + 54,301 + 6,658) \times \frac{464,670}{11,50,159} = 30,923$

(d) *Monetary working capital adjustment*

	₹
31-12-2019 Debtors ₹ 1,56,000, Creditors 1,30,000	= 26,000
31-12-2020 Debtors ₹ 2,00,000, Creditors 1,50,000	= 50,000
31-12-2019 = $₹\ 26,000 \times \frac{123}{112}$ = 28,554 – 26,000	= 2,544
31-12-2020 = $₹\ 50,000 \times \frac{123}{134}$ = (45,896) + 50,000	= 4,104
	6,658

(e) *Fixed assets revalued at current cost*

	Historical Cost ₹	Factor	Current Cost ₹	Increase ₹
Land at cost	50,000	revaluation	1,20,000	70,000
Building cost	1,50,000	revaluation	2,70,000	1,20,000
Depreciation	(30,000)	270/150	(54,000)	(24,000)
	1,20,000		2,16,000	96,000
Plant and machinery				
Cost 1-1-2018	1,50,000	170/120	2,12,500	62,500
Plant cost 1-1-2020	2,50,000	170/150	2,83,333	33,333
	4,00,000		4,95,833	95,833
Plant Depreciation				
1-1-2018	(45,000)	170/120	(63,750)	(18,750)
1-1-2020	25,000	170/150	28,333	3,333
	(70,000)	92,083	(92,083)	(22,083)
	3,30,000		4,03,750	73,750
Total	5,00,000		7,39,750	2,39,750

(f) *Stock revalued at current cost* 31-12-2020 ₹ 3,50,000

31-12-2020 ₹ 3,50,000 $\frac{134}{130}$ = ₹ 3,60,679

(g) *Capital maintenance reserve*:

(1) *Revaluation Reserve:*

			₹
Land			70,000
Buildings	1-1-2019		1,20,000
Plant and Machinery	1-1-2020		62,500
Plant and Machinery			33,333
Less: Depreciation buildings			2,85,833
$22{,}500 \times \frac{270}{120} - 22{,}500$		= 18,000	
Less: Depreciation Plant			
and Machinery $30{,}000 \times \frac{170}{120} - 30{,}000$		= 12,500	30,500
			2,55,333
Less: Deferred tax 52%			1,32,733
			1,22,560
P&L A/c Adjustment:			
Cost of sales (No. B)			54,301
Closing stock revaluation			10,769
Monetary working capital (No. D)			6,658
Less: Gearing (See No. C)			30,923
			1,63,365

Current Cost P&L A/c
For the year 31-12-2020

		₹
Sales		20,00,000
Profit before interest and tax on historical cost bias		2,50,000
Less adjustments:		
Depreciation	15,583	
Cost of sales	54,301	
M.W.C.	6,658	76,542
Current cost operating profit		1,73,458
Interest payable		24,000
		1,49,458
Gearing adjustment		30,923
		1,80,381
Less: Taxation		1,01,897
		78,484
Less: Extraordinary item (net)		20,000
		58,484
Less: Dividends		70,000
Over distributed current cost profit		(11,516)

Balance Sheet
As on 31-12-2020

Capital		₹	Fixed Assets		₹
Preference shares	1,00,000		Land		1,20,000
Equity shares	4,00,000		Buildings	2,70,000	
		5,00,000	*Less*: Depreciation	54,000	2,16,000
			Plant & Machinery	4,95,833	
Share premium		20,000	*Less*: Depreciation	92,083	4,03,750
Capital maintenance reserve		1,63,365			7,39,750
P&L A/c		62,484	*Current Assets*		
Debentures		2,00,000	Stock	3,60,769	
Deferred Tax		1,44,670	Debtors	2,00,000	
Taxation 2020		90,000	Cash/Bank	70,000	6,30,769
Creditors		1,50,000			
Proposed Dividends		1,90,000			
		13,70,519			13,70,519

Notes:

(1) The extra depreciation is the difference between the annual charge on a current cost basis and a charge in the accounts on a historical basis catch up or backlog depreciation is ignored. It is the difference between depreciation provided actually and that should have been provided i.e. on current cost and average current cost.

(2) The cost of sales adjustment is the difference between the figure based on the replacement cost of items sold at the date of sale standard costing variances may be used to calculate current costs.

(3) The gearing adjustment is the application of the gearing proportion to the extra depreciation and cost of sales adjustment. Assuming liabilities exceed monetary assets, the proportion is calculated as follows:

$$\frac{\text{Net monetary liabilities}}{\text{Equity capital + reserves + net monetary liabilities}} \times 100$$

Balance sheet figures used are cost of sales adjustment and those for the beginning and of the year averaged. Profit is increased by this gearing adjustment and offsets the reduction in profit for depreciation and cost of sales.

(4) Monetary working capital adjustment will normally cover debtors and creditors an allowance being made for cash and bank overdraft where this is necessary to avoid giving a misleading result.

ADVANTAGE AND DISADVANTAGE OF CURRENT COST METHOD

Advantages

1. It provides a better measure of efficiency. While general level of prices may be increasing, specific items may be decreasing. This system takes into account that.
2. It is an approximation of the service potential of the asset.
3. It provides for maintenance of physical capital.
4. It provides an assessment of future cash flows.

Disadvantages

1. It is subjective because it is difficult to determine the exact current cost of all items at any point in time.
2. The maintenance of physical capital is not the function of the accountant.
3. It is not always an approximation of the fair market value. It does not measure the increase in the service potential of that asset.

PROFESSIONAL PRONOUNCEMENTS

Owing to the relatively high rate of inflation experienced world-wide during the seventies and the expectation of continued significant inflation, several countries have undertaken studies to find better ways to report financial position, earning power and cash flows. U.K., U.S.A., Canada, Australia, Germany, France, Holland and Brazil are few of them.

U.S.A.

The first significant work on price-level accounting in the United States was published by Henry W. Sweeney[1] in 1936. His book, *Stabilized Accounting*, established the framework for later studies and official pronouncements. In 1961, the Accounting Principles Board Authorized a study of the price-level problem which resulted in the publication of *Accounting Research Study No. 6*[2] (*ARS No. 6*) recommended that the effects of price-level changes should be disclosed as a supplement to the conventional financial statements. Six years later, the Board issued *Statement of the Accounting Principles Board No. 3*, which outlined detailed procedures for the restatement of financial statements to recognize changes in the general price level.[3]

---

1. Henry W. Sweeney, *Stabilized Accounting*, Harper & Brothers (New York: 1936). Reprinted in 1964 by Holt, Rinehart and Winston, Inc., New York.
2. *Accounting Research Study No. 6*. "Reporting the Financial Effects of Price-level Changes", authorised by the staff of Research Division, AICPA (New York: 1963).
3. *Statement of the Accounting Principle Board No. 3,* "Financial Statements Restated for General Price-level Changes", AICPA (New York: 1969).

Then in 1976, the Securities and Exchange Commission issued ASR No. 190, which required a modified form of current value accounting. Large publicly held companies were required to disclose the cost of replacing inventories and plant and equipment and to show what their cost of goods sold and depreciation expense would be if computed on current replacement cost basis. Upon issuance of ASR No. 190, the Financial Accounting Standards Board (FASB) began to re-valuate its position concerning accounting for price-level changes. In 1979, FASB issued statement No. 33 "Financial Reporting and Changing Prices" which requires certain large, publicly held enterprises to disclose supplementary information on both a constant dollar basis and a current cost basis. In order to encourage experimentation in the development of techniques for accumulating, reporting and analyzing data on the effects of price changes, the requirements of statement No. 33 are more flexible than is customary in Board statements. The Board indicated that no major changes should be made to the primary financial statements at the present time, but something must be done to argument them with information about effects of price changes. Balance sheets and complete statements of income on the other a current cost or a constant dollar basis are not required, although their presentation is encouraged. Certain enterprises are required to report (a) income from continuing operations, (b) PP gain or loss on net monetary items, (c) income from continuing operations on a current costs basis, (d) current cost amounts of inventory and property, plant and equipment at the end of the year, and (e) increases or decreases in current cost amounts of inventory and property, plant and equipment, net of inflation. In addition, a five-year summary of selected financial data must be reported. Little guidance is provided in statement No. 33 for companies who which to present comprehensive financial statements. But it had simplified the matter by (a) restatement is necessary only for inventory, property, plant and equipment, cost of goods sold and depreciation and depletion expenses; sales and other revenues and other expenses do not have to be adjusted, (b) the average for the year dollars instead of year and dollars be used, and (c) no distinction is made between realized and unrealized holding gains and losses. A total holding gain or loss, net of inflation referred to in the statements as the excess of the increase in specific prices over the increase in the general price level, only need be presented. In 1985, the FASB decided to retain FAS 33.

U.K.

There has never been a strong feelings about upward revaluation of assets in U.K. and the British Companies Acts expressly instructed companies to revalued fixed assets where their current values were substantially different from their historical costs. It was in 1970, the British Accounting Standards Steering Committee applied itself to the question of inflation accounting and in 1973, produced Exposure Draft

(ED) 8; Accounting for changes in purchasing power of money. This advocated the used of current purchasing power accounting. The ASSC again published in 1974 Statement of Standard Accounting Practice No. 7: Accounting for changes in the purchasing power of money (details follow). SSAP 7 has persuasive force only because in 1974, the government has set up a committee, headed by Francis Sandilands, known as "Sandilands Committee" to consider the effects of inflation on financial statements (details given in this section). The committee published its report in 1975 and SSAP 7 was withdrawn. The committee came out firmly in favour of a form of replacement cost accounting for the basic financial statements and against the continuance of historical financial statements. The (renamed) Accounting Standards Committee set to work on a new standard to give effect to Sandilands proposals. The committee set to work on a new standard to give effect to Sandilands proposals. The committee produced ED 18 in 1976: Current Cost Accounting, but ED 18 was withdrawn in 1977. The ASC has to begin again and as an interim measure issued its interim recommendations on inflation accounting, famous by the name of "HYDE" guidelines (details given later in this section). In 1979, again there were some proposed amendments in "Hyde" guidelines, called ED 24. Finally the SAC issued SSAP No. 16 in 1980.

Other Countries

In Germany, before June 20, 1948, all items appearing in historical cost financial statements were to appear in revalued statements. This was because new currency was introduced after World War II and from which new price indices were to be calculated. After 1948, the German Companies Act and commercial code returned to historical costs and German Laws do not permit revaluations. Similar post war revaluations were permitted by Belgium, Italy and Japan.

In France, the law of 28-12-1959 put a date line on revaluation, which in view of the stabilization of France affected during 1959, was believed to be necessary after 30-6-1959. Firms were given until Dec. 31, 1962 to accomplish their revaluations, which were obligatory for all business, whether public or private the revaluation coefficients to be used were two sets of indices, one for fixed assets and depreciation and other for stock and shares and obligations.

The Dutch system adopted a replacement value accounting, which differs from replacements cost approach under it non-monetary assets are valued for balance sheet purposes. However, in recent years there has been considerable criticism of this in Holland and accountants are in favour of replacement cost approach as of U.K. and U.S.A.

In Australia, the Mathews Committee in its report in 1974 recommended current cost approach to income measurement. It rejected the recognition of PP gains and losses on holding monetary assets and liabilities.

In 1964, Brazil adopted inflation accounting into tax laws an adopted a system of monetary correction, called indexing, as the basis of financial reporting. Chile, Peru and Uruguay had also permitted regular voluntary revaluation of assets during the 1960s. In Netherlands also complete readjustment for financial statements is a practice with some companies. From 1974, Argentina has, by law, adopted price-level adjusted financial statements.

INDIA

The Institute of Chartered Accountants of India and the Institute of Cost and Works Accountant of India recommend CCA method, as CPA method does not ensure the maintenance of operating capability of an enterprise.

International Accounting Standard No. 15

The IAS Committee, founded in 1973, by nine countries *viz.,* U.S.A., U.K. (including Ireland), Australia, Canada, France, West Germany, Japan, Mexico and Netherlands. India is also an associate member of this committee (Total 30 countries). IAS are not mandatory. In 1976 IAS 16 was issued about "accounting treatment of changing prices".

This standard appears to be very permissive, merely requiring additional information in financial statements, on the basis of either current purchasing power or current cost accounting or some combination of both. There is not yet an international agreement on a single systematic response to the problem of changing prices. IAS 15 was withdrawn w.e.f. 1.1.2005.

INDIAN EXAMPLE

Many companies are showing current cost accounting as a part of their financial statements. Here is example from NTPC.

Notes on the basis of revaluation/conversion of account to current cost for the year ending 31st March, 2015.

Current Cost Accounts

Inflation which is persistent phenomenon in the recent decades has significant impact on the performance and financial structure of an enterprise. Summarized current cost accounts showing the impact of price changes on its working results and the financial position based on principles enunciated in the Guidance Notes on Accounts for Changing Prices, issued by the Institute of Chartered Accountants of India, have been worked out.

The current cost adjustments have been made on the basis of specific indices for various items, taken from the detailed indices comprising the whole-sale price index published by the office of the Economic Advisor, Ministry of Industry, Government of India and Central Statistical Organisation. The base year for price index has been changed from 1991-1992 to 2001-2002 with effect from 2010-2011. Accordingly, 1991-

1992 indices have been converted into 2001-2002 base year wherever the same were not available from government agencies.

Fixed Assets

Fixed assets are stated at their gross current replacement cost by applying the relevant specific indices to the gross book value of each category of fixed assets. The net current replacement cost has been arrived at by charging depreciation on the gross current replacement cost at the rates specified under the Electricity (Supply) Act, 1948.

Capital Work-in-Progress

Since the gestation period is 3-5 years for each Project, capital work-in-progress has been stated at its current replacement cost.

Inventories

Inventories are stated at their value of the business which is the lower of their current replacement cost and net realisable value.

Others Assets and Liabilities

Cash, sundry, debtors, loans and other liabilities have not been revalued since these are already expressed in current monetary terms.

Depreciation Adjustment

The depreciation adjustment represents the difference between the amount of depreciation computed on the current cost of fixed assets and the amount of depreciation actually charged in the accounts.

Cost of Sales Adjustment

The cost of sales adjustment has been made on the basis of averaging method. The opening and closing stocks have been brought to a common average stock price on the relevant price indices and the revised cost of sales compared with the historical cost to arrive at the cost of sales adjustment. Since holding of component and spares has increased, cost of sales adjustment has been made on these items based on nine years weighted average during this year.

Monetary Working Capital Adjustment

The monetary working capital adjustment has also been made on the basis of the averaging method. The opening and closing monetary working capital have been brought to a common average on the basis of the relevant price indices. The increase in monetary working capital at current cost has been deducted from the increase in monetary working capital of historical cost to arrive at the monetary working capital adjustment.

Gearing Adjustment

As a part of the operating assets of the corporation is financed through borrowings which are to be repaid in the same monetary amount irrespective of changes in prices, the full impact of price changes as reflected by the above-mentioned adjustment (viz. depreciation adjustment, cost of sales adjustment and monetary working capital adjustment) has been reduced by adding back a proportionate amount while determining the current cost profit attributable to shareholders.

Current Cost Reserve

The current cost reserve represents unrealised revaluation surplus on fixed assets and inventories, adjustment in respect of depreciation, cost of sales and monetary working capital and the gearing adjustment.

Taxation

As the liability for taxation is determined with reference to profits on historical cost basis on adjustment in this respect is required to be made in the current cost accounts.

Analysis

The major observations emerging out of the preparation of current cost accounts are summarized below:

(1) The estimated replacement cost of the fixed assets of the Corporation is approximately ₹ 40,925 crores which in the historic books of accounts are carried at ₹ 22,727 crores.

(2) The capital work-in-progress as per historical cost is ₹ 1,928 crores whereas as per replacement cost its value is ₹ 3,379 crores.

(3) The total depreciation provided on the basis of the historical cost works out to ₹ 5,566 crores and depreciation worked out on current cost basis comes to ₹ 9,966 crores.

(4) Profit for the year as per current cost is ₹ 597 crores as against profit of ₹ 1,679 crores as per Annual Accounts of the year on historical cost basis.

(5) The balance sheet in current cost terms shows capital employed as ₹ 37,371 crores as against ₹ 20,642 crores at historical cost. Net worth of ₹ 29,629 crores is as per current cost which comes to ₹ 13,799 crores on historical cost basis.

Current Cost Ratios

	2013-14	2014-15
Value Added/Turnover	51.86%	53.65%
Value Added/Capital Employed	13.68%	14.66%
Turnover/Capital Employed	26.38%	27.33%
Operating Profit/Capital Employed	3.20%	4.64%
Profit After Tax/Net Worth	2.02%	3.33%
Debt/Equity	0.31	0.35

Current Cost Balance Sheet as at 31st March, 2014

(₹ in Lakhs)

		As at 31st March, 2015	As at 31st March, 2014
Net Assets employed:			
Gross Block	40,92,467.16		32,00,700.13
Less: Accumulated Depreciation	9,96,595.48		6,60,400.51
Net Block		30,95,871.68	25,40,299.62
Capital Work-in-Progress		3,37,894.91	8,30,672.12
Construction Stores		25,561.22	24,606.00
Advances for Capital Expenditure		36,560.25	27,546.97
Investments		6.81	1.94
Net Current Assets, Loans and Advances			
Inventories	1,97,482.13		1,65,969.69
Other Current Assets	6,48,007.50		5,32,536.80
	8,45,489.63		6,98,506.49
Less: Current Liabilities and Provisions	2,04,280.05		1,70,384.65
		6,41,209.58	5,28,121.84
Miscellaneous Expenditure (to the extent not written off or adjusted)		363.25	291.66
		41,37,467.70	39,51,540.15
Financed By:			
Shareholder's Funds:			
Share Capital	7,40,377.94		7,33,496.94
Current Cost Reserve	16,63,954.22		14,80,003.08
Other Reserves and Surpluses	7,65,885.19		6,93,279.98
		31,70,217.35	29,06,780.00
Loan Funds:			
Secured Loans	3,27,219.46		3,21,713.09
Unsecured Loans	6,40,030.89		7,03,423.47
		9,67,250.35	10,25,136.56
Deferred payment liability		—	19,623.59
		41,37,467.70	39,51,540.15

As per the detailed note on basis of revaluations attached.

Current Cost Profit and Loss Account for the year ended 31st March, 2015

(₹ in lakhs)

	For the year ended 31st March, 2015	For the year ended 31st March, 2014
Profit before interest and finance:		
Charges and taxation (on historic cost basis)	2,81,580.66	2,30,202.50

Less:			
Depreciation Adjustment	1,18,290.36		73,014.68
Cost of Sales Adjustment	12,687.36		8,108.87
Monetary Working Capital Adjustment	31,303.07		6,210.34
		1,62,280.79	87,333.89
Current Cost Operating Profit		1,19,299.87	1,42,868.61
Add: Gearing Adjustment		54,076.37	31,068.30
		1,73,376.24	1,73,936.91
Less: Interest and Finance Charges	1,09,302.57		94,929.25
Provision for Taxation	4,334.95		12.15
		1,13,637.52	94,941.40
Retained Current Cost Profit Attributable to Shareholders		59,738.72	78,995.51

As per the detailed note on basis of revaluations attached.

However, the company adopted format as prescribed by schedule ITI of companies Act 2013 w.e.f. from year ending March 2016.

QUESTIONS

1. Explain the meaning of (a) monetary items and non-monetary items, (b) holding gain, (c) conversion, (d) gearing adjustment, (e) monetary working capital adjustment.
2. (a) If the GPL is rising steadily, which of the following would be most realistically valued for balance sheet purpose—(a) stocks in trade, (b) debtors, or (c) property.
   (b) Clarify each item as monetary or non-monetary items:
   Stocks in trade, discounts on debentures, accumulated depreciation on machinery, bills receivable, equity share capital debentures, deposits with company.
3. (a) Under each of the following a company gains or losses:
   (i) The company maintains an excess of monetary assets over monetary liabilities during a period of price level increases. Is it same if it maintains the same during the price of price-level decrease?
   (ii) A company maintains equal amounts of monetary assets and monetary liabilities during increase in price-level.
   (iii) If an excess of liabilities over monetary asset during a period of increase in price-level.
   (b) Explain three commonly advocated concepts of current values.
4. What are the major advantage of current cost accounting? How does it differ from replacement cost accounting?
5. For each independent situation below, calculate general price-level gain or loss, assuming that assets and liabilities remained unchanged during entire period. The general price-level rose by 4% during the period.

		₹
(a)	Monetary assets	1,00,000
	Current liabilities	40,000
(b)	Monetary assets	1,50,000
	Current liabilities	1,00,000
	Long term liabilities	2,50,000
(c)	Cash	50,000
	Debtors	60,000
	Bills receivable	90,000
	Stock	1,00,000
	Investment	1,00,000
	Plant and machinery (net)	6,00,000
	Liabilities	5,75,000
	Shareholders' capital	5,25,000

6. In its accounts for the current financial year Janata Dal Ltd., had opening stock valued at ₹ 25,000 and closing stock valued at ₹ 2,00,000 and sales ₹ 4,00,000. Appropriate stock index numbers were 100 at the beginning of the year and 110 at the end of the year. The average index for the year was 105.

   You are required to state (i) following current cost accounting principles, the gross profit both on the historic cost and the current cost basis. What double entry adjustment is recommended in the historic revenue account to adjust it to current cost.

   The following entry appeared in the company's Balance Sheet at the end of the current financial year ended 31-3-2015 for furniture and fittings.

Historic Cost	Accumulated depreciation based on historic cost	Net Book value
₹ 1,040	₹ 680	₹ 360

   The furniture and fittings were acquired:

   (i) During year ended 31-3-2013 at cost of ₹ 600, accumulated depreciation 31-3-2015—₹ 480.

   (ii) During the year ended 31-3-2014 at a cost of ₹ 440, accumulated depreciation 31-3-2015—₹ 200.

   Depreciation charged in the year P&L Account on furniture and fittings was ₹ 280 (₹ 180 on 2013 purchased and ₹ 100 on 2016 purchases). Relevant price indexes were 150 for 2013 and 200 for 2014 and 225 at 31-3-2015.

Calculate the depreciation charge for furniture and fittings based on current cost accounting principles, to be entered in 2015 P&L Account. Also show the entry for furniture and fittings in current cost accounting balance sheet as on 31-3-2015 and the amount credited to furniture and fittings revaluation reserve in the balance sheet.